Agnes Macphail:
Reformer

Agnes, soon after winning the 1935 election

Agnes Macphail: Reformer

Canada's First Female M.P.

Doris Pennington

Simon & Pierre

TORONTO, CANADA

We would like to express our gratitude to The Canada Council and the Ontario Arts Council for their support.

Marian M. Wilson, Publisher

Photos, collection of the author, pages 15, 18 (top), 21, 28 (bottom), 68 (bottom), 238 (both); courtesy of Macphail family, 54, 87; courtesy of James Palmer, cover and 208, opposite title page, 68 (top), 166, 172, 185, 25; National Film Board of Canada, 18 (bottom), 223; National Archives of Canada, 28, 112, 147, 231, 234; courtesy of Rockwood Terrace, 122; courtesy of Shaver Homestead, 150; Toronto City Archives, 129.

ISBN 0-88924-212-7

2 3 4 5 • 93 92 91 90
Second edition
Canadian Cataloguing in Publication Data

    Pennington, Doris, date
    Agnes Macphail, reformer

    ISBN 0-88924-212-7

    1. Macphail, Agnes Campbell, 1890-1954.
    2. Canada. Parliament. House of Commons -
    Biography. 3. Women legislators - Canada -
    Biography. 4. Feminists - Canada - Biography.
    I. Title.

    FC541.M27P46 1989   328.71'092'4   C89-093911-X
    F1034.3.M27P46 1989

Cover design: Christopher W. Sears
Editor: Peter Goodchild
Printer: Gagné Printing

Printed and Bound in Canada

Order from
Simon & Pierre Publishing Company Limited/
Les Éditions Simon & Pierre Ltée.
P.O. Box 280 Adelaide Street Postal Station
Toronto, Ontario, Canada M5C 2J4

To my sisters Jean and Blanche,
and in memory of our parents,
Robert and Viola Tucker

Acknowledgements

Many friends and relatives of Agnes graciously contributed their time and memories to assist in this project. I thank in particular Agnes' nieces, Mrs. Jean Huston, Mrs. Jean Clunas, and her great-niece, Mrs. Joan Burrows. Thanks especially to James Palmer: as friend, protégé and advisor of Agnes Macphail, his help was most valuable and was generously given. He shared his pictures, clippings and memories of Agnes, and gave much time to discuss various points. It is greatly appreciated, and my debt to him acknowledged. The late Farquhar Oliver, another friend and protégé of Agnes and one-time leader of the provincial Liberal Party, answered promptly and kindly when asked for information.

Thanks to editor Peter Goodchild, for his expertise, and to my husband, John, for his unwavering support.

My thanks also to the following for permission to quote from articles in their papers:

Chatelaine
The *Dundalk Herald*
The *Durham Chronicle*
The *Durham Review*
The *Owen Sound Sun Times*
Saturday Night
The *Toronto Star*
The *Woodstock Daily Sentinel-Review*

Contents

Illustrations

Preface

Agnes Macphail, Canada's first female Member of Parliament, descended on
Ottawa in 1922 and was as welcome as an unexpected guest at a dinner party.
Colleagues in the House of Commons hoped she would go away or, if not, sit
quietly in a corner. No such luck. She came armed with youthful idealism, strong
opinions and a stubborn independent streak, determined to set Parliament on its
ear if necessary to get a fair deal for farmers and women in particular.

Alone she faced the scorn of members and learned to give a little better
than she got. To the horror of colleagues she criticized the military, meddled with
the penitentiaries, lectured on economics as if she knew what she was talking
about, quoted experts they scarcely recognized — and to make matters worse,
turned back $1,500 from her salary for four years in a row. She fought for peace
in an age that glorified war. And she fought for reform — economic, social,
prison and parliamentary. She earned the reward of most reformers: abuse.
Nevertheless, when she died, it was widely recognized that there had been little
good social legislation in the past thirty years in which she had not played a part.

In her fight she was aided by a mellifluous speaking voice — calm, low,
and capable of reaching the farthest corners of the House of Commons — a dry
wit, and an ability to squelch hecklers, which earned her a wary respect.

Canadians have benefited from the pioneering work of Agnes Macphail, but
we scarcely realize it, as women's accomplishments tend to be invisible, and
even if recognized at the time, quickly disappear from history. In 1928, when a
reporter wrote that women had never done anything great in politics, it made
Agnes "very angry," not for herself but for her sex. "Such nonsense," she said.
"When have they ever had the opportunity?" Agnes had the opportunity and she
made the most of it. Those who knew her recognized her as a great personality.
As journalist Marion Fox said: "The women of Canada have very good reason to
be proud that their first representative in the House of Commons is brave,
fearless, true to principle Agnes Macphail."

John Diefenbaker said Canada had produced five outstanding politicians and
that Agnes was one of them.

I knew Agnes Macphail as a friend of my parents. I remember her visits to
our home and the real enjoyment obvious in their conversations interrupted
frequently by hearty laughter.

Agnes grew up near my father in the hamlet of Ceylon. At one time in their
youth they were engaged to be married. But the thought of relinquishing her
freedom and losing control of her own destiny probably caused her to turn from
marriage and apply her abilities to a broader field — for which we Canadians
can be thankful.

Throughout the book the name Macphail is spelled as Agnes preferred, with
a small "p." She claimed it was easier to spell this way. Her family spelled it
with a capital "P." On the family tombstone it is spelled minus the "a": McPhail.

Doris Pennington

Chronology

1890	Agnes Macphail born on March 24 in Proton Township, Ontario
1906	Begins school at Owen Sound Collegiate Institute in September
1910	Graduates from Stratford Normal School with teacher's certificate
1918	Women who have a vote in provincial elections are granted the right to vote in federal elections
1921	Agnes elected to her first term in Federal Parliament, as member of the Progressive Party; Mackenzie King begins first term as Prime Minister
1925	Agnes re-elected to Federal Parliament
1926	Agnes elected to third term; her parents, Dougald and Henrietta Macphail, retire to Ceylon, Ontario
1929	Agnes goes to Geneva as delegate to the League of Nations; New York stock market crashes
1930	Death of Agnes' father
1930	Agnes wins her fourth term in Federal Parliament; R. B. Bennett elected Prime Minister
1931	Beauharnois power-project scandal
1932	Founding of CCF in Calgary, Alberta
1935	Agnes elected to fifth term in Federal Parliament; Mackenzie King returns as Prime Minister
1936	Archambault Commission to investigate prisons
1937	Death of Agnes' mother, Henrietta Macphail
1939	King George VI visits Canada; Canada declares war on Germany
1940	Agnes defeated by Walter Harris
1943	Agnes elected CCF member for York East in Ontario Legislature
1945	Agnes loses her seat in the Ontario Legislature
1948	Re-elected to Ontario Legislature
1951	Ontario Legislature passes legislation on equal pay for women; Agnes defeated in election
1954	Agnes dies on February 13

Chapter I
The Early Years
1890-1920

When Agnes Macphail died in Toronto on February 13, 1954, her body was sent home to Grey, the county that had nurtured her and sent her off more than thirty years before on a splendid quest for social justice.

A snow storm raged that Tuesday; visibility was poor; side roads were blocked and main roads barely passable. Trains were hours late.

"It was the most ungodly storm you ever saw," said James MacArthur, who with his brother, Donald, spent most of a day digging the grave of the area's most noted citizen.

Many people, like the Honorable Walter Harris who came from Ottawa to honor the woman he had defeated in the 1940 election, arrived late. Some made it in time only for the burial. Others, including one pall-bearer, did not arrive at all.

The wind and snow were still blowing fiercely when the service at Priceville ended, but a township plow had spent much of the day breaking open the road a mile south to the McNeil Cemetery.

Pallbearers struggled through the last five hundred feet. Friends and relatives followed and huddled together against the cold.

"She came in on a Grey County storm and she's bloody well going out on one," observed an old farmer to no one in particular.

Some thought it only fitting that one who had "created many a storm during her career, went to her last resting place in a fierce storm, this one provided by Mother Nature." [1]

Agnes herself would not have been surprised. Nothing in her life, or that of her ancestors, had been gained without a struggle.

Her paternal ancestors, the Macphails, came from Kilmartin, near the Firth of Lorne, Scotland. In her autobiography, "My Ain Folk," Agnes says that

> progress has passed it by. The little stone church is still lit with great hanging sconces of oil lamps. A quarter of the grave-stones are moss-grown and scoured by the sea winds to illegibility. But inside the building the brass plaques commemorating the famous dead are kept gleaming, and the stained glass windows throw rainbows on the pavement . . . .
>
> The country . . . is very beautiful. The Macphails must have hated to leave it. They must have been driven by economic desperation. My great-grandfather Macphail was head shepherd on a large estate with thousands of sheep. He lived with his wife and twelve children in a small stone cottage at the foot of the mountains. His eldest son, my grandfather, helped him, but there was no future for the others in Kilmartin, no way for the family to keep together, and the land was not their own. About 1846 the Macphails decided to emigrate . . . .

Grandfather Macphail was sixteen when the family settled between Galt and Guelph. They prospered and eventually built a fine stone house of material not unlike what they might have found on a Scottish hillside. But when young Alexander, turned twenty and ready to settle down, came to look for a farm, he walked up to what is now Mount Forest and east to Proton with his bundle in a bandana to squat on land which he later acquired legally. It was the twelfth concession of the township, just over from the Campbells [her maternal ancestors], who were on the fourteenth. Here he begot and raised his own twelve children, or left the job to the eldest, Dougal, my Father. [2]

In "Women Pioneers of Proton," Agnes writes that her "grandmother Macphail [Jean Jack] came from Scotland to Hamilton with her parents, when she was a small child. The whole family stayed in Hamilton for a couple of years, and then moved to the 9th Concession of the township of Proton.

"Grandma was eleven years old when they came into the bush. They hired horses to take them the first part of the way. When they were in the bush a year, great-grandmother died, and little Jean Jack, a child of twelve, was left as the house-keeper for her brothers and father and the foster-mother of little Anzel Ainsworth, a baby one year old." [3]

At twenty-one, Jean Jack married Alexander Macphail.

Agnes' maternal ancestors, the Campbells, were landowners and came from Ayrshire. Her grandfather Campbell was a "typical stubborn Scot," according to Agnes, and his wife, Jean Black, a "sonsy merry farm dairymaid, with whom his elder brother, the master of the farm, was also in love." They travelled to Canada in the "Heather Bell" on a voyage which lasted for ten miserable weeks, during which time their infant son died of a "bloody flux." Agnes writes:

In this gallery of my ain folk, perhaps one figure stands out particularly. My Grandmother Campbell was brave and bonny. She could work in the slash with the men and rush home a few minutes early to prepare the bannocks and bacon . . . . Completely fearless, she several times drove off bears that were threatening the stock, and she never shed a tear when a gang of "swamp angels" took all her food, turned her and Great-uncle Geordie's wife and their children out of their painstakingly built log homes, and burned the little dwellings. My Grandfather and his brother were away hunting, but Great-uncle Tam always kept a protecting eye on the bonny lass who'd turned him down for his younger brother. He trailed them through the bush and drove them off with a shotgun, single-handed. Grandmother said she couldn't cry, she was so angry. . . . The daughter of a coal miner, who died when his five children were still almost infants, Jean Black had few worldly advantages, but she had an indomitable spirit. . . . She could do everything a woman is supposed to do and do it better than most women, and she could do most things a man is supposed to do and do them as well as most men. That's not unusual in a farm woman, but I idolized her for it. [4]

On March 18, 1889, the eldest Campbell daughter, Henrietta, married the eldest Macphail son, Dougald, in the manse of Esplen Presbyterian Church. The young couple, both twenty-five, set up housekeeping in a three-room log cabin on a 100-acre farm: lot seven, concession twelve, Proton Township. Here a year later, on March 24, 1890, Agnes Campbell Macphail was born.

She was to become Canada's first female Member of Parliament.

The Macphail family: left to right, Agnes'
father, Dougald; sisters Gertha and Lilly;
Agnes; and Agnes' mother, Henrietta

"She was," said relatives, "the crossest, most restless baby you ever saw . . . . As a child and growing girl she was hard to manage, and always, once embarked on any achievement, bound to see it to its finish."[5] A good thing, too, for as she recalled later, "being the only woman in the House of Commons was sometimes almost more than I could bear. Had I known how bad it was going to be I wouldn't have gone through with it. But once in, I wouldn't give up."

Agnes and her sisters, Gertha, born July 26, 1893, and Lillian, born December 18, 1897, grew up in a close-knit family, full of "the old Scottish clan spirit." In "My Ain Folk" Agnes described her parents:

I have no consciousness of being brave . . . but if I am, I got it from my Mother. . . .

Mother had the sterling quality of standing by her beliefs, whatever the cost. This was early impressed on us as the very foundation of life, and I do not think any of us have ever backed down from a stand we had taken as a matter of conscience. . . .

A rigid disciplinarian, Mother was harder on herself than on anyone else. She was a very good housekeeper, the kind a maid, in the later days when we had help, used to call "killing clean." My two sisters are like her, but I, like Father, am content if things are handy and comfortable. My Mother was hard-working and thrifty, but I am impatient with clutter and delay and have become a thrower-outer. At the same time I am more sentimental than my Mother, who had no time for nonsense like holidays, and washed on Christmas Day the same as any other day, if it happened to come on a Monday. . . .

Mother was not the retiring kind. She always raised chickens, and her flowers were beautiful, both indoors and outdoors. She had fine taste, with a great eye for colour and balance expressing itself not only in horticulture, but in interior decoration, and the selection of clothes. . . .

My sisters and I were taught to control our feelings, and Mother seldom sympathized with childish hurts, or the troubles of older life either. Some pretty bitter attacks were made on me at various times in my parliamentary career, and only once did she say she was sorry for me — when Hugh Guthrie made such an attack on me for demanding prison reform, calling me the companion of sex perverts and suggesting that there was something depraved and unwomanly in anyone who could interest herself in such a topic. . . .

People say I have a ready tongue, and I know I have a passion for public service. The first part of that description would fit my Father whose jollying ways and stimulating personality made him so successful an auctioneer that people said he could sell haggis to an Englishman on St. George's Day. But his father had been the second reeve of Proton Township and for years had spent more time and energy than he could afford on municipal work . . . . Father used to say that Grandfather looked after all the widows and orphans for miles around and had no time to look after his own family. He wasn't going to make the same mistake. . . .

Father, perhaps because of his many outside contacts, was more tolerant and flexible than Mother, and here again, in many ways, I think I resemble him. . . .

As an auctioneer Father was known all through South Grey. People used to come from miles around to hear him sell, and his popularity was a great political asset to his eldest daughter. . . .

With my Father I had a particularly close kinship, as is not unusual with eldest daughters where there is no son. If I have any insight or wit or understanding I owe them to him. He was a man of great ability, and his death saddened me less than his apparent failure to reach his potentialities. I like to think that I did some of the things he might have enjoyed doing if he had not had to take on such heavy family responsibilities so early. But perhaps I could do them only because of the qualities I inherited from Mother as well as those I inherited from him. Perhaps if I owed him the ability to get into Parliament I owed her the ability to stand it when I got there.[6]

The Macphail farm near Ceylon

Henrietta Macphail hated the log house she had come to live in as a bride. Agnes, however, recalled it with affection. "I can remember the home-made table, used in the cellar in my day, which would seat twelve people. . . . [The house] was hard to heat in winter, and the kettle, which would be boiling when we went to bed, would be frozen solid in the morning. But the kitchen was big and attractive, and we children loved it. Father built a fine new barn, but he never got around to a new house, and eventually, when I was twelve, we bought a much better farm near Ceylon. There, with his work as auctioneer, cattle dealer, and farmer, Father really prospered, and at sixty-two was able to retire to a small chicken ranch in the village itself." [7]

In 1904 Agnes passed her entrance examinations and planned to continue her education at Owen Sound Collegiate Institute. She was shocked and angry when her parents told her that they needed her at home. After two years of helping her mother she became so difficult that her parents relented. Ecstatic, Agnes ran, as they had no phone, to a neighboring farm, rushed in and cried: "Jack, I'm going, I'm going."

"There was no need to say *where*. They all *knew*," recalled her sister Lillian Bailey.

In 1906 Agnes took off by train for Owen Sound Collegiate, thirty miles away.

The collegiate had earned a solid reputation for scholarship since it opened in 1880. It consistently led the province, as indicated by the results of departmental examinations, and had attracted so many students from outside Owen Sound that by the year Agnes attended, four large classrooms, a typewriting room and a gymnasium were being added.

The original school was a three-storey brick building whose roof line was broken by a tower and the ornamental windows of the Assembly Hall. Windows in the first and second storeys were tall and narrow with rounded tops. There were ten classrooms on the first two floors and the large Assembly Hall on the third. The Hall could seat 600 people and contained a stage, waiting rooms and piano. It was used for school gatherings, literary society meetings and entertainments and no doubt looked immense and exciting to youngsters like Agnes who had attended a one-room school house.

Each week there were written exams in which "printed question papers" were used and there was a "regular course of supplementary reading to encourage in pupils a love of literature, and to beget a habit of thoughtful reading."

There was little room for frivolity. The Literary Society was looked on as an opportunity to secure training in "Elocution, Declamation and Public Debate." Agnes probably belonged and took part in the debates, adding her own special sparkle and wit to subjects such as, "In awarding the franchise there should be no discrimination on account of sex."

At Collegiate, too, she quite possibly formed her first unfavorable impression of the cadet corps where young boys were drilled and trained in the use of guns and other military matters. While the cadets were being instructed in the spring, other students had their only spare. And, said a writer in the anniversary year book, "Although the girls had to stay inside, there was much craning of necks to watch out the windows."

It is unlikely that Agnes would be one of the group. More likely she would be remarking on the stupidity of training boys in the art of war. She was not in Parliament long before she vehemently voiced her opinion on the subject.

The school had a Glee Club and Bible Class. A picture of the "Collegiate Bible Class 1906" shows forty-five young men dressed in their Sunday best, formal and serious in dark suits and high stiff collars. Included in the picture are Agnes' friend from home, Bob Tucker, who was later to become her suitor, and Norman Bethune, who was to become a national hero to the Chinese for his work as a doctor during China's war with Japan in the 1930's.

The school also had a football club and an evening once a year when, to music, the young people walked around the auditorium in couples. When the music stopped, the boy escorted the girl back to her seat and chose another partner for the next "promenade." At the last promenade the partners enjoyed a dish of ice cream together.

It is probable that when Agnes arrived in Owen Sound in September of 1906 she had never been in the town before, except possibly with her parents to look for a boarding house.

No doubt the town fascinated the country students with its brightly lit streets and shops, its substantial homes and churches, its location on the frigid waters of Georgian Bay and the rocky hills of the Niagara Escarpment. Still it was a big change for a sixteen-year-old farm girl to be transplanted from the protection of her parents' home to the cold anonymity of a boarding house in a large and seemingly inhospitable town. Delighted though Agnes was to be at school again, she was shocked and offended to discover the social gulf which existed between the town and rural folk.

It had to do with money. Around 1900, students from outside Owen Sound paid ten to twelve dollars' tuition, depending on the class of certificate they wanted. Added to this would be the cost of books, boarding house fees, and train fare. As Agnes said: "When I saw how the daughters of the city people could afford so many things while it was an actual pinch for my people to send me to Owen Sound, I began to wonder, and reached the conclusion that the town and city people made their money easier than we did."[8] She saw that she and other boys and girls from the country were not as well dressed as the other young people. Even worse, she saw that many town boys and girls, and even some teachers, thought them inferior.

In an interview with the *Woodstock Daily Sentinel-Review* after her election to Parliament in 1921 she said: "I found that in the class room I was on an equality basis with anyone else in the class. But outside of school at social events, I was not their equal and I was made to feel it. That was because I was a farmer's daughter. I decided then, that I would, in my own small way, do what I could to better rural conditions."[9]

Later she told a reporter from the *Family Herald and Weekly Star* that when she went home from Collegiate

> *the sight of her grandmother's hands did something to her —
> they seemed to sear her soul. Those old hands were not soft and
> white like some hands she had seen there in town. They were all
> knotted and calloused. And her grandmother was such a wonder-
> ful woman . . . why had she not had the cultural, the educational,
> the money advantages of those other women! Why had she all her
> life to work so hard and receive so little material gain? Why*

Durham Road School, which Agnes attended from ages 12 to 14

Agnes during the time she attended Owen Sound Collegiate

were her own parents doing this? Bit by bit she reasoned it out —
it was just because they lived in the country; because they were
farmers — and farmers were not having fair play in the world! [10]

This struck Agnes as totally wrong and in years to come, not only farmers, but all disadvantaged people, were to benefit from her strong sense of fair play.

In the meantime, Agnes dealt with the perceived discrimination at school in her own way. When a teacher tripped over her outstretched feet and asked rhetorically, "Now, I wonder, Miss Macphail, why I tripped over your feet?" Agnes answered promptly: "Probably because your own are so large."

Shock and stifled laughter filled the room. Boys, in particular, who had felt their ears flattened for less, were impressed by her impudence. There was no record of her suffering any untoward consequences and the story became legendary in the school.

Agnes did well in her studies but after her first year decided to continue her schooling at Stratford where she boarded with a relative. The OSCI's anniversary year book states that "Agnes' strong will clashed with that of Principal [Thomas] Murray, and so she moved to Stratford to complete her secondary education before entering Normal School there."

"That could be," said a neighbor, "but I've always heard she went to Stratford because her friends Roy Fletcher, Bob Tucker and Hattie Coleman were going and she wanted to be with them."

Whatever the case, she graduated from Stratford Normal School in 1910 with a second-class teacher's certificate. She applied for her first job and "just in order to be safe I applied for five and was accepted for all five. That was no compliment to me; it was merely that teachers were scarce."

Her Normal School days had been enjoyable. Her interests had broadened and she was recognized by students, teachers and principal alike as an outstanding young woman. She could often be seen holding discussions with male students in the library. These discussions were not interrupted as they might have been with less serious students.

Pictures of the time show her oval-faced, serious, slim, with dark, wavy hair parted in the centre and often held at the back by a wide bow. She wears small steel-rimmed glasses that do not detract from her beautiful dark eyes. Her Sunday dresses are dark with high necks, long skirts and sleeves, and are usually adorned with a white lace collar, a brooch, a small corsage of cloth flowers or a long chain which falls below her small waist. There is a sweetness about her eyes and mouth.

Agnes taught first at Gowanlock's School, four miles east of Port Elgin; then at Kinloss, between Walkerton and Kincardine; later at Honeywood and Bothwell Corners; a few months at Oyen, Alberta; and finally at Sharon, near Newmarket, Ontario. She was offered town schools but felt she should work in the country. Of her teaching skills she said: "I do not now feel that I was any huge success as a teacher . . . at least not in the sense of pouring in facts." [11]

She took part in all community affairs, "entering heartily into everything that she felt was for the betterment of the community and farm home," and initiating many activities herself. Once she got a note from a pupil's mother saying: "Dere teacher, Julie can't go to school no more for Jimmy Jones kicked her in the stomach when her back was turned." [12] Agnes said nothing to either child but spent an evening with each family and as a result formed a neighborhood club which met once a week. Both families joined, their feud forgotten, and Agnes directed activities.

In this she was in her element. She liked to be in charge. "She would come to a meeting," said a friend, "and move people around like chessmen. She didn't want her audience to be scattered or to sit at the back. She'd tell them, by name, where to sit and they'd move."

Another friend agreed that Agnes thought she knew what was best for everyone. "When my father died, Agnes came to visit my mother and said: 'Now, Gerty, this house is too big for you. You'll have to move.'"

Years later, when she was in Parliament, a reporter figured that it must be "swell" to be Agnes Macphail because she was always certain she was right. In fact, he said, she was also "persuaded, convinced, positive and sure" she was right. "Swift intelligence rides upon a brow that is high, wide and handsome. Assurance moulds the chin. Determination sets the lips a thought too thinly. Self-confidence swaggers; only a little, but it does swagger; in the angular ease of a country woman's stride. Add a joy that neither eye-glasses nor pacifist principles can quench; the unmistakable joy of battle to light eyes the color of storm clouds. You can see at once that it's swell to be Agnes Macphail, joint leader of a new party. And right." [13]

Her self-confidence did not bother her friends.

Remember [said one], *if she'd been different — if she'd been soft and gentle — she'd never have been able to do what she did. We liked her and enjoyed listening to her talk about her schools. We would be cross when Bob or Roy came and took her away. She was kind-hearted. One time when we were little and mother was ill, she washed our kitchen floor. Then she went home, made two lemon pies and brought them back to us.* ["Didn't know she knew how to make pies," commented another friend.] *She didn't enjoy sitting around discussing babies and recipes. She wanted to be with people who talked politics.*

Agnes' sister Lilly agreed. In a CBC tape she said that at parties it was the custom for women to visit in one room, men in another, while the young people gathered in a third. Agnes was generally to be found with the men, "discussing such things as farm prices." Lilly would go after her and say, "Why don't you come in with the rest of us? We're playing cards." [14] But Agnes would generally stay with the men.

Now that Agnes had her own money she enjoyed spending it. In her first year she made $500 and "thought it was a tremendous amount of money." With her first pay cheque she bought gifts for her family and a new hat for herself. Her parents scolded her for her extravagance and reminded her that they expected her to help pay for her sisters' education. This Agnes did, fully repaying her father for the cost of her own education. Years later she told colleagues in the Legislature that in her day, "children of farmers were expected to pay their fathers back and it did not hurt anybody." [15]

She went home often for weekends, when she enjoyed buggy rides with her boy friends, dances and visits with relatives and friends.

Bob Tucker and Roy Fletcher were now medical students at Queen's University in Kingston. They too went home when their pocketbooks allowed, and both courted her. Eventually Bob became the more serious suitor.

Robert Tucker, a lifelong friend

Dark of eyes and hair like Agnes, he was tall and slim with a farm boy's large hands; serious, as were many children of pioneers, but with a ready twinkle in his eyes. He played the piano after a fashion and sang duets with his younger brother Jack at school and church concerts. They also spent many evenings singing with friends around the piano in neighborhood homes. No doubt Agnes was frequently one of the group who sang the sentimental and military songs popular at the time — "In the Gloaming," "After the Ball," "Comrades," "Tramp, Tramp, Tramp, the Boys Are Marching," "England Expects That Every Man This Day Will Do His Duty."

More conservative than Agnes, Bob was amused by Agnes' strong opinions and outspoken views, and if he did not always share them, he would say nothing to discourage them.

"Bob and Agnes were good friends," recalled Bob's brother. "She dropped into our house whenever she passed, which was pretty often. Our white horse turned automatically into the Macphail lane."

"Theirs [the Macphails'] was a very hospitable home and Bob visited there and she [visited] at the Tucker's who lived about a mile away," said Roy Fletcher. "At Collegiate, since Bob was ahead of her, he was, I suspect, her guide, philosopher and friend until she knew her way about, as he was mine also."

She and Bob, the "boyfriend of my youth," became engaged before he went overseas in World War I. In his little diary he often mentions "writing to Aggie." His first card was sent from Montreal on board the boat that was to take him and other members of the Twenty-first Battalion to England: "Arrived in Montreal 5:30 a.m. Turned out and went immediately to boat where our quarters were assigned us. Breakfast at 9 a.m. consisting of a little meat and bread with margarine. Dinner, soup and hash. Pretty punk. Supper ditto. Sent Mother and Aggie a card. The night is beautiful. The band is playing. Passed historic old Quebec and we all gazed at the lights as we passed."

Eventually the whole class of Queen's medical students that had joined up at the same time, was sent back to Canada to finish medical training.

Agnes got the news and dropped in on a friend. They sat in the kitchen, Agnes with her feet on the open oven door.

"Well, I guess I'll be getting married soon," she announced. "Bob is coming home."

But it was not to be. On his return Bob went to see his mother in Paisley before going to see Agnes and ostensibly this led to the breaking of the engagement.

In 1955, after the death of both Agnes and Bob, Dorothea Deans, a former Owen Sound *Sun Times* reporter, not realizing that Bob had died ("Strange, I heard so many people refer to him brightly and warmly that I just naturally presumed that he was here. . . ."), wrote asking for information on his early relationship with Agnes:

> Your name, Dr. Tucker, pops up constantly in Agnes' early years
> and appears in her own writings practically to the last. Letters to
> friends in her last years tell of visits with you and your wife at

*your home, and how you and she recount old memories with
laughter, and how your wife joins in. . . .*

*Now she was asked many times, particularly in her first
election campaign, if she had any beaux, any proposals. She
always laughed and passed it off. But, she kept old letters and I
know that she was a very popular young woman. . . .*

*I want to ask you directly if you would have any objections to
your name appearing in Agnes' biography. I would like to go
further and say that you are accepted among her contemporaries
and old school friends to this day as her chief beau. Her sisters
do not know what, if anything, came between you.*

Since what came between them was relatively minor, it is reasonable to
suspect that at least subconsciously Agnes had already rejected the idea of
marriage and that her interests had become too broad to confine herself to
one man. But as Deans said, the two remained lifelong friends and Agnes
would drop in on Bob and his wife, unannounced, generally alone, and stay
for a visit and a meal. That they enjoyed these visits was apparent in the
rapid-fire conversation interrupted by frequent gales of laughter. The visits
continued until Bob's death in 1948.

Agnes' interest in politics increased during her stay in the tiny hamlet of
Kinloss. This was due largely to the influence of her landlord, Sam Braden.
Braden's store stood at a crossroads a mile or so from Agnes' school and
was a gathering place for farmers of the area. The family lived over the
store, and Braden, a strong Liberal, often called Agnes downstairs to help
him debate his mainly Conservative neighbors. Agnes, too, was Liberal at
this time. She used to sit on the counter top, her tongue flying as fast as
her legs, which she swung back and forth in the excitement of the debate.

"One day the question of tariffs came up and Agnes realized her
ignorance of them," said friend and protégé James Palmer. "The farmers
laughed at her and ridiculed her, for they believed [the subject] was beyond
the ability of any woman. 'It was their laughter as much as anything else
that strengthened my determination and kept my nose to the fiscal grind-
stone,'" Agnes told Palmer. [16]

Liberal though he was, Braden taught Agnes to examine both sides of a
question before making a decision. "He taught me to read editorials in the
then *Globe* and the then *Mail* and by taking some central position between
them it would probably be the truth, and from that time to this I have
always read different opinions in different papers," Agnes told the House
years later.

Although her interest in politics was certainly stimulated in Kinloss, it
was not until several years later that she became actively involved, when
she was teaching at Pegg's School in Sharon, about forty miles from
Toronto.

It was here that she met John C. Ross, editor of the *Farmer's Sun*, the
newspaper of the United Farmers of Ontario (UFO). Ross introduced her to
public life in Canada. She had written a letter to the *Sun* on rural boarding
houses for school teachers. [17] The letter interested Mr. Ross, and further cor-
respondence and an interview followed. He persuaded her to speak on

behalf of UFO candidates, including his brother, D. M. Ross, the UFO candidate for North Oxford.

She made her first appearance on a political platform on October 10, 1919, when UFO President R. W. E. Burnaby asked her to speak on behalf of Sam Foote, the UFO candidate for North York. She was unprepared and answered: "Oh, I can't do that — I've never made a speech on a public platform." But then she thought: "They all say that — if this movement is to succeed, lots of us have to do things we don't want to do and have never done before." [18]

Sam Foote was the "'farmeriest farmer I ever saw — and I decided that if anything was to be told someone would have to go along with him,' since farmers as a class had little opportunity for self-development along the lines of public speaking." [19]

Her speech was roundly cheered, and from that time on she spoke almost every night of the campaign and taught during the day.

Just how quickly she became favorably known is indicated by the fact that in April, 1920, she was nominated in North York as the UFO candidate in the forthcoming election. Her opponent was no less a personage than the Honorable W. L. Mackenzie King, Leader of the Liberal Party. Agnes discreetly withdrew in favor of R. W. E. Burnaby, who must have been somewhat startled by his protégé's popularity. The *Globe* wondered facetiously whether Mr. King would have been gentlemanly enough to give up his seat to a lady as he had been taught to do, had she won. "But just how near Honorable Mr. King came to having his manners tested could only be estimated by those present who witnessed the enthusiastic reception given Miss Macphail Saturday," [20] said the *Globe*.

In December she spoke before a large audience when the UFO chose her, along with another woman and several men, to represent them at a Tariff Commission which was to be held in Toronto's City Hall. The Commission, headed by Canada's Minister of Finance, Sir Henry Drayton, had been touring Canada for three months, hearing delegations from different interests. Industrialists wanted high tariffs but farmers were convinced they needed low ones to enable them to sell their produce.

Agnes' speech, according to the *Toronto Star*, "enlivened proceedings" and "occasionally drew peals of laughter from her audience." She had kept her promise to study the tariff and now she was challenging Canada's Minister of Finance.

"'We need no more funny papers since the tariff commission began,' declared Miss Agnes C. Macphail, 'a plain farmer's daughter and proud of it,' who flailed the tariff and its supporters, even the representatives of the commission in semi-serious comic vein. . . [She told Sir Henry Drayton that it was the first time she had been in the presence of a real knight.] 'Farm women wear out early,' she said. 'Farm women are done at 50 years of age. . . . So hard is the tariff on the farmers that girls hesitate to marry their sons. I do,' she frankly admitted." [21]

On August 5, 1920, the *Dundalk Herald* reported an address she made at a UFO meeting in Orono. She said in part:

> *You can't get a house or a room in Toronto, while at the same time the country stands empty. On one concession in Proton Town-*

ship, not an isolated place by any means, there are 1000 acres on which are living today five men and four women, some of the men being over 50 and one of the women over 90. If in all Canada we had our people spread out as butter is spread on bread you would have but two people to the square mile, while in Toronto half a million people are crowded in narrow streets. We are building a colossal top on a very flimsy foundation. Some day there is going to be a crash and a lot of people are going to be hurt.

We have heard questions raised as to why farmers do not do this and do not do that, until we are sick and tired of the hearing. Why do not farmers have hot and cold water, baths and electric lights? Why? Because, speaking broadly, every farmer expects to sell his farm some day and when selling time comes, he knows he will have to throw the house in for nothing. It is not a case of "is the farm to be sold" but "when is it to be sold." Why this unanimous desire to sell? The answer is in the bent backs, calloused hands and limited rewards. To farm is the most arduous and most poorly paid of all occupations.

We were told that rural mail and rural telephones would check the exodus from the farm. We have these things today, but still the movement from the land is greater than ever. There is only one thing that will check the movement and that is stated in one word and that word is MONEY.

Farmers work 12 hours a day to feed people who work eight hours and still some people call that a square deal. Too many are eating 16 hours a day and working eight. Some who eat three meals a day do not work over one hour.

Still farmers are called profiteers! Profiteers! How can a farmer be called a profiteer when he goes to market with his hogs, cattle or wool and asks "How much?" How can he be called a profiteer when he goes to buy a pair of boots and asks, "What is the price?"

Farmers occupy the same position today economically that the Indian did years ago in trading his furs at the Hudson Bay post. The dealer, not the producer, fixes the price both in buying and selling. As the furs of the Indians were worth a great deal more than the trinkets received in exchange, so are the products of the farm worth more today than that which the farmers receive in exchange.

Addressing the women she said, "Do not let any minister, any lawyer, or even your own husband do your thinking for you. Use your own brains." [22]

Around this time the *Durham Review* suggested that Agnes Macphail would make the best representative for South East Grey in the coming election: "She was the product of their own district; she had championed the cause of the farmer for years, no man had done more for the country people; she, herself, had come from the farm and spent all her life in rural communities, therefore she knew whereof she spoke. . . . The idea of a woman sitting in the House of Commons was so new to them that at first some of her most ardent admirers laughed. At last it seemed to many of the farmers of Southeast Grey that the only person who could properly represent them . . . was: Agnes Macphail." [23]

Agnes herself must have felt comfortable with the idea, for she resigned her school in June, returned to Grey County, moved in with her Grandmother Campbell and began making speeches in the riding.

At Varney she told the crowd that the keynote of the farmers' movement was unselfishness and they would get out of it what they put into it. She gave figures on rural de-population and said curtly: "People don't run away from a gold mine." She pointed out that only one per cent of farmers made enough money to pay income tax.

The UFO believed in the League of Nations, a good relationship with the Mother Country and the immediate reduction of the tariff.

She criticized the school system and said: "We have no public school system [in the country]. We have a town system in the country." She stressed the importance of women's clubs and advised women to learn about the government of their country.

In reporting the speech, the *Durham Review* said she had a "good voice and platform manner ["She stood on the platform very erect with one hand fingering the inside of a wide belt she usually wore" — *Durham Chronicle*] and her grasp of public questions has few superiors in the riding, male or female."

Chapter II
Entering Politics
1921-1922

On September 26, 1921, at a farm-labor convention held in Durham Town Hall, Agnes Campbell Macphail was chosen UFO candidate for South East Grey in the federal election. The *Durham Review* said

> one hundred and fifty delegates were present — all men — from every part of the riding — and these men, out of at least 24 nominees, have chosen a woman as their representative. Truly the world do move.
>
> Miss Macphail spoke and opened with a jocular drive at the men because not a single woman delegate was present. Women had been given rights and the will of the people should be reflected in the assemblage. The issue in this election was not the tariff alone, but democracy. She had heard J. A. M. Armstrong in North York trying to fasten the cry of absolute free trade on the UFO and she was sure on polling day he would be knocked into the initials of his name.
>
> She was going to let her name go to the vote, a statement greeted by applause, as previous speakers had been "reserving" that decision. "I am going to let my name stay for the sake of the women who are here today. I will not contribute to any fund, national, religious or otherwise more than I gave in private life. To do so would be buying your vote before I go and if I could stoop to that, I might sell it after." She added: "I will not kiss babies nor smile at the men" — after a pause — "more than I have done as a private citizen" — a sally that caused a hearty laugh. Again stating her firm adherence to the (UFO) motto "Equal rights to all, special privilege to none" she sat down amid applause.[1]

Years later, discussing her nomination with the *Family Herald*, she said: "It didn't seem that I had the ghost of a chance along with those ten men, but, my — it was exciting!"[2] In fact it was the greatest thrill of her political life, she said in 1936. She told the *St. Louis Post-Dispatch*:

> I began to lead; on the seventh I won. A solid block of Proton Township delegates — from the land of my fathers — swung the convention. I telephoned the folks at home. When I told my father that I had been nominated, he said simply, "I am sorry." But in the campaign which followed and throughout my public life, my parents have been with me heart and soul.
>
> Many of the delegates almost had heart failure when in the cool of the next morning they realized that they had chosen a woman. "Are there no men left in South East Grey?" one indignant neighbor asked a delegate. The atmosphere grew chilly. At the first executive committee meeting it was positively frigid. Some even suggested the

Agnes at age 31

Durham Town Hall, where Agnes was nominated in 1921

calling of another convention. I was against that. The campaign warmed things up. The committee and the defeated candidates were magnificent. They worked like Trojans. Loyalty to a cause held us together. Curiosity brought the people out.[3]

Agnes was opposed by Robert J. Ball, Conservative, a manufacturer from the town of Hanover, and by Walter Hastie, Liberal, a well-known farmer from the Township of Egremont. When Hastie was selected as the Liberal candidate, the *Owen Sound Sun Times* wrote: "It is tonight conceded, even in quarters friendly to the UFO, that his acceptance of the nomination probably spells disaster for Miss Agnes Macphail, who in a two-party contest stood a good chance of securing the seat from sitting member R. J. Ball."[4]

But Agnes had just begun to fight. Interviewed after her victory, she explained how she organized her campaign. The riding consisted of nine townships, two towns and five incorporated villages. The UFO had thirty-seven clubs and one labor union within the riding, and an organization with a supervisor was set up in every polling subdivision. Each week they put advertisements in local newspapers, posted bills of meetings and used the telephone a great deal. "I distributed three hundred special numbers of the Farmer's Sun, and there were no halls that were large enough to hold the crowds. . . . I mounted a map of the riding on the lid of a box," Agnes told the *Toronto Daily Star*, "and put in a large black-headed pin at each place where I held a meeting, and the putting of these pins, and covering a large part of the map was the joy of my life."[5]

On October 7, 1921, the *Durham Review* reported that Miss Macphail had fired "the first gun in the campaign." The *Review* said:

> *The Town Hall was filled on Thursday afternoon last to listen to Miss Macphail and J. J. Morrison, the well known UFO Secretary in Toronto. The meeting was announced only by bills a few days previous; the day was a disagreeable one, yet in Durham where no club (UFO) exists, the hall was filled.*
>
> *In becoming a candidate Miss Macphail had only one object, to assist in cleaning up public affairs along the lines of honesty, economy, truthfulness. She had heard strange stories were going around; she assured them that on her part there would be no personalities.*
>
> *The issue to her was, shall we send to Ottawa a Parliament unbiased, free from malign influence and wholly bent on doing the people's will.*
>
> *Both Morrison and Miss Macphail spoke at length. When the meeting dispersed, not a few claimed that the speech of Miss Macphail was the better of the two.*

Later that month at a meeting in Hanover Agnes promised that if elected she would not take her full salary. The *Hanover Post* reported:

> *Miss Macphail was warmly greeted as she stepped forward to speak. Right off the bat she expressed her intention if elected not to take one cent over $2,500 for her services instead of the members' indemnity of $4,000 per session. "The rest is 'dirty money' — I won't touch it," she said and added that she took this stand not merely to win approval. The country was "up to its ears" in debt and Parliament*

should set the example of economizing and reducing expenditures.
She felt that a Member of Parliament should keep in touch with his
or her constituents, not only during recesses but also during the
session.

Gossip said she wore $14 boots. She said: "In the first place I
haven't any $14 boots and in the second place, if I did have them, it
would be nobody's business but my own." [6]

Fifty-five meetings were held in the seven-weeks campaign and Agnes spoke at all of them, "always for an hour or an hour and a quarter." She had little outside help but the meetings always had musical entertainment and sometimes recitations. "We indulged in no personalities," she said, "and asked no one for a vote. We rested the cause on its merits absolutely."

She toured her constituency in an old Ford car which she said would take her "either to the House of Commons or the House of Refuge." Often the car broke down. Once she and her companion walked "in the blackness of a starless night" almost five miles to her destination. Another time her car's radiator froze and she waited in a farm house for hours until it thawed. Again, she had a narrow escape from death when the driver of her car had to swing it into a ditch to avoid being hit by a train. They continued to Mount Forest where she spoke on behalf of T. A. Crerar, Leader of the Progressives.

Formed in 1920, the Progressive Party was a coalition of Ontario, Western and New Brunswick farmers, and a few disenchanted Liberals who opposed the high tariffs favoured by the Liberal Party. Through her federal years Agnes describes herself variously as UFO, Progressive — and whether or not under the Progressives — as an Independent, voting always according to her own conscience.

In the case of the frozen radiator, Agnes exulted that they lost nothing by the experience, "for when the votes in that locality were counted we had two hundred and two; the Liberals seven and the Conservative candidate twenty-three."

She had enemies, however, and after the near-miss with the train, certain reporters sent a telegram to Mr. Edward Beatty, President of the Canadian Pacific Railway, and asked him to fire the engineer because "he missed hitting Miss Macphail."

A serious challenge came from within the UFO itself when one of its directors, John Cooper of Hanover, resigned because Agnes was a member of the Church of Jesus Christ of Latter Day Saints.

In a letter to the *Hanover Post* in November, 1921, Cooper wrote that he was tendering his resignation as a member of the UFO-LP political organization of South East Grey. He said that the interests of the UFO were still his interests and he was resigning "entirely and only" because the UFO candidate was a member of the Church of Latter Day Saints. He could not give "any such a one my support in this election campaign."

The UFO's President promptly defended Agnes: "[The Directors have] confidence in the honesty, sincerity and ability of our candidate, notwithstanding the different view taken by our disgruntled ex-director." [7]

Sermons were preached on the subject, and letters to the editor appeared regularly in riding papers. R. H. Ledingham of Durham wrote that he felt it a cowardly business to "run down the religion of any denomination" and said that if she were a candidate "in the interest of the manufacturer and the moneyed men, her religion would never have been mentioned." He went on: "Just think of all the slandering statements made against her when she should be upheld especially by the women of Canada, when she is trying to make a road [for them] through the forest." [8]

The controversy disturbed Agnes because she wanted to concentrate on legitimate issues and run a clean campaign, free from personal remarks. She was raised a Presbyterian but became a member of the Church of Latter Day Saints because that was the faith of her beloved Grandmother Campbell. In her essay "My Ain Folk," Agnes tells how her Campbell ancestors became associated with the Latter Day Saints.

> [My] *descendants might still be living in Ayrshire if they had not decided to grow potatoes. The Presbyterian Church then regarded these "imports of heathendom," sponsored by Catholic clergy and nobles, as the cause of palsy, scurvy, leprosy, and what not? The Campbells grew fat and healthy on the forbidden diet, and made money selling the "devil's tubers" to the near-by garrison. When the parson refused to baptize James' grandson, the parents took little Tommy to the garrison chaplain and stopped contributing to the church. . . . A distrust of sanctimonious intolerance became a family inheritance and no doubt persuaded the Campbells of later days to accept the simple evangelical doctrine of the Latter Day Saints when missionaries brought it, purged of its undesirable features, to the neglected pioneers in the Canadian bush.*

In later years Agnes joined the United Church and taught Sunday school there. But she always felt the Church of Latter Day Saints was the church with the greatest social conscience and during this, her first election campaign, defended it with youthful fervour.

Ceylon, Ontario,
November 11, 1921

To Whom It May Concern: —

> *In reply to the charge made by Mr. John Cooper, R. R. No. 2, Hanover, I wish to say that Mr. Cooper has been throwing cold water ever since I was nominated — first, on my manner of speaking; second, on account of the fact that I was a woman, and third, because he feared I was a Mormon. I only hope that Mr. Cooper's concern for our dear Homeland, Canada, is as real as he would have us think.*
> *Chief Justice Armour of the Canadian Court, with other Judges concurring, said when an attempt was being made to confuse the Reorganized Church of Jesus Christ of Latter Day Saints with the Mormon Church of Utah — "I have read the evidence over, and find nothing contrary to the doctrine of Christ in the teaching of the Reorganized Church of Jesus Christ of Latter Day Saints. The great trouble is the Latter Day Saints' doctrine is Christian in the highest sense and the rest of the religious world is opposed to them because they (the Saints) cling so closely to the Bible. It seems as though it is jealousy, not justice that moves the action in this case. These people teach that one man should have one wife only, and they stand for*

that. I am surprised to see this trial; it seems as if some of the Christians are wanting to go back to the dark ages; they would have us try heresy here. This is not prosecution — but persecution."

Again in Canadian Court in 1893 the judgment of the Court was delivered by Armour, C. J., as follows: "There is nothing contrary to Christianity in the tenets of this body. It is true they have something supplemental to the Bible, but that is the case with every . . . denomination. The Church of England has its creeds and the Presbyterian Church its confession. That does not make the church an anti-Christian one. The fundamental law of the country makes no distinction between churches or denominations. Every person is at liberty to worship his Maker in the way he pleases. We have, or ought to have, in the country, perfect freedom of speech and perfect freedom of worship. Conviction quashed."

Blessed are ye, when men shall revile you, and persecute you and shall say all manner of evil against you for my sake." St. Matthew 5:11.

It has been the proud boast of the U.F.O. that in it people of every race, colour and creed can meet on terms of perfect equality.[9]

Yours Happily,

Agnes C. Macphail

Throughout the campaign Agnes continued to do her share of the housework and always made sure the 145 Wyandotte chickens were fed before leaving for a political meeting. Most often she wore a sailor hat, a blue serge suit and a light cloth coat. When the weather turned cold she wore a man's fur-lined overcoat, a tam, warm woolen gloves, rubbers and spats. Various newspapers described her:

The Family Herald and Weekly Star reported:

She is quite tall and dark — hazel eyes behind horned-rimmed glasses; she has a good head of dark hair — unbobbed, waved and worn back from her forehead, giving the impression of rather a long shaped head.[10]

The *Woodstock Daily Sentinel Review* said:

When the writer looked for her as the train pulled into the Grand Trunk Station on Friday morning, only one person stepped off the train. She was a woman of slight stature, dressed neatly and smartly in a fawn coat of attractive design, and wearing a black velour tailored hat. . . . Her back was turned, so the writer looked again at the coaches of the train, to see if any other woman would descend. But no other came, so he came to the conclusion that this slip of a woman was the woman about whom all Canada was talking, and so it was. . . . She is . . . deep-chested and strongly made, so that the reserve of physical strength is greater than appears at first to the casual observer.

Miss Macphail is 30 years old, but looks rather more mature in features. Her hard life on the farm and her struggle for education and for advancement have told on her, and already a few streaks of grey are appearing in her hair. . . . None of her published photo-

graphs do her justice. At the close of the meeting which she ad-
dressed at Princeton on Friday evening, one young man was heard
to remark to a companion: "Why, she's good looking." Miss Mac-
phail is decidedly good looking. Her features have none of the
severity which seems to be apparent from her published portraits. . . .
Her eyes have a kindly expression, and in them there is a good-
natured twinkle which never seems to leave them. Her forehead is
high and wide . . . the nose is well formed and straight and her lips
have a happy knack of curving into the faintest suggestion of a smile
when least expected. Her chin is firm . . . and the whole aspect is a
pleasing one.

[She dressed] very plainly, but neatly and becomingly. She can in
no way be classed as dowdy. . . . her taste in clothes is excellent,
and she knows how to dress smartly without in any way following the
example of the ultra-fashionable.

Agnes' own opinion of fashion appeared in the same interview: "The fashions of the so-called smart women of today are a positive disgrace. They dress for the North Pole from the knees up and for the equator from the knees down. I have seen women in Toronto wearing furs and Hudson seal coats which came to their knees, and below that they had nothing but a pair of transparent silk stockings and a pair of summer pumps. They spend a thousand dollars on their coats and probably before spring they will pay as much again in doctors' bills." [11]

The campaign continued with almost no outside help. However, riding newspapers enthusiastically reported her activities. The United Farmers inserted advertisements, explaining their platform, and Agnes herself inserted a personal message.

A UFO advertisement in the *Durham Review*, October 27, 1921, asked:

WHY IS THE UFO IN POLITICS?

1. To establish the personal responsibility of the elector
2. To promote honest debate of public questions
3. To establish honesty and economy in public business
4. To secure fair treatment for farmers as producers (lifting embar-
   goes, finding markets, lowering freight rates and duties, etc.)
5. To establish a fair representation for Agriculture
6. To insist on the fulfillment of pledges made by governments
7. To secure real responsible government — not government by
   Orders-in-Council

Our motto is: EQUAL RIGHTS TO ALL — SPECIAL PRIVILEGES
TO NONE

And she placed an advertisement in the *Durham Review* on December 1, 1921:

Ceylon, Ontario, November 28, 1921

PROGRESSIVES

You have done a great work. All Canada has been stirred as never before. But there is one more battle to fight, one more victory to win. The date is December 6th and the sword is the ballot. Vote early and vote right and by 6 p.m. our country will have been redeemed from the greedy hand of the spoiler.

At the height of the campaign, twelve days before the election, Agnes' Grandmother Campbell died. This was one of the great sorrows of Agnes' life. Her beloved grandmother had been deprived of yet another joy — seeing her favorite granddaughter elected to Canada's Parliament.

The *Durham Review* reported:

> There died on Thursday of last week, November 24th, after only two days' illness, Mrs. Jean (Black) Campbell, wife of the late Jock Campbell, concession 15, Proton, aged 91 years. The funeral was held on Sunday to the Latter Day Saints Cemetery.
>
> Mrs. Campbell was born in Scotland, October 31, 1830, and there spent her girlhood. Sixty-nine years ago she married John Campbell and shortly after set sail on an immigration ship for Canada. Both found employment on the Grand Trunk Railway — Mr. Campbell on the road and Mrs. Campbell in camp. Later, they and two sons came to Proton. . . . Two daughters and four sons were born here. She was of a bright and cheerful disposition and the smile still on her face in death . . . will be a sweet remembrance to her family. [12]

A year earlier Agnes described her grandparents' lives in an article in the *Farmer's Sun*. She told of how her Grandmother Campbell and a sister-in-law, Lizzie Campbell, walked with their husbands eighteen miles through thick bush to reach new homes in Proton, the men driving oxen hitched to jumpers and carrying all their goods with them. "The women walked and carried a baby each and drove a cow and five pigs. One of the babies was only nine weeks old."

Her grandmother thought the new shanty a good one. However, the chimney smoked so she "tore it down. She then dug a hole in the ground and with her bare feet tramped water into the clay until she had a suitable mortar, then alone she rebuilt it and it never smoked again."

There was only one window, and "the house was so dark that the sewing was done by the fireplace where the light came in through the chimney. . . . [A] man made a frame for another six-paned window and Grandma got the glass for it . . . but she could never get the men to saw out the logs and fit it in." With the help of her three-year-old son she finally "got the logs cut out and the window in."

The women made thimbles by "getting a 'thumb' of cedar, boring a hole with a half-inch auger and punching holes over the outside with an awl. For pins they used the 'jags' of the hawthorn and they made their first brooms out of birch, cut fine and tied with strips of leather wood [the bark of a bush by that name]."

Her grandmother worked in the field, raking and binding, often with a baby strapped to her back. "When she could cover her shadow with one big step as she stood with her back to the sun, she knew it was time to go in and prepare dinner."

"The rugged honesty, the devotion to duty and the real Christianity of these early settlers makes us look very small. We do not realize how great is the debt of gratitude we owe them. . . . They built the foundation of the country [strong] and true, and if we sit around and let 'captains of industry' so undermine it that this land for which they toiled so hard is taken out of our hands by the fiscal policy of this Dominion, we are not worthy of our heritage." [13]

Years later Agnes explained to an American reporter how her love for her ancestors and the land inspired her to do something about it: "My intense love of agriculture is the heritage of 10 generations of farm folk. It is not a thing assumed; it is part of my life. My parents are poor. My farming ancestors in Scotland were poor. I feel that it is my duty to do something for the farmer. My inspiration has been the thought of my two wonderful grandmothers, wives of farmers who fought the Canadian wilderness. They were great women. They were pioneers, yet they did not get the fruits of their labors. As a young girl, I decided that there must be something wrong with an economic system which withheld the comforts from those who toiled." [14]

On December 6, 1921, Agnes Campbell Macphail was elected to the Fourteenth Parliament of Canada on the Progressive ticket in South East Grey. She had a majority of 2,575, the largest Progressive majority in Ontario.

Agnes learned of her victory in the Macphail farm home where friends filled the lamp-lit kitchen and took down results over the telephone.

The Liberals under Mackenzie King had a bare majority in the new Parliament with 116 seats. The Progressives under T. Alexander Crerar had sixty-five seats, and Meighen's Conservatives, who had been swept from power, had fifty. There were two Independents.

There was no mention of Agnes Macphail's historic election on the front page of the *Toronto Globe*. On page six under the heading "Old Faces and New" it reported, "The House gets a real thrill through the election of Miss Agnes Macphail in South East Grey, the first woman to enter the Canadian House of Commons. Miss Macphail carried on a remarkable campaign, being exceptionally capable on the platform and being in request in many constituencies." [15] At the bottom of the same page was a short item headed: "Ontario Gives Parliament First Canadian Woman M.P."

There were few facts regarding the new member; they did not know her age, "one good reason being that the lady has not figured among those listed in the *Parliamentary Guide* of the *Canadian Who's Who*." Most dailies did not interview her at the time.

Commenting on this "astigmatism" of Canadians towards their own, the *Beaver* of November 7, 1929, noted that the editor of the *Cleveland News* had learned that a school teacher was going to run for Parliament:

> He sent a special representative to Durham, to report the nomination — which was more than some Ontario dailies, that were supposed to be enterprising, thought of doing, even though Miss MacPhail was the first woman candidate for the House of Commons.
> The report . . . praised the young woman, in anticipation of whose advent multitudes came to Durham, and so overcrowded

the Town Hall that recourse had to be made to the skating rink, which, on the a cold day had to be warmed by platform and people. There the school teacher put it all over the old-line party men, who soon saw that it was not they the concourse had come to hear.

The "Cleveland News" editor realized that something new had entered Canadian public life; and steadily followed the career of the Parliamentary neophyte. He also followed . . . the Canadian reaction to this new portent. One day he asked his Canadian representative to get pictures and reading material about the rising apostle of feminine wisdom in Canadian national affairs. "If we had such a personality in our political life," he said, "we should make much of her. But your papers seem to ignore her, as if she had no distinctive quality. Can you explain the Canadians' seeming indifference toward their own eminent people? This girl is full of personality, brains, and statesmanship — and courage. Why don't your newspapers give her her due? Is there some sort of a blight on Canadian patriotism?" [16]

Not in South East Grey! Riding newspapers like the Durham Review were jubilant. They had sent the "first and only lady M.P. in Canada" to the Dominion Parliament and they were pleased and proud.

The *Durham Review* reported: "The uncertainty is over; the victory is decisively won and the honors go to the Maid of Ceylon, now Miss Agnes C. Macphail, M.P."

At the victory celebration, supporters in the Durham Town Hall listened politely to various speakers, "but," said the *Review*,

expectations were fixed on another speaker who was looked for from the east — Miss Macphail herself, and she did not disappoint them. At a quarter to ten her well-known figure appearing in the doorway amid the surging crowd on stairs and landing was the signal for a great outburst of cheering and no warmer welcome was ever accorded a victor in a political contest in South East Grey.

She had come by car with father, mother, two sisters and other friends. When they left Ceylon, her majority stood about 400. When they reached Durham it had grown to over 2000. She was allowed time to rest a little, the interval being taken up with hearing returns, and songs from Mr. Wm. Rammage whose "Man Behind The Plough" suited the audience. The way the audience joined in "Rule Britannia" which followed was refreshing.

Great applause again greeted her as she came to the front of the platform. "The long lane has at last been turned," she said and thanked all and sundry for the warmth of the welcome. "I was coming to Durham whether I won or lost. . . ." She admitted disappointment in returns for the province but believed if the Progressives numbered even 30 to 50 and stood firmly together they would accomplish good for the country. She did not want them to congratulate her, but "I must congratulate you on a magnificent victory." The many friends who stood by her in the "little trouble" (the disagreement over her religion) she would never forget. "I will endeavour to represent all the people of South East Grey, town or country, with fairness along the line of our slogan — Equal rights to all — Special privilege to none. No one through me at Ottawa will get special privilege."

She asked them not to let the interest awakened in this election die — keep it up. Everybody follow the doings of the House at Ottawa and the discussions of public questions. She rejoiced that from their standpoint the election had been fought absolutely clean. If the Progressives had been the largest party in the new House they would have placed on the statute book a law to disclose where funds came from and where they went. (Her own campaign funds amounted to about $600. "Of these expenses I became liable for one-third and the United Farmers for two-thirds. We got our funds in one dollar bill subscriptions.") With thanks again for the warmth of her reception she retired amid applause.[17]

Her parents' reaction was restrained. Her father said that his campaign job — "keeping the fire on at night to have the house warm for the return of his busy daughter" — was over.

"I'm sure you're proud of her."

"Yes, I'm proud of the way people stuck by her. And the mother is equally appreciative."[18]

A reporter from the *Woodstock Sentinel Review* was also sure her parents were proud of her. Agnes answered: "Oh, I think they are, but they have never said anything about it to me. They have never discussed my election or my campaign, but they are Scotch, and the Scotch are not given much to praising their own children."

She told the *Review* that she did not intend to try to set the House on fire.

I have no intention of doing anything sensational. I am a newcomer and I am going to keep quiet until I learn the ropes and know exactly the proper forms of Parliamentary procedure. If there are going to be mistakes made by new members, I prefer to have someone else make them, and not myself. But I am going to try to set one precedent in the House and that is to introduce into Parliament a simplicity, a sincerity, and an honesty which have not heretofore existed there. The old parties might as well have been represented by rubber stamps. All that was really necessary in the old system was a leader for the parties, with the names and the photographs of the members at their benches, and then, when the party whip cracked, then they came in to record their votes. I tell you, there is no party whip that can crack loud enough to make me jump. I intend to do my own thinking, instead of having the party leader do it for me.

Proposals had been made that the Progressives join the Liberal Party but Agnes was determined to remain a Progressive. This determination stayed with her during her years in Parliament when she was offered every post in Cabinet — except that of Prime Minister and Minister of Finance — if she would switch her allegiance and join the Liberals.

"If Mr. Crerar decides to join hands with Mackenzie King and if he is the man I think he is, he won't, then he can't take the Progressives with him. He belongs to us, and we do not belong to him. If he joins the Liberals, we will simply elect a new leader and carry on as the Progressive group. And even if the Progressives go over with him, I will remain independent, even if I am the only independent member of the house. I have no use for Mackenzie King, and never did have any use for him. I believe honestly that if the Progressives join hands with the Liberals, it means that the Progressives are doomed to extinction" — a prophetic statement, as it turned out.

The *Review* asked how it felt to be the first woman elected to Parliament and suggested she would be in great demand socially.

"Why should being elected M.P. make any difference to me? I am just the same person I was before. Life will go on just the same as ever, only I may have to work a little harder than I have ever done . . . . I am going there to work, and I am going to have nothing to do with the social side. I wonder if an invitation to visit with the Governor-General amounts to a command?" she asked with a little twinkle in her eye and the suggestive curve on her lips.

"I will have to be careful. . . . I know I am no foolish young girl, but I will be watched by all the people of the country and until I find my level in Ottawa, I must walk warily."

The *Review* said that Miss Macphail was richly endowed with good common sense. It said that she knew she would not be able to make political history all at once, but she had one aim and that was to be worthy of the expectations of the women of Canada and to act in such a manner in the House that it would not be long before she had other women there "to help her fight the battles of womanhood." [19]

Deluged with invitations to address meetings, Agnes visited Ottawa for the first time in January, 1922, while campaigning in the area for other UFO candidates. She registered at the Russell Hotel and then went to see the Parliament buildings.

The *Ottawa Journal* reported that while she was impressed with the buildings and "agreed that the dignity of the state must be maintained to a certain extent," still she found them "very lavish." She wished that all the people of the country might have such comfort as had been arranged in the new buildings. Her own private room in the House had not been chosen and Miss Macphail said she had no indication where it would be.

When Premier King heard that Miss Macphail was visiting the House he left his rooms in order to welcome her with cordiality. Col. H. W. Bowie, Sergeant-at-Arms, did the honors and personally showed the new woman member distinctive features of the building. [20]

Agnes in front of the Parliament Buildings,
1922

Chapter III
First Years in Parliament
1922-1925

The Fourteenth Parliament of Canada opened on March 8, 1922, with a new Governor General (Lord Byng of Vimy), a new Prime Minister (Mackenzie King) and a new Speaker (Honorable Rodolphe Lemieux). The first week, as members spoke in reply to the Governor General's address, they welcomed Agnes to the House. The welcomes varied — formal, patronizing, self-serving. Some expressed expectations that would daunt a Churchill.

Arthur Meighen, Leader of the Conservatives, said:

> I add especially a word of welcome to the first lady member of the House of Commons. The last Parliament, by a very large majority, almost by a unanimous decision, conferred the franchise on women and conferred on them as well the candidature for the Commons of Canada. To be the recipient of the first expression of confidence by a constituency is a historic honor and I know I express the feelings of all, when I put into words the hope that she will vindicate the confidence that the last Parliament has reposed in her sex, do credit to herself and to the constituency that she represents.

Prime Minister Mackenzie King added:

> May I also, Mr. Speaker, join with the right honorable friend (Meighen) in welcoming to this Parliament the lady member who has come to us from South East Grey. I could not but think that my right honorable friend's remarks would have been more felicitous had he not been a member of a government which at a previous election denied to a very large proportion of the women of this country the right of the franchise. It is still more unfortunate that among the women of this country who were denied that privilege and right was the honorable member for South East Grey who is sitting in this House of Commons tonight. My right honorable friend has at last received his answer from the women of this country to the action which disenfranchised such a large percentage of their number in the election of 1917.

(Women whose next-of-kin were soldiers on active duty had been given a vote in 1917. In 1918 the franchise was extended to all women who already had a vote in provincial elections.)

R. J. Woods, Dufferin, who was like Agnes a newcomer to the House, and who referred to himself as "a member from the back concessions of rural Ontario," said:

> It is gratifying to me and I believe to a great many people in this Dominion to know that in the election campaign which terminated on the sixth day of December last, women of this country had an oppor-

tunity to cast their ballot. I think we in this country were very slow in coming to the point where we recognized the worth of the women of our land. I think we were very slow in granting them the franchise and according them their proper place as citizens of this great Dominion. They contributed no less a part than the men in the construction and pioneer life of this country. Many of them came to Canada from the Old Land when this country was a wilderness and they helped their husbands hew out a home and raised families which were a credit to this Dominion. They contributed their part in the home life and also in the social-religious activities of the community. And yet for years and years they were deprived of their franchise. But at last the women have been accorded their proper place as citizens of this country and I join with the previous speakers in expressing gratification that the House is today honored with the presence of a lady member, the honorable member for South East Grey.

Thomas E. Ross, North Simcoe, gave her a half-hearted welcome:

In the first place I would like to refer to the fact that we have with us in this Parliament the first lady member of the House of Commons of this Dominion of Canada. . . . I am glad to know that the young lady member of South East Grey belongs to this large Progressive group of which I myself am proud to be a member. I consider that is as it should be, owing to the fact that the rights of our Canadian womanhood have been won for them by the organized farmers of Canada. The honor for bringing this about is due to the Canadian Council of Agriculture; it was through the pressure that they brought to bear that our Canadian womanhood at last received what I always contended was only their just right of which they had been deprived so long.

And C. H. Dickie, Nanaimo, said:

As regards the lady member who represents South East Grey, I hope she will find political life pleasant and will exercise a refining influence on our assembly. . . . I may say that a great many of us in the West did not at one time view with pleasure the granting of the franchise to women . . . we thought, perhaps in an old-fashioned way, that it might detract from their charm if they entered the field of politics. We believed that the sex for whom we have so much admiration and love were not temperamentally fitted to cope with the intricacies and intrigue of public life and at that time we would rather have seen these engaged in an occupation less open to unpleasant influences.[1]

In spite of the public welcome, resentment was never far from the surface and Agnes was only too aware of it. She confessed to James Palmer that her first session was a miserable time. "I was intensely unhappy. Some of the members resented my intrusion. Others jeered at me, while a very few were genuinely glad to see a woman in the House. . . ."

"Everywhere she went she was on display, and was pointed out and discussed and dissected until eventually . . . she lost some 20 pounds," said Palmer.

Ottawa women cut her. She was not invited to a banquet for the British M.P. the Duchess of Atholl. The Duchess was so indignant that Prime Minister King arranged a luncheon where the two could meet.[2]

Mrs. M. A. Hamilton, a British Labour Member, who met Agnes at the League of Nations in Geneva in 1929, told Thelma Williams of the *Zontian* that when Agnes first went to the Commons, "opposition to her was extreme; criticism of her unjust and continuous. The men resented deeply the fact that another sanctity had been invaded."[3]

Arthur Hawkes, writing in the *Beaver*, said, "To some extent it was fashionable to discount the first female Canadian M.P. The discounting was done, though not consciously, because she was a woman; because she was an innovator; and because she had the courage to think, and say what she thought."[4]

Looking back on her early days in Parliament, Agnes told the *St. Louis Post Dispatch*: "A bouquet of roses welcomed me to my desk when I first entered the House. . . . Those roses, I thought, were a kindly thought, and I wondered who sent them. The name on the card meant nothing to me. I discovered later that some unlucky bachelor, sure that I would be defeated had bet roses against a new hat. He lost his bet. These ironical roses were emblematic of my reception to a House hitherto sacred to men."[5]

"When I was first elected, everything I said was wrong; everything I wore was wrong; everything I did was wrong, to hear comments about them," she told a Boston paper. "Bouquets were not thrown at me because I was the only woman in the House. Brickbats were what I got. The men did not want me in Parliament and the women hadn't put me there. You can imagine how they felt when one morning they woke and found a girl from the country had been elected and they hadn't had anything to do about it. Men and women were both mad because they did not know anything about me. I had entered as an Independent and everybody was critical. The papers were full of it."

She had come to Ottawa, young and idealistic, with excitement barely restrained at "meeting for the first time the men whose names [were] familiar in every household of the Dominion — Mackenzie King, Meighen, Bennett, Geo. Graham, Fielding." When she first met them as fellow members "it seemed," she said, "as if one were meeting Plato or Ruskin."[6] What a let-down to find that they were ordinary individuals with opinions and characteristics which she neither shared nor admired.

Nor could she understand the hostility she met, particularly from female reporters.

At a reception given in Ottawa for Lady Astor, Britain's first female member of the House of Commons, Agnes gave her a rose from her small corsage. That night she was pleased to see that Lady Astor still wore the rose while speaking to a large gathering in the Russell Theatre. Her pleasure was spoiled the next day when she read a report of the incident in the *Ottawa Journal*: "Agnes Macphail, who attended the reception for Lady Astor yesterday, was the proud possessor of a dozen American Beauty roses and generously gave Lady Astor one."

Commenting on the incident, Agnes said:

> It seemed strange to me and it does still, that women who had a pen in their hands or who had the public ear in any way, used it in those early days to make my life more difficult. They didn't know me; it couldn't have been any personal dislike. What was it then? Even if

I did things they were displeased with, I at least had opened a door which had always until then been closed to all women. Surely that fact alone should have arrested their criticism and called out their sympathy. In the women of the farms it did.

I am sure that my plain serge suit, my horn-rimmed glasses and my prim attitude frightened a good many of the members. . . . I did not think I could mix in the social life without weakening my convictions. I had not learned the small talk by which a clever politician says little and learns much. I was determined to do my duty at whatever sacrifice I thought necessary. I know now that this was the wrong attitude. If one's convictions are not strong enough to withstand the social atmosphere they are weak indeed. [7]

Pictured on the steps of the Parliament building soon after her arrival in Ottawa, she wore the fabled blue serge dress. It hung several inches below her brown coat. The coat was belted loosely and its hem was slightly down at the right front. She held an envelope-style purse and obviously new gloves. Her straw off-the-face hat had a stitched and veiled brim and concealed most of her dark curly hair. She stood in the winter sunshine in sturdy Oxfords, a tenuous smile on her face. Sweetly and vulnerably unfashionable on the outside, she was soon to show that she was years ahead of her colleagues in her social ideas.

The House of Commons has been referred to as a battlefield where one must come well prepared to fight for one's beliefs, and as a football game where cabinet ministers carry the ball and the speaker is the referee. "It's a fight. It's war," said one member. Most approach their first speech with fear and trembling — some put it off indefinitely. The ornate surroundings, the formality, the traditions — everything conspires to intimidate.

Agnes herself said that a spirit of awe and timidity hung over the House, and when she got up to ask a simple question she was afraid her heart would go out of her mouth. This did not keep her from speaking. She set forth her ideas with confidence, and colleagues who tried to patronize her were subjected to withering sarcasm. "She lit into people in a way to rip their hide," said Wilfred Eggleston, Director of Carleton College School of Journalism. [8]

Parliament was open only three weeks when Agnes first rose to speak. It was the first of many speeches on women's rights that she was to make in the House. The debate concerned a change in the Election Act which would permit foreign-born women married to Canadian men to vote without making special application. Agnes spoke against it because she wanted women to be treated as independent persons and not as the personal property of men:

Mr. Speaker, I think that what women really want today is perfect equality with men and therefore if the striking out of section 29 of the Dominion Elections Act in its entirety does not confer upon women perfectly and entirely equal rights with men, then I think it is not going far enough. To me it would seem that if a woman were herself a naturalized Canadian it would not matter whom she married, or whether she was married at all, because she would still be permanently a Canadian, a naturalized Canadian.

On the other hand, if she were not a naturalized Canadian herself, it would not matter whom she married, or whether she was married

*or not — she would not be a Canadian citizen. If that is not true
then women must simply be deemed to be part of the goods and
chattel of men — she is not an individual at all. . . .*

*I think that in the very few remarks I have made I have voiced the
opinion of Canadian women. I think women just want to be individuals, as men are individuals — no more and no less. And so I would
like to see that principle embodied in the law, rather than that a
woman should be made a citizen by marriage to a man who was
himself a citizen.* [9]

In Parliament that day was Genevieve Lipsett-Skinner, the special correspon-
dent for the *Montreal Star* in Ottawa. She talked to Agnes "in her little private
office on the 6th floor" — an experience Genevieve called "delightful."

*She has made her room quite homelike with growing plants. The
members have a certain discretion in choosing the furnishings for
their quarters — they may select from the rugs and furnishings on
hand. Miss Macphail's can be taken as an index of her quiet good
taste. The furniture is substantial oak of early English finish and the
rug of rich brown tones harmonizes with it. There are dainty cur-
tains, and flowers in radiant bloom indicate the feminine occupant.*

*The pioneer of the Federal Parliament dresses as any other smart
business woman of the present day. She favors dark cloth frocks on
tailored lines. Sometimes when she is going out to tea she brightens
up the Gothic Chambers with a dash of flame colour. She detests
wearing a hat; says she cannot think properly with a chapeau pressing her brains.*

*Miss Macphail takes the position that she does not represent the
women of Canada in the Canadian Parliament. She represents the
men, women and children of South East Grey, which is her constituency. "There wasn't a single woman delegate at the convention
which nominated me as Progressive candidate. There were eleven
nominees and I won out. It would be ungrateful for me to say I
represent only women and children and forget the men of South East
Grey," she remarked with a smile.*

*While in Ottawa Miss Macphail shares an apartment in the Queen
Mary apartments with Mrs. Quay who is chief of the senatorial
stenographic staff. They do their own housework — whoever gets in
first puts the kettle on and sets the table. About the only recreation
Miss Macphail has had time to indulge in since coming to the Capital is walking.*

*I must confess that I felt very proud of Miss Macphail the other
day when she stood up in her place and told Mr. Speaker that the
women of Canada did not want to marry a franchise — that they
were willing to qualify on the same basis as men — that all the
women of this country asked was nothing less than equality and
nothing more than equality.* [10]

Newspapers now vied to interview her. They wanted her impressions of
everything from Parliament to marriage and quickly realized that she was good
copy. They praised and chided her, advised and quoted her, and as she said in

the following letter to the *Halifax Sunday Leader*, they also "horribly misrepresented" her:

> *Your letter requesting my first impressions of the House of Commons received. I have been so horribly misrepresented in the daily press that I hesitate to burst into print. I understand, however, that what you want is not something senseless, but a little of that unfamiliar thing — Truth.*
>
> *My impressions of the House of Commons have changed from time to time. I think the very first impression that I got was the great stress that was laid on formality; that is, the form seems to be of more outstanding importance than the spirit which it was supposed to enshrine. I was happily impressed with the very kind reception given me by all sections of the House, and for the sake of all women who are to come after me I very much appreciated it.*
>
> *In all groups of the House I find people of valour, and in all groups their opposite. For those who come to the House of Commons enthused with the idea of changes coming immediately because they are so necessary and so sensible, the sensation is very much the same as attempting to batter down a wall by hitting it with your head. This, of course, will either produce unconsciousness or sense enough to use more sensible tactics, such as the very careful cutting out in this wall enough space to let the reform through.*
>
> *I am much impressed too with the great amount of detail work to be done and the little result which it brings. I had looked for much free time to study when the material for study was at hand, but find that in the hurry of trivialities real concentration is almost impossible.*
>
> *I concluded that there is no need to fear radical action in Parliament because the whole tendency is away from it, and the real fear is that there will be no action. You see the broader one gets the flatter one gets until finally there is nothing left but a large expanse of polished surface.*[11]

An editorial in the *Ottawa Evening Citizen* advised her to be wary of encouraging fellow members to smoke in her presence unless she was quite sure "as the forerunner of other Canadian women representatives in parliament that she can fittingly afford to waive such amenities as the convention about smoking in a lady's presence. In the next parliament there may be some gentle women — old-fashioned they may be called — who cherish just such nice little marks of distinction." [12] (These "nice little marks of distinction" worried Agnes to death. "What we women want is not deference but equality. This old-fashioned chivalry is all hollow. It means nothing, except that men think women inferior.") [13]

The next day the same paper said that Agnes was entertaining the nation by her descriptions of Parliament and that she was "losing no opportunity of letting the cat out of the bag." Since she was a woman, "her point of view [was] not shared by anyone else in the House . . . and therefore was of more than passing interest." Her humor was "biting" but mixed with "much wisdom." [14]

The *Ottawa Journal* interviewed her in March and said she talked of many things —

> *of school teaching on Oyen on the Goose Lake line of the CNR, of summers baking bread and churning and attending UFO picnics in*

North York, of the books she liked (now mostly economics [15] but when she had time, Nellie McClung and Agnes Laut), and the music (something solid and not jazz all the time) and the plays for which lately she has not had time, of her grandparents, of economics, and the blare of brown and green and red that is her rug in Room 605. She likes to ride, having learned on the farm and out west and she plays all the usual games including dancing, though she says she does not do the modern dances. . . .

"Yes, I've done a woman's work on the farm — baked bread, washed, scrubbed, milked cows, hoed the garden and hitched horses — I didn't go into the fields, because father said when the women had to do that it would be time for him to quit. . . ."

Room 605 is not without its feminine touches for a pink tulle bow hangs from the window curtain and on the ledge hyacinths and primroses bloom. [16]

Once launched in the House, Agnes spoke often. [17] In the following speeches from Hansard she covers subjects ranging from capital punishment to rural de-population to equality for women in divorce.

On April 11, 1924, Hansard reported a debate on capital punishment, during which she said:

Just twice in my life have I come closely in contact with capital punishment. The first time was the day that I wrote my entrance to normal examination. I will never forget that day; it was in Stratford, Ontario, and as we passed the jail on the way to the collegiate institute the black flag was at half mast and I knew of course that this meant that capital punishment had been executed, that the extreme penalty of the law had been enforced that morning. I have not forgotten the feeling I had then. I felt that society as a whole had deliberately contemplated and taken the life of this man, who, it is true, had taken the life of another. The second time I came closely in contact with capital punishment was last week and I am not likely to have forgotten the fact so quickly. I was reading about a week ago that they used to hang people in England at one time for picking pockets. They had public executions and the picking of pockets at these executions became so prevalent that they had to abandon the public execution of pickpockets. When we are trying to teach children to be truthful do we lie to them? I think not. Or if we want to teach people to be honest, do we steal? If we want to teach the hater to love do we hate him? Well, then, if we want to teach people to respect and revere human life, that which we can take away but cannot give, can we do so by taking human life? It seems to me that if we are really going to reverence human life we must as a society refuse to take it; we must come to the view that punishment should be of a reforming character rather than revengeful. . . . To me life is sacred, and because it is such a sacred thing that I personally could not take the life of anyone, even though that one had taken the life of another, I support wholeheartedly the bill that is before the house.

On April 13, 1923, Hansard recorded Agnes' comments on rural de-population:

> *When the honorable member for Glengarry (Mr. Kennedy), who has just spoken, said that the farmer, his wife and family work and the farmer gets the money, he stated the truth. It is true that farmers work hard; it is true their days are long and their pay is poor. But it is also infinitely true that the farm woman's day is longer and her pay poorer. With all due deference to the superior wisdom of men, one mistake that I think the men continually make in the House is that of treating the problem of rural depopulation as a man's problem and a man's problem only. Hon. members talk about the boy getting an education, as if when you have talked about the man and the boy you have finished the family — but you have not. You want to remember that the girl is also getting an education. The girl has seen her mother work as that mother does not want her daughter to work and as the daughter herself does not want to work. If you go over a rural community to-day — take your own constituency for example — and tabulate the results of your observation, you will find more young men on the land than young women; the girls leave first, and that is a pretty sure indication that the boys will leave later. I have noticed so often that the matter is looked at from the man's point of view. When a man is forced to quit farming, if you go into the case carefully you will find — and this applies to over half the cases — that he quit because of inability to carry on the work any longer. It is because the wife or the housekeeper in that house is broken down in health, or because of the woman's rebellion at the drudgery of her life. So I feel that the other view of it, the feminine view, the woman and girl part of the household will have to be considered before the problem of rural de-population is to be solved.*
>
> *I am glad the Minister of Trade and Commerce (Mr. Robb) is so optimistic; it is easy for people who are not farming to be optimistic. Our farm at home has no mortgage against it; there are no sons in the family or there would be a mortgage against it. There is some little money coming in besides that which is the direct result of farming, but we did not break even last year and will not this year. How long can anybody go on under those conditions?*

On March 25, 1924, members were to vote on spending an extra $600,000 to complete the Memorial Tower on the Parliament Buildings. The expenditure was to cover such things as electrical wiring, roofing and special lighting fixtures. Agnes thought the amount of money requested exorbitant and voted against the expenditure, which, nevertheless, was granted. Canada had lost over 63,000 soldiers in the First World War and most Canadians thought it was an insult to their memory not to finish the tower. Agnes reasoned differently:

> *I am against the principles of a memorial chamber. I know that is not a popular attitude to take, nevertheless that is my view. I think we have too many stone memorials throughout this country*

*and not enough sympathy in the hearts of the people for the
wrecked humanity that is the living memorial of the late war. If this
money were spent in helping the soldiers and their dependents; if
the Pensions Board and some others were advised to treat the
soldiers sympathetically; if the money were put into a fund that
would be used to help desperate cases against which the law seems
to be almost too hard, it would be more sensible. . . .*

*The fact of the matter is that in this Chamber we are apt to get
too far away from the people, even those who pride ourselves on
being near to them. The people not only want economy, they will
have it, and if we do not give it to them they will send people here
who will. The whole thing is atrocious and silly the amount of
money it takes to do government work. I am against this vote of
$600,000.*

On July 18, 1924, Hansard reported a debate on cadet training, with
Agnes' comments:

*I am not in favor of cadet training and while I do not intend to
make a speech, I wish to make a few remarks on this subject. . . .
The fact that many men in high places declared that the last war
could have been prevented by open and above-board methods, the
slowing down of the industrial machine since the war, and the
realization that scientific discoveries will leave no part of the world
safe in future wars has led many groups of people to seek the
causes of war and to strive to remove them. . . . Possibly one who
has not been reading this sort of thing can scarcely believe the
tremendous strides which the peace movement of the world has
made. . . .*

*The youth of the world are accepting the challenge of Sir James
Barrie[18] when he said it was time for them to begin to think seriously
and to find out the truth about war, that while their elders played for
stakes, the youth played for his life. Youth has nothing to gain by war
and everything to lose. War is not glorious. The object has been to
associate in childish minds these three things — soldiering and honor
and glory. Those who have inculcated this idea have carefully kept out
of sight the waste of human life, the lowering of moral standards, the
increase in disease, the assertion of brutality, and the general falling
away from the high standards of the Prince of Peace — in short, the
retrogression rather than the progress that results from war. . . .*

*Cadets, to me, is the most terrible part of all this business of
national defence. We are spending on national defence $11,000,000
and yet I hear today that the pension bill has again been spoiled by
the Upper House. We build monuments to glorify war and to encourage young men to emulate the deeds of those who died in order,
as we are told, that we might have liberty; but when it comes to
something worthwhile that we might commemorate, Parliament fails
to measure up to the occasion. $11,000,000 is a great deal of money.
It is much too much money to spend on teaching Canadians to fear
and dislike and distrust humanity in other parts of the world. The rest*

of humanity is just the same as we are; just as good; no better, no worse. If you read history, as I am sure all of you do, and I feel at a disadvantage because I do not know as much about it as a great number of you do — you know that the superiority of nations is really the sole excuse for war. In 1914 every school boy thought that his nation was unconquerable. We are all national egotists. Everybody thought his own country was right and the other fellow's wrong. That, you know, is bunk. . . . You spend $11,000,000 on building up a defence against someone. But who in this world is any worse than ourselves; who is any more foolish; who has any more nonsense going on in his country? We are spending $11,000,000 to prepare for another war, and at the same time we have failed to look after the poor fellows who are maimed in the last war. . . . We should be teaching our young boys to see the vision of what humanity really is; to think that the world is one — for we have made it so by invention and commerce. Instead of that we are teaching them the idea of war. . . .

Why should we take young boys, dress them in uniforms and teach them to strut along to martial strains with their foolish little guns and swords at their sides until they think they are manly? We are teaching them to get ready to kill some fellow in another country, some fellow who loves the same games and who is just as clean and just as mean as they are themselves. . . .

If the getting ready to kill somebody in some other country, on account of some misunderstanding that may occur between rulers, be patriotism, I want to say frankly that I am no patriot. If living each day cleanly and striving to the very last ounce of our ability to help our community, our province and our dominion, to help youth see a vision of service to humanity — if that is patriotism, then I want to be a patriot. . . .

Military drill for boys — cadet training — is increasing. In 1912 there were only 12,000 cadets in Canada; in 1922 there were 105,000. So we are getting on very well. We will soon be ready to go to war with somebody, and I suppose when we are ready we will go. . . .

It is true that what the schools are today the nations will be tomorrow. There is a definition of citizenship here which I want to give as my own: "Citizenship today must be broader than nationalism. There must be an international consciousness; there must be an international heart and a world mind. This world mind is largely an attitude or habit of thinking in the larger units of the world and the habit of regarding the nations as co-operating parts of the great whole. . . ." So I wish to move, seconded by the honorable member for Bow River (Mr. Garland) that item 89 of the national estimates be reduced by the sum of $400,000 [from $450,000].

The entire budget was approved, but Agnes' speech was commended by members and the press.

In March of 1924, Mr. Joseph T. Shaw (West Calgary) proposed that the divorce law in the four western provinces be changed from the English Matrimonial Causes Act (1857) to place the wife on an equal basis with the husband as regards the grounds on which divorce could be obtained. Several members opposed the bill but Agnes defended it, as Hansard, March 19, 1924, recorded:

Mr. Shaw: Translated into ordinary English this section means that while a husband may secure a divorce from his wife on the ground of adultery, the wife must, in order to succeed, be able to substantiate one of the following charges: 1. Incestuous adultery; 2. Bigamy with adultery; 3. Rape; 4. Sodomy or bestiality.

That is the English law as it stood in 1870, and those are the grounds only on which a married woman could secure a divorce from her husband. Why was equality denied in England, you may very well ask, at this particular time? Well, the debates of that day indicate that one of the main reasons was that men made the law, and the second reason given was that adultery was considered a more grievous offence against the wife than against the husband because of the possibility of the introduction of illegitimate children into the family. . . .

Miss Agnes Macphail (Southeast Grey): I did not intend to speak on this question because I feel it is an injustice against woman brought about by man, and I want the men unassisted by what I say to remove that injustice as I am sure they will do. The member for George Etienne Cartier told the exact truth when he said that the cause of this was that the law had been made by men. When you read the laws, not only this but a great many more, and read history, you will find they are everywhere the handiwork of men, describing their own actions and forgetting that after all they are only half of the great human family.

Mr. Logan: The worst half.

Miss Macphail: I would not say that. The honorable member who sits across the way is anxious that divorces should be made fewer instead of more. I had written on a piece of paper here just the question that the honorable member for East Calgary (Mr. Irvine) asked my honorable friend when he was speaking, that is, would he be willing to put men on the same basis in the four western provinces as women are in regard to divorce? If he is willing to do that it will remove restrictions and result in bringing about equality between the sexes. The very fact that men would take this step to place women on an equal footing with themselves will in itself have the effect of bringing about a feeling of good will. I think men hardly realize how deep in the heart of women is buried the resentment which they all feel against what they know to be an injustice, not only in this particular matter but in other things. That is one of the causes for the great woman's movement throughout the world. Women have felt that only by organizing and influencing public sentiment in this way could they obtain justice for themselves. I therefore ask honorable members to adopt this resolution out of a sense of justice for women and a proper regard for the spirit of fair play.

Mr. Casgrain: The honorable member for South East Grey (Miss Macphail) spoke just now on this subject to vindicate the rights of women and claim justice, equal rights for all. I sincerely congratulate her on the way she unfolded her arguments in the name of all those whom she has the honor to represent, and whose interpreter she is for the whole Dominion, being the only representative of her sex in the Canadian Parliament. . . . I congratulate her, but I cannot entirely side with her, because notwithstanding all legislation or law which might be adopted, aiming to grant women the same rights as men, there will always remain a difference, something which will not be identical. The difference exists since the creation of man. There has always existed and there will always exist in women, an inborn weakness, a marked inferiority. I am not saying this with the idea of depreciating woman, because we have all had mothers. And we know that if woman, notwithstanding her nature and weakness, may render services to her country, we are also aware that she is unable to accomplish as much as men. On the other hand, woman is looked upon — and with reason — as the angel of the home, as a gentler being than men. . . .

In spite of our granting the franchise to women, in spite of our placing her on the same footing as man, in all spheres of action, notwithstanding that we grant her the same rights and the same privileges, it is not less certain that you will never make woman equal to man. The latter will always have that superiority which characterizes him and places him at the head of society. And even in the home, although woman is the queen, although she is the one who brings up the children, although she is the one who, very often, through her advice, prevents her husband from blundering, is it not finally, man that is the master?

Miss Agnes Macphail: When I hear men talk about women being the angel of the home I always, mentally at least, shrug my shoulders in doubt. I do not want to be the angel of any home; I want for myself what I want for other women — absolute equality. After that is secured then men and women can take turns at being angels.

The debate was adjourned without the question being put.

Since her election all eyes had been on this lone woman. According to reports of the time, she had not only done well, she had out-performed most of her male colleagues.

The *Boston Herald* said that she spoke well — "much better than the ordinary man member — better indeed than any we have been listening to for the last two days." [19]

The *Family Herald and Weekly Star* said she was "quite a forceful speaker, making her points clear-cut, and with a considerable touch of humor, neither does she omit sarcasm which she uses as a very telling weapon against her opponents." [20]

The *Labor Advocate*:

In nothing has her triumph been greater than in the sheer efficiency with which she met her difficulties in addressing the House. Imagine the

*most experienced and skilful orator facing an audience hostile to the
point of dislike and contempt, an audience in which even friends were
patronizing rather than partisan. What would become of his best-
rounded periods, his finest bursts of eloquence? By ability and personality Miss Macphail has made for herself a recognized place as a
speaker in the House. Her success is due mainly to one simple fact —
she knows her facts and she has carefully thought out her reasons. Her
style is usually semi-colloquial, yet somehow without loss of dignity. Her
voice, a deep contralto, enables her to make herself heard even in the
large Commons chamber and in this she has a decided advantage over
many of the men.* [21]

Agnes made every effort to educate people in her riding. A friend agreed
but said that once *she* asked her a question about politics and Agnes said, "Now,
Emma, you're a nice girl but you don't know a thing about politics." And that
was that.

Nevertheless, said a writer for the *Flesherton Advance*, Agnes was a "leader
of the people. . . . Her independence of thought, her courage in championing
progressive ideas in advance of public opinion, her ability to inspire others to
better things and her skill in imparting information on which others may form
their conclusions are her qualifications for the title."

In addition to a weekly letter to newspapers — which she later called a
"pernicious habit" — she organized clubs for young farmers, sponsored debating
and essay contests, wrote to schools and provided each with a picture of the
Parliament buildings.

The object of the debating club was "to encourage the serious study of
problems of national or local interest, especially pertaining to agriculture; to
provide through the medium of public debates an interesting and profitable form
of entertainment for the people of the community and to foster among the young
people of the riding a spirit of friendly co-operation and to afford opportunities
for bringing them together."

Even her campaign speeches were used to educate the people. They "generally [took] on the form of classes or discussions on economics, democracy and
co-operation. Often she . . . overlooked mentioning the election." [22]

She wanted a book written on government especially for children. "They
haven't the faintest idea that government is anything in which they have any
concern." [23] She therefore chose political topics for the debates and essays.

In 1924 a twelve-year-old Markdale girl, Maxine Lyons, won the prize — a
trip to Ottawa for the Opening of the House — for speaking on "How We are
Governed." The *London Advertiser* asked: "Would any august male member ever
dream of giving such a sumptuous prize?"

Maxine chose the trip rather than a medal, said the *Durham Review*, "and
that she had a delightful and interesting trip may be gathered from her diary
which she has kindly forwarded to the Review for publication":

Wednesday, February 4th

> *The train left Markdale at 4:18. The school children and three of
> the teachers came down to the train to see me off. My mother ac-
> companied me as far as Shelburne. Miss Macphail got on the train at
> Flesherton. When we got to North Toronto Station we hired a taxi*

and went to Union Station where we checked our grips. We had three hours to wait and spent the time at a vaudeville show. Then after a light lunch at Walker's Cafeteria, we got the train about 10:30. I had never slept on a train before and it was quite an experience, but I think I must have been excited and the train was warm, so I did not sleep well, and the night seemed quite long.

Thursday, February 5th

We arrived at Central Station, Ottawa, shortly before eight o'clock and went directly to Miss Macphail's apartment, where after breakfast we rested and got ready for the opening in the afternoon. We went to the Parliament Building about 2 o'clock. I liked Miss Macphail's office. After looking at the House of Commons Chamber, the Library and a few other principal rooms, I was given a seat on the floor of the Senate.

Already many ladies in formal evening dress were in their place, and they kept coming continually until 3 o'clock. It was a brilliant spectacle, much more wonderful than I thought it would be. The floor of the Senate was packed with people as was also the galleries. At 3 o'clock the Governor General and Lady Byng came. Lord Byng sat in a large red chair at the upper end of the room. Lady Byng was quite near him, exquisitely gowned in wine-coloured lace with court train and on her head a diamond tiara in maple leaf design.

Maxine told of the Speech from the Throne and then continued:

At the conclusion of the speech . . . Miss Macphail waited for me, and we went to two receptions, the first given by the Speaker of the Senate and Mrs. Bostock. We were asked to lead the procession in. The tables were beautiful. We had some lemonade. We then went into the Gallery of the House of Commons. Two members have died since the House arose, and the Prime Minister, Mr. Meighen and Mr. Forke paid a tribute to their memory. I asked Miss Macphail if they would say nice things about her if she were dead, and she said, "Yes, if I were dead."

From there we went to Mr. Lemieux's reception. When Miss Macphail told Mr. Lemieux who I was he kissed me in his courtly French way. We went to a dinner party that night and to the movies afterwards.

The next few days Maxine viewed Ottawa from the roof of the Parliament buildings, ate in the parliamentary dining room, met members, listened to speeches in the House, walked around Fairy Lake, had tea at the Woodsworth's. Her final entry was on Tuesday, February 10.

I packed my things in the morning and went through some of the shops. I met the Prime Minister; he was gracious, and the Hon. Chas. Murphy. He gave me a flower and showed me his lovely office. We spent a few minutes at Mr. Meighen's office and he gave me an autographed book of the speeches he made while in England. . . .

It was my birthday and Miss Macphail gave me a dinner party for six with a birthday cake in the centre of the table. The chef of the House of Commons made it. It had twelve candles. We had a gay party.

Everyone was wonderfully good to me. The trip was better than any medal could possibly be. I was sorry to leave but glad to go home to see my mother and father and little brother and school mates once more. [24]

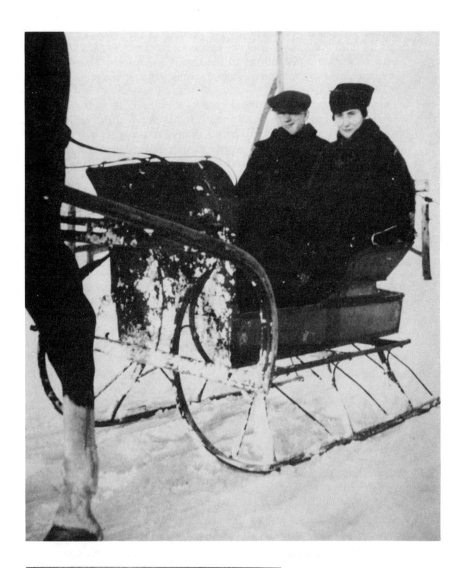

Agnes in cutter used for transportation in winter

Out of Agnes' debating clubs came many young people of promise. One, James Palmer, a Dundalk boy, won both the essay and debating contest in 1931.[25] Four years later while at McMaster University, he managed her 1935 election campaign and Agnes credited him with helping her win the election. Palmer became a student and teacher of history and later a school trustee in East York. An exceptional teacher, he persuaded many prominent politicians to address his classes in St. Catharines, East York and Toronto. Among them were Louis St. Laurent, Pierre Trudeau, Tommy Douglas, Ed Broadbent and John Diefenbaker, who said there had been five outstanding politicians in Canada and "Agnes Macphail was one of them." Agnes, too, spoke to his classes. "In St. Catharines," said Palmer, "she spoke to 1,000 students. Her topic was 'Out of My Life.' She spoke, as usual, without any notes and kept us spell-bound. When we re-played the tape, fully half of it was taken up with laughter and applause."

Palmer became her trusted friend and adviser. When she was defeated in the election of 1940 it was he who drove her from Ceylon to Toronto, Toronto to Sharon, Sharon back to Ceylon as she sought to distance herself from her defeat and gain time in which to regain her emotional and mental balance. They corresponded when he was overseas in World War II, and at the last of her life he was a pall bearer at her funeral.

Farquhar Oliver was another protégé. A neighbor's son, he too got his start in Agnes' speaking contests. In 1925 Agnes asked him to help with her election campaign. He worked all day in the fields and accompanied her to meetings at night. Agnes predicted that the twenty-year-old would go far. He ran for the provincial UFO Party in 1926 and with Agnes' help was elected on December first at the age of twenty-two. Judith Robinson, *Toronto Telegram* columnist, said that Agnes Macphail could almost be said to have invented Farquhar Oliver politically. He and Agnes campaigned for each other through the years until Agnes was defeated. Farquhar then switched to the Liberal Party, much to Agnes' disgust. He later became leader of the party. When they were both in the Ontario Legislature, Agnes was not above taking the odd verbal swipe at him, but he did not hit back. A true disciple of Agnes, while serving as Minister of Welfare and Public Works, he brought in free medical care for old age pensioners, the blind, recipients of mother's allowances and those on relief. He raised old age pensions and started the first day nurseries for mothers engaged in war work.

Letters which Agnes sent to riding schools dealt with history, parliamentary affairs and current events. One, which caused a furor, was on the Chinese Opium War and the Boxer Rebellion. Toronto's *Globe* branded the letter "a specious tissue of half-truths and untruths and a despicable attempt to misrepresent and discredit Great Britain and British policy in the eyes of school children."

Ottawa, March 28, 1927

Dear Teacher and Pupils:

> *This letter we will talk about the Chinese war. The Chinese use a great deal of a drug called opium. It is a very bad drug, much worse than liquor on the person who takes it. It gives them pleasant dreams. They live in a sort of dream world, and are very happy, but when the influence has worn off they are nervous wrecks and are sick. Then they want more opium to make them nice dreamers again, and if they do this for some time, it spoils their health, and they are not good for anything.*

There was a war in China between 1839 and 1842 which is called the Opium War. The Chinese wanted to make the use of opium in China illegal, to keep it out of China, but Great Britain insisted that the Chinese Government make the use of opium legal, because Great Britain owned India — and India sells opium to China. This made the Chinese angry. Then, too, nearly all the great ports where the big ships come in are controlled by Great Britain, or by some other great power like Japan, and in these Chinese cities the Chinese have no vote. The police are foreigners, the whole show is run by people who are not Chinese, and the Chinese have no rights.

The Chinese revere their dead, and their graveyards are a very sacred place. When Western civilization came they ran railroads through the graveyards. This made the Chinese mad, and caused them to rebel. This rebellion was called the Boxer Rebellion. The Chinese were defeated in this rebellion and were made to pay money called an indemnity, and Great Britain, to make sure she got this money, imposed a five per cent tax — that is five cents on the dollar — on goods coming in. This is called Customs tariff. She also controls the post offices.

Many countries, Japan, Great Britain, and before the war, Germany, had factories in the big cities of China. The living conditions in these factories were horrible. The children work as young as six years old, and are often hurt and killed. The Chinese Government can do nothing because these are European factories and the owners of the factories will do nothing.

A group of Chinese students walked the streets of one of their big cities about a year ago as a protest against the awful conditions of the children in factories, and the British police shot them down. You can quite easily see how all these things made the Chinese determined to put the British out of their country, to bind their many provinces together in one Federal Government, to control their own customs tariff and their own post offices, their own railways, etc. Russia, seeing that a rebellion was coming in China, wisely gave up all her rights within that country, and the Chinese are very grateful. There is little doubt that Russia is urging the Chinese to rebellion, but the conditions in China are so bad that one cannot wonder that these people rise in revolt. Germany used to have much control in China, but according to the Peace Treaty of the Great War, she was forced to give up her privileges.

I wish very much that Canada, who is a member of the League of Nations, would protest against what has been done in China. We have a right to try to stop anything that is breaking the peace of the world. We must remember that it is only a few very rich people in England who want to do these dreadful things in China; that most of the British people are very sad and grieved over what is being done and that meetings are being held there in protest, and some of the leading papers are saying that the action of the Government and the big interests is all wrong — and so we are in good company if we do say that we think the Chinese are being unfairly treated.

Many of the patriotic Canadians say over and over again: "We want Canada for Canadians," then if that is true, why do we not want China

*for Chinese. We sent missionaries to teach them of Jesus and His Love,
but unless we love them and act as brothers toward them, how can they
know that we believe in Jesus and His love to all.*

*Thursday was my birthday and I had a lovely birthday party. We
have two hours for dinner between 6 and 8 o'clock. I had a party of
fourteen. I got lovely flowers, three dozen roses, three boxes of candy,
some nice maple sugar, handkerchiefs and all sorts of good things. I had
a very gay time. My office has been much brighter with the flowers. The
gardener of the House of Commons always keeps flowering plants on
my window, but the roses are even more beautiful than they are.*

I must close for this time.

After the *Globe*'s attack on the letter, the UFO's paper, the *Sun*, came to her
defence saying that if Miss Macphail's letter had lauded British policy in China,
"even though the letter contained not a single element of truth, there is little doubt
that the jingo press would have applauded the writer. . . . The fact is, Miss
Macphail does not misrepresent Great Britain to anything like the same extent the
Globe misrepresents Miss Macphail. . . . But all this by the way. The point at issue
is this: Have Canadians the right, or have they not the right, to discuss British
foreign policy with an open mind without being branded as traitors and scally-wags
by such papers as the Globe? Advocates of that priceless possession, freedom of
speech, are entitled for a little more justice from a paper of the Globe's calibre." [26]

Agnes welcomed such support but did not depend on it. She made a spirited
defence of the letter, both to a *Toronto Star* reporter and in Parliament.

She told the *Star* that when she was asked about a thing she said what she
thought even if it wasn't the popular thing to say. "I do not worry over what others
may say as to my views." [27]

In Parliament she explained that the "opium" letter was one of a series she had
written to schools in her constituency trying to educate the children in the ways of
government. Normal schools had ordered them by the hundreds and teachers had
asked that they be put in book form for use in the schools. She had run out of
governmental topics and asked the children to name subjects they would like her to
discuss. Ten or twelve students wrote and asked her what she thought of the
Chinese War.

"I have no apology to make for that letter," she said. "There may be one or
two inaccuracies in it in detail, but it is substantially correct. . . .

"In 1830," she said, "permission was given by the Lieutenant-Governor of
India to extend the cultivation of the poppy with a view to increasing the supply.
This alarmed the Chinese emperor of that time. He knew it was a growing evil in
his country and he instructed Commissioner Lin to go from Peking early in 1839 to
Canton, and his orders were to get rid of the opium evil. Mr. Lin did go there and
he took from the British merchant 20,283 chests of opium and destroyed them. This
led to the war." [28]

She cited authorities who agreed that the war was unjust and a disgrace to
Britain. She said that anyone who believed in Christianity must blush with shame to
realize that the same treaties legalized the sale of opium and gave privileges for the
"propagation and practice of Christianity. . . . I think that if Great Britain had been
as anxious about her Christianity as she was about her opium — not all of Great
Britain, but the ruling faction — China would not have had to defend herself while
trying to get rid of something harmful to her own people. Who gave us the right to

trot around the world settling difficulties and quarrels, or imaginary difficulties of the different countries?"

For China's resistance to Britain,

> *a load of debt was imposed and foreign officials appointed to collect custom duties to meet the interest due. . . .*
>
> *The treaty that closed the first opium war was called the Treaty of Nankin, 1842. By it China had to pay $6,000,000 for the cost of the opium destroyed, $12,000,000 for the expense of the war, and $3,000,000 for debts due to English subjects in addition to $6,000,000 already paid for the ransom of Canton. Hong Kong was ceded to us for refitting ships and four additional ports were opened to trade. . . .*
>
> *In regard to the Boxer Rebellion it is said I should have guarded myself by saying that it was really a civil war, rather than a rebellion. How could it be a civil war with foreign powers backing one faction and exacting very heavy indemnities from the section whose army was defeated? . . . It is as true to say that crossing sacred ground with railways aroused the Chinese populace to anger as to say that the Boston tea party was the cause of the American revolutionary war . . . or that slavery was the real cause of the Civil War. There is no doubt that the Chinese were ignorant and that they did not understand the real causes of the war, but I may say to this House that the people of any country never understand the real causes of a war while that war is proceeding. . . .*
>
> *The Hon. member for Kingston (Mr. Ross) had scorn in his voice when he said that in my letter I stated that living conditions in the factories* [in China] *were horrible.*

She quoted excerpts from the *Globe* in which the paper told of conditions in China where children of eight or nine years of age were standing between double rows of whizzing unguarded machinery, steadily but wearily feeding the machines. "One mite, perhaps eight years of age, was curled in an exhausted heap on the cement floor, sound asleep. . . . In one small hospital there were one day this winter three children under ten years old. The arm of one had been caught in an unfenced machine and was all but torn off. The leg of another was smashed from hip to ankle by the teeth of a machine. The third, a little girl, had been caught by the hair in her machine and her scalp torn off. Such are the terrible conditions in Chinese industry. . . ."[29]

Agnes continued to cite the *Globe*, which told of women working ten hour days for six cents an hour, of boys working from 5 a.m. to 11 p.m. with no pay but their food.

"It is in the interest of all nations," she said, "that industry in no nation should be built on sweated labour."

She finished her well-documented speech: "I want to say, regardless of what the hon. member for Kingston (Mr. Ross) and the hon. member for Frontenac-Addington (Mr. Edwards) may think, that I consider myself a patriot. I have no desire in the world to mislead the school children of South East Grey, or the school children of Canada, or the people of Canada on any question whatever. To the extent that any details of the letter were inaccurate I regret it, but the spirit of the letter was true, and I stand by it, be the consequences what they may."[30]

In 1925 Agnes started what was to be a long campaign to reform Canada's penitentiaries.

James Palmer said that no one would ever know the tremendous sacrifice and heartache which was involved in her struggle for a fair deal for the convict.[31] Their fate was of little concern to most Canadians at that time. Why then did Agnes take on this unpopular cause?

According to close friend Muriel Kerr, it was "because she was always interested in people who needed help. She was horrified at such things as prisoners' dishes being washed in bathtubs."[32]

E. B. Jolliffe, one-time leader of Ontario's CCF Party, and another good friend of Agnes', said it was only one aspect of her wide interest in all human beings.

This interest took her to Kingston Penitentiary to see conditions for herself. She presented herself at the gate but was told no ladies were allowed.

"I'm no lady," said Agnes. "I'm an M.P."

She was admitted — the first woman to tour Kingston Penitentiary — and became a "thorn in the flesh" of authorities until she got what she wanted — a Royal Commission to examine conditions in Canada's penitentiaries.

It took years, and obstacles were constantly put in her way. During one of her early speeches on the subject (March 18, 1925), the Speaker had to call for order: "There is too much conversation going on in the House. I can hardly hear the speaker." Unperturbed, Agnes introduced a resolution to amend the administration of penitentiaries. She wanted sufficient productive work to keep the inmates employed, and a share of the proceeds to go to dependents, and in case of no dependents such share to be held in trust until release.

She argued that productive labor would make the task of discipline easier. It would help the unfortunate and blameless dependents. "And," she said, "it would also have a tremendous effect upon the prisoner himself if he felt that he was still of some account, that he still had responsibility; because often it is true of us — and it must be true of those who are confined in prisons — that responsibility will hold us to a task when nothing else will. . . ."

She quoted a document prepared by the Secretary[33] to the Prisoners' Welfare Association which said that the prisoner "comes out of the penitentiary with almost no money, and very often with no skill for any trade, and it is difficult for him to get back into society. This embitters him, and the result very many times is that the man in desperation in the first few weeks after his release turns back to crime. . . ."

She continued that

> quite apart from the remaking of the men and the caring for their dependents, there [would] be a very great material gain. This plan of work with pay has been tried in very many places with success. . . . Mr. C. E. Vasaly speaking for the Minnesota Penitentiary Board says: "We make a great deal of money, but we make something in the prison much more important than money, and that is the making of men. . . . In the first place, our prison earns its support; it saves the state something like $360,000 a year in that respect."

She ended with a plea:

> It seems to me that we in this House, who really are the guardians of these wards of the Dominion Government, must find in our treatment of this resolution a test of our own intelligence and our own humanitarian

*instincts. Surely, we in this generation should crystallize into legislation
and into the administration of these institutions, the best principles we
can. If we do not do that we are not fair to succeeding generations and
succeeding Parliaments. We are not taking advantage of our privileges if
we do not adopt the best features in penitentiary administration which
past experience has developed and put them into operation. If it is
possible for all the honorable members of this House to help in the re-
making of men, to save suffering to those who have really caused no
harm to the state, to sweeten the lives of very many people and over and
above that to effect a large economy in public expenditure, why should
we not pursue a course that will bring about these happy results?*

The House adjourned without putting the resolution to a vote.

A continuing issue was the bitter strike in Nova Scotia and Cape Breton Island
between miners of District 26, United Mine Workers of America, and the British
Empire Steel Corporation. Miners' hardships were discounted as Red propaganda.[34]
The miners *had* applied for membership in the International Red Labor Union —
headquarters, Moscow — but had withdrawn when threatened with a loss of
support from American headquarters.

As in the case of the penitentiary, Agnes wanted to see things for herself. She
went east and came back with a report that distressed some members and angered
others. Nova Scotians in particular thought Agnes had "slandered" the province and
that her report was prejudiced because "she was guided around town by the Labor
mayor and the truant officer."

She gave her report to Parliament on March 31, 1925, and for the first time
spoke for the allotted forty minutes. It was late in the day but members did not
leave. They sat and listened with increasing interest and some discomfiture. The
speech gave notice that Agnes Macphail's interests had spread beyond farm problems to include all primary workers, all disadvantaged people.

She described the unequal struggle between the giant steel corporation ("They
have received . . . subsidy, bonuses, protection by tariff and militia") and the
miners, who had not had regular work for four years, were deeply in debt to
company stores, and were "actually fettered as securely as though the links of the
chain that bound them were visible." Credit had recently been cut off at the stores,
and the men saw this as a means of forcing them to accept a ten per cent reduction
in wages.

In Glace Bay, Agnes visited hospitals, schools, relief stations, the headquarters
of the United Mine workers, and the Savoy Theatre where she met "at least 2000
miners." She "went to inspect the colliery towns in a Ford sedan that succeeded in
getting through the mud. It spluttered and stuttered but it got through." She went
into some of the "squatty, unpainted houses" and talked to the people. "In one
house the roof leaked and the plaster was falling off. . . . There was the kitchen
and one bedroom in which the mother, the father and the six children slept." In
another "the wife was wearing a clean calico dress which was all she had . . . a
little child was wearing a coat but no dress and a pair of stockings that the mother
had made out of cloth." In a third "the man, wife and two children were actually
obliged to sleep in one three-quarter bed, although . . . the woman was suffering
from tuberculosis."

She told of a woman who came to the relief station "in an old sweater and
skirt, without any shoes, and with a very bad blister on her heel as a result of

having to wear old rubbers." Another woman whispered in her ear that she and her husband were simply out of clothes — they had provided for the children rather than for themselves.

"I never saw anything so devoid of beauty as Glace Bay in the spring." The section of town where these people lived "had no electric lights, no sewers, only open gutters flowing on each side of the roads . . . no sanitary conveniences at all. Just now in the springtime it is a bog hole, and when night comes the place is plunged in absolute darkness. . . . Yet," said Agnes, "these homes were on the edge of the sea, only a few yards from the wholesome sea that is at our eastern gate, as we read when we come into the entrance to this building." (Inscription over main entrance to Parliament Buildings: "The wholesome sea is at her gates, her gates both east and west.")

Agnes was disgusted that neither the provincial nor federal government would intervene to help the miners, but left it to private citizens. She was disgusted, too, that the miners had been persuaded to turn down "a gift of $5,000 sent to them by Russia. . . . I think it is a very dubious compliment to Canadian intelligence that the miners of Nova Scotia and those who are working with them thought it necessary to turn down such a substantial gift in order that those people . . . might remain respectable in our eyes. We are indeed a smug, self-righteous people."

She admitted that she had more than usual sympathy for these people because many of them bore Scottish names that were dear to her, and she sent money, clothes and other supplies to them out of her own pocket.

She concluded that the whole situation was caused by the fact that we put commercial values ahead of human values.

In the House Agnes again took up the question of divorce, this time in reply to Thomas Vien (Lotbinière) who had introduced an amendment to the Divorce Act in which he proposed that divorced parties would not have the right to marry again.

On June 4, 1925, Agnes said:

I believe it is the desire, Mr. Speaker, of everyone in this House that the home should be preserved. I believe the preservation of the home as an institution in the future lies almost entirely in the hands of the men. If they are willing to give to women economic freedom within that home; if they are willing to live by the standard that they wish the women to live by, the home will be preserved. If the preservation of the home means the enslavement of women, economically or morally, then we had better break it, and for that reason I will support the bill and I will vote against the amendment. I would ask men to think of that and think of it seriously. I do believe that the economic freedom of women is one of the things that is causing increasing divorces, because women will not tolerate what they once had to tolerate. You can smile about it if you like, but I know a lot of men talk very learnedly on a subject like this and who want women to be very pure and chaste when they themselves are not fit to associate with a chaste and pure woman. So, when we have a single standard for men and women, both morally and economically, we shall have a home that is well worth preserving, and I think we can be quite sure it will be preserved.

Chapter IV
Campaigns and Causes
1925-1929

By 1925 Mackenzie King was increasingly unhappy with having to depend on the support of Progressive members. Dubbed the "Ginger Group" by the Parliamentary Press, the Progressives had held unusual power since 1921. "At that time," Agnes said, "the two political teams were playing a baseball game. Alternately one team was at bat and the other on bases. It was a bit disturbing when the 'gingerites' broke up the game." Obviously King agreed and in September in what the *Durham Review* called "his great speech to his constituents at Richmond Hill in historic North York," he called an election for October 29.

On September 17, 1925, the *Durham Review* reported that Agnes Macphail was again the choice of an enthusiastic convention in South East Grey for the next Dominion Parliament.

In her acceptance speech Agnes "nailed a lying rumor that she had only once refused the full indemnity, and that if she had refused it, there was some means by which she could reclaim it." Agnes replied that the money was in the National Treasury and showed receipts to prove it. "Someone in the audience wanted to know 'if she could never touch it no more' and she assured them that this was true. She had decided, however, that in the future she "would not take less than any other member."

(The *Flesherton Advance* of September 16 reported that a member of the audience asked: "Don't you think you were a fool to return it?" "I think I was a complete fool," replied Agnes.) [1]

"We are out," she said, "to seek representation for agriculture, not for power. . . . Progressives had given many constructive ideas to the other parties. . . . The two old parties were in the grasp of the money group — the Progressives stood solid for social reform and were sometimes despised for it. . . ."

The *Review* said many thought it the best speech she had ever made — that she had won the love and loyalty of her followers as few candidates had and that any candidate who hoped to beat her "had his work cut out for him."

On October 29, the Liberals and Progressives lost heavily. The Conservative party doubled its strength and was now the largest group. It was still short of a majority over the combined Liberals and Progressives, however, and King decided to carry on.

Agnes had survived the slaughter and back in Ottawa promptly chastised Mackenzie King for holding on to office. The *Durham Review* reported that "on rising to speak she got a storm of applause from all parties and proceeded to give both parties a tongue thrashing." She described the situation as one in which no party had been returned in numbers to form a government.

I think the King Government played atrociously poor politics when
they continued to hold office after the first of the year. (Conservative

applause.) The effect is increased resentment of the people of Canada against them, which will continue until some change takes place.

Certain passages of the Speech from the Throne show ingratitude and ungraciousness. I want to say quite plainly that I have no confidence in the King Government. (Conservative applause.) I am not pleased with their past performance, nor am I pleased with their promise of future actions. . . . On the other hand, I am not in accord with Conservative policies nor in sympathy with their mental outlook and I view with alarm the return of a great many old war horses to the fray. I believe it is true of both parties, especially in Ontario, that their method of financing and conducting elections does much to lower the tone of public life. I believe they have grown fat off my class and I cannot support their party, but I still have the safe ground of supporting each piece of legislation on its merits. [2]

Writing to the *Farmer's Sun* in July, 1926, Agnes gave her account of the session:

The fifteenth Parliament just closed was the shortest Canadian Parliament, consisting of one session of six months. During this Parliament the two historic parties waged a fierce struggle for power. Neither having a majority, the support of other groups in the House had to be secured by the governing party. The Farm, Labor and Independent groups agreed to support the King administration on a legislative program the chief items of which were re-evaluation of soldiers' lands, rural credit, land settlement bill, amendment to the Grain Act, the Hudson Bay Railway, amendments to the criminal code, old age pensions and a budget at least partly suitable to us. . . .

King was back where he started from before the election and even more dependent on the Progressives.

After the election there was another round of Agnes stories. Intrigued by the fact that she was one of only two survivors [3] of the Progressive Party in Ontario, F. G. Griffin of the *Toronto Star Weekly* did a full page story entitled "How Aggie Did It." The article ran in November, 1925, and was illustrated with six pictures. One was an unflattering head and shoulders picture of Agnes, hair drawn primly to either side of an unsmiling face and small steel-rimmed glasses perched on her nose. Others showed her hunched over the wheel of an ancient-looking car and feeding a flock of white chickens — variously described as Leghorns and Wyandottes. A picture of the Macphail home with its large well-maintained barn showed apple trees leaning across the fenced laneway. There were cut-out pictures of her parents and of F. J. Oliver, her young (twenty) "principal lieutenant" in the recent campaign.

Her parents stood together, her mustachioed father in a heavy high-necked sweater, work pants and rubber boots; her mother, white hair neatly arranged on top of her head, ample in a dark loose-fitting square-necked house dress.

Tom Gilchrist, Ceylon blacksmith, told Griffin why he thought Agnes survived the general slaughter of the Progressive Party. In the past four years she had stayed one of the people and never forgot it was her own folk that sent her to represent them. "She's absolutely honest — with herself and everyone else and her word is as good as Rockefeller's bond," said Gilchrist. "She's an awful good mixer . . . I've known her since the Macphails first came here in 1904 when she was a girl going to school and I don't see a whit of difference in Aggie. She's one of the few women who would drop into the shop here for a chat, yes, long before she ever thought of running for Parliament. . . . If she went into your house and felt hungry, she'd say she was, and if she felt like it, ask you right out for a piece of pie. . . . If she was driving along the road and saw you walking she'd give you a lift — it didn't matter if you were man, woman or child. I know four Conservative votes she got this election by just giving a man like this a lift during the summer."

Griffin wondered how she won when there were still "whisperings against her because she belonged to the Latter Day Saints" and rumours that she had said she "didn't care a whoop if all the factories closed down." [4]

Her parents said she won because she worked hard and "stuck to her word." Farquhar Oliver said it was because of her "personal popularity — and she's a fighter through and through."

Griffin thought also that it was because she "came face to face with her constituents for approval or criticism." She studied economics and politics so she could represent her people well and he wondered how many members took Parliament seriously enough to "grind and cram" as Miss Macphail did. "She is given credit for all this in the constituency. 'They can't catch Aggie. She's got her facts and figures right on tap.'"

People were her first hobby. "One of the most gratifying things to me is the tremendous love that surrounds me in this community. . . . I hold the trust of the people as my most sacred possession. Nothing else matters."

Griffin said she pointed to a picture of "a strong old face full of character and experience. 'That's the woman from whom I got my desire to serve — Grandmother Campbell — my mother's mother. She was from Scotland — what other countries would call a peasant, she went to work when she was nine. But she taught herself. And I was devoted to her. She was a woman who always put first things first. She never got her values mixed. And she taught me something of that at an early age. For she loved people with a great love. . . .'"

Agnes ran her campaign from her home with the help of a stenographer, she told Griffin. In the evenings she and Farquhar Oliver went to meetings, sometimes two in one night. She would get home between 12 and 2 a.m., have a bowl of puffed wheat and cream and fall into bed. In spite of snow storms she never missed a meeting.   On election night she listened to returns on the radio and then went to Durham with young Oliver to celebrate. [5]

In January, 1926, Cornelia, editor of the women's page of the *Toronto Telegram*, wrote a gratuitously "catty" column on Agnes. She reported that even Ontario's UFO Openings were not as "undress" as the Opening of Canada's Fifteenth Parliament. "Only one lady present wore her best clothes — may she not be read out of her party — she was Miss Agnes Macphail.

"At her debut in the House of Commons, Canada's first woman member wore a simple blue serge one-piece dress. But today Miss Macphail seemed to have dressed for the 'Land of Afternoon.' She wore one of the latest models with the cutest puff sleeves in apple green crepe and satin with lace in the V neck and a pearl necklace. She also wore beige hosiery and substantial brown Oxfords." [6]

At first Progressives supported the new government but trouble soon appeared. Alberta members were upset with how the government handled their natural resources — they wanted to control their own resources. Rumors of irregularities in the Customs Department surfaced and added to the general unrest and King asked Governor-General Lord Byng [7] to dissolve the House. Byng refused, so King resigned on June 28. Meighen formed a government but was defeated on July 2. Parliament was dissolved and another election called for September 14.

Agnes was again chosen to represent the UFO at a nominating meeting in Durham Town Hall "without another name being proposed," said the *Durham Review*.

"Two Proton delegates, John Aldcorn and R. Cronin, moved the name of Agnes Macphail and from all parts of the hall the delegates proclaimed they wanted no further nominations. The second unanimous nomination for Miss Macphail was greeted with great applause and the final motion made." [8]

The Conservatives were meeting to select a candidate but the *Review* considered it unlikely that the Liberals would enter one. "Furthermore," said the paper, "with Miss Macphail's strength in this riding, it is almost a forlorn hope from the start for any candidate." [9]

As Agnes stumped the riding, enthusiasm was high. "The Town Hall was crowded, many standing, more turned away," reported the *Durham Review* of a meeting held in Durham. "The hall was adapted for pre-car days and is now obsolete, for anything that appeals to town and country proves it quite inadequate." (Durham Town Hall looks much the same today: the narrow stairway and small auditorium where Agnes pushed her way through the crowds, the platform from which she spoke, the upright piano, old-fashioned hanging lights that dimly lit the room, the shuttered windows and quaint arm chairs nailed to the floor.)

"We have seen political meetings in years not so far gone when half a dozen women would have caused comment, now with the franchise and good leading, they make half the audience.

"On the platform with Chairman Joe Crutchley were Miss McKessock of Massie, Mr. Farquhar Oliver of Artemesia and Miss MacPhail. All four did their parts well and it was pointed out that in a sense the three first named are a product of the 'Farm Youth Movement' which was created and has been fostered by Miss MacPhail as everyone knows. The meeting in its every part was very good, and left no doubt in the minds of the audience that Miss MacPhail's work is reaping fruit." [10]

A meeting the following week was held in the rink, the only building in town large enough to hold the crowd. Seating arrangements had been made in preparation for a planned meeting for Premier Meighen the following night. "Most were comfortably seated and in addition to the sea of faces on the floor, the balconies were filled also. It was without doubt the largest meeting ever held in [a] Durham building, estimates of the number running from 2,000 to 3,000. . . ."

Miss Macphail, said the *Review*, dealt with the Alberta Natural Resources problem, prohibition, the customs scandal, the tariff. She gave proof that it was impossible to protect farmers whose products had to meet world competition. "Don't fool yourself that protection is a blessing. . . . Sir John A. Macdonald brought in protection for infant industries, but they were still clamoring to be propped up." She justified her votes for and against King: she had been accused of being a Liberal yet forty times she had voted against King and twenty-three times with him. "I voted with the Liberals when they voted for our program and not otherwise." The Senate was there to defend "special privilege" and "it tends to business well." Accused of not having leaders she answered: "God gave us brains; we don't need leaders." [11]

Meanwhile, on the Liberal-Conservative side, her opponent R. T. Edwards criticized her constantly and asked for someone to name one thing Agnes had done since she went to Parliament. He no doubt wished he had not asked, for Agnes obliged with a list of her accomplishments which was published in the *Durham Review* on September 9:

> *I secured approval of Parliament for prison reform — by which prisoners will have productive work to do. They will first pay for their keep, thus relieving the people of the burden, and when cost of maintenance is met a prisoner will receive a small wage which will go to keep his dependents; if he has none, money will be held for prisoner until release, thus helping him to get an honest start in life.*
>
> *I seconded Mr. G. C. Coote's resolution for reduction of tariff on automobiles.*
>
> *I have spoken, voted and worked to have military training removed from our schools and physical training substituted instead.*
>
> *I have spoken and worked for change in form of government to allow questions to be debated on their merits [12]; the defeat of a government measure to mean only defeat of the measure and for the right of third or fourth groups to move an amendment to the Budget.*
>
> *Assisted in attempt to secure ruling that directors of big concerns who become ministers of the crown, should, while they are ministers for the crown, resign their directorship.*
>
> *I tried twice to have the indemnities of members of Parliament reduced.*
>
> *I helped to secure continuance of Crows' Nest Pass agreement.*
>
> *Supported attempt to prevent legalized gambling on race track.*
>
> *Helped pass through House of Commons an amendment to the Criminal Code making it no longer possible for a British subject to be arrested and deported without a trial.*
>
> *I tried to prevent vote of five million for Quebec harbor.*
>
> *Worked for the right of Western grain growers to ship grain to any terminal elevator they liked (including the pool terminals) and have weight and grade of grain guaranteed.*
>
> *We got through the House of Commons Old Age Pensions, single transferable vote, senate reform and rural credits.*
>
> *I assisted in putting women on the same basis as men in regard to divorce in the western provinces.*
>
> *I assisted in lowering taxes and in lowering tariff on many articles; helped on co-operative marketing when I could.*
>
> *Spoke and worked against state-aided immigration policy.*

Spoke and worked for international harmony and active good will; talked and practised economy and supported every effort toward reduction of debt.

I supported every effort worthwhile to secure markets.

Voted on the merits of all questions.

Answered hundreds of requests for information, help, etc.

Sent 500 letters every month to South East Grey on the work of the Session.

Made 200 speeches in South East Grey on national issues.

Helped young people and children to develop themselves and to be alert citizens.

Gave all assistance I could to organizations of women and men.

Had several mail routes extended and changed to better serve people's needs.

Had several railway crossings improved.

Got electric lights in Holstein station and cattle rates from Holstein reduced.

Got many soldiers and their families pensions and hospital treatment for soldiers.

Secured vote of $25,000 in 1926 estimates for Durham Post Office.

Returned $5,060 [part of her salary] *to Dominion Treasury.*

I handled alone large delegation of women from Oshawa.

Visited Washington as a representative of the Women's International League for Peace — chosen as the only Canadian delegate to Dublin.

I tried by my actions to smooth the way for women who came after.

I strove to serve Canada truly and thus raise the tone of Canadian public life.

I am not ashamed of my record.

On Election Day, September 14, Agnes told the *Toronto Evening Telegram* that she was spending the day "laying down the law to deputy returning officers and scrutineers. . . . So far I have not had a chance to do anything else. . . . I think it is high time the entire election machinery was taken out of the hands of partisans and some experts permanently engaged who know the election law. I am having no end of trouble ever since the polls opened. They are challenging names of voters regularly on the lists, apparently just because they have been visiting out of the riding for a short time. It is quite ridiculous, for the law is very clear. I am doing the best I can to straighten the matter out over the long distance phone." [13]

Agnes said she planned to spend the day "chiefly at the telephone directing her forces and in the vicinity of her home poll." She would receive returns at her home in the early evening and go to Flesherton and Durham about 9:30. The *Telegram* said that Conservative workers were very hopeful of defeating Miss Macphail.

As the *Durham Review* predicted, it was a "forlorn hope." Agnes was returned with a majority of 1722. The Conservative Party was defeated and Meighen retired. The Liberals secured a clear majority and formed the new

Agnes in the garden, Ceylon, Ontario

The Macphails' home in Ceylon, Ontario

government. The Progressives were in disarray. Robert Forke had resigned the leadership and with several other Progressives pledged to support the Liberals. Now he accepted the post of Minister of Immigration in the King government.

Commenting on the election, the *Durham Review* said it

> *was one of the keenest in many years. The Conservative leaders made a strenuous effort to defeat Miss Macphail, they brought Meighen into the riding, sent Hon. Hugh Guthrie to Hanover and Feversham, and some party hangers-on with unwise zeal tried a whispering campaign, that recoiled on their own heads. Miss MacPhail will, we think, consider this her greatest victory, considering the odds against her. . . .*
>
> *Great interest was shown as returns came in. The Conservative Committee rooms was a busy spot, so was the telephone office, till at last the Town Hall was secured and there the winners of the day assembled, filling the hall even to standing room. Miss MacPhail was sent for and until she came an impromptu program was conducted . . . [with] community singing . . . and at intervals returns from the Country were received.*
>
> *At last the well known figure of Miss MacPhail appeared in the doorway and as she with some difficulty made her way to the front, tremendous applause greeted her, continued as she stood before them, the victor of the day.[14]*

In 1926 Dougald and Henrietta Macphail retired to Ceylon. They bought an attractive ginger bread trimmed house on the main street. It sat on top of a steep hill and the grounds were large enough to have the gardens that Mrs. Macphail loved.

Before they left the farm, neighbors gathered for a last evening in the old home and presented them with a "beautiful pyrex casserole in a silver stand." Mrs. A. Hincks read an address which concluded, "As neighbours and friends you were unsurpassed — a joy to know, ever ready to give a helping hand, sharing your joys and lightening our cares. We treasure that high and noble friendship.

"Mr. and Mrs. Macphail are widely known and respected and Agnes has shown her ability and genius in her untiring and painstaking service as our worthy M.P. We may well be proud of the distinction she has brought to this community."

The *Durham Review* said the evening was spent in "music and chat" and Agnes gave "a short sketch of her trip to Boston where she had been invited to speak to exclusive clubs on 'Canada, your neighbour' and 'Canadian elections.'"[15]

Back in Ottawa Agnes told members it was quite time more women came to the House.

> *They could not do worse than the men have done; of that I am fully convinced. At least they would not talk quite so much, and when they did it would be about something. The mountain of words that overwhelms the most trivial business in this House is a perpetually amazing thing to me. I hope the time is not far distant when women*

will sit in this House representing the sentiments that the different parties now represent. I do not believe in a woman group, much as I believe in groups, but I do believe that women should now come to the House of Commons, because they will take direct action, because they are interested in human welfare more than in making long speeches that are very difficult to follow.

On April 6, 1927, she spoke for the second time on the naturalization of women, arguing that women should not lose their nationality by marrying an alien and expanding on the original plea she had made in her first speech in the Commons:

Miss A. C. Macphail: Mr. Speaker, there are many Canadian women who resent the injustice which women who are British subjects, but married to aliens, suffer in regard to naturalization. A woman may be a Canadian, she may be the grandchild of Canadians, but if she marries an alien she ceases to be a British subject. She may not resume her British nationality until her husband chooses to become naturalized; and if he dies or the marriage is dissolved the woman remains an alien until she makes a declaration and obtains a certificate from the Secretary of State. It would seem that such treatment makes naturalization of small account. It must be of little importance if adults can be naturalized without satisfying the condition as to desirability and without being required to take the oath of allegiance, and it certainly is insulting to women to assume that their allegiance can be transferred without their own consent.

Under the present law marriage and citizenship are very much mixed up. I don't think the two should be so closely related, if related at all. There are scores of British women resident in Canada who, having married aliens, find themselves citizens of no country, unable to claim the protection of any government, unable to vote, unable to teach or accept any civil position should the need arise, and, in the event of their husbands' death, unable to participate in the mother's allowance for the benefit of their children. Because of their statelessness they find it almost impossible to obtain a passport. I have a letter from a woman in Ontario received when the resolution in regard to this subject appeared on the order paper. She lives in Prince Edward county and pays taxes, but at the last election on December 1 not only herself but twenty-five other women in the county were prevented from voting. She tells that her great grandfather was an officer in the Revolutionary war and a British subject and she describes how loyal they had always been; yet after marriage to an American, although they live in Canada and she owns large property and pays taxes, she finds herself unable to vote in any election in this country. She writes protesting such treatment.

Last year I tried to get a passport for an Ontario girl who was married to an alien. I could not obtain the passport and she had to cancel her trip. Many other members of this House could tell similar stories. I have heard them in private conversation. . . . When it is considered that, in western Canada particularly, we are receiving from many shores aliens who are marrying women of British nationality, this is a matter of vital concern to Canada.

The right of women to retain their British nationality although married to aliens was enjoyed until the year 1870. . . . In that year the law was changed to provide that a married woman should be deemed to be the subject of the state of which her husband for the time being was a subject. When this change was made the women of Great Britain — for this is British law — were not consulted at all, and the subject received very little debate in the House of Commons, through which it passed very hurriedly. . . .

In the British Nationality and Status Act, 1914, women gained the principle, excluded since 1870, that a woman might be of different nationality from her husband. . . .

In 1922 Lord Danesfort brought forward a bill, which passed its second reading, containing two important principles: first, British women should have the right to retain their nationality when they married aliens; and second, that an alien woman should not by the mere act of marriage with a British subject become a British subject. Dissolution of Parliament prevented anything further being done, but in 1923 a select Committee of the Lords and Commons was appointed to consider the subject. This committee, comprising five commoners and five lords, agreed that a change was necessary. But, one of the lords dissenting, no recommendations were made when the report was presented. The objection advanced by this dissenting lord was that the change would result in trouble in the home. Men and women, it was urged, were one. We all know that, but the thing I want to know is, which one? If it is going to disturb the harmony of the home to have any change of nationality on the part of either husband or wife, let the husband take the nationality of the wife. It is as fair that way as the other. I have no great fear that the home will be disrupted if women are given the vote, or if they go to work, or if they retain their nationality. Every advance made by woman has been frowned upon because of this very fear of the home being disrupted. Men are always worried about this consequence, but it does not happen, for the simple reason that the real home is a community of interests so strong that it will take more than any change of nationality, more than the vote or any of these things to disrupt it. We need not worry about the home on that account.

The matter was brought forward again in the British House of Commons in 1925, when Major Harvey introduced a resolution, which was carried, to the following effect:

> *That in the opinion of this House a British woman should not lose or be deemed to lose her nationality by mere act of marriage with an alien, but that it should be open to her to make declaration of alienage.*

I believe that public opinion in this country favours a change. . . . From the beginning we can conclude that the British House of Commons on various occasions had wanted to do something about

*the matter. . . . I cannot see why they did not hear from our Domin-
ion, and I think it is time the Parliament of the country took whatever
steps are necessary to make it possible for British women married to
aliens to retain their own nationality. . . .*

*A Canadian girl who marries an American ceases to be a British
subject and does not become a citizen of the United States, and is
therefore a citizen of no country. . . .*

*Resolutions asking for this change have been passed by women's
organizations in Canada for many years past, among those outstanding being the National Council of Women, who have time and
again asked that women be naturalized of their own right, and that
marriage to an alien should not affect them in any way. The Canadian Council of Agriculture have presented this question to the
cabinet almost times without number. The Womens' Institutes of
Canada have taken a firm stand upon it, together with the Social
Service Council of Canada. The Alberta legislature on two occasions
adopted resolutions dealing with this problem, one of which was
introduced last session by Hon. Irene Parlby and seconded by Mrs.
Nellie McClung, but no action was taken in this House. As I have
already pointed out, Great Britain adopted Major Harvey's resolution
in 1924, and I do not see why the parliament of Canada has not taken
some stand on this question.*

*I realize that this is an international matter, but after all it will
not be dealt with in an international way until all the countries
affected deal with it first, and I appeal to the members of this
House in the name of the womanhood of this country to see that
this injustice is removed and that women have the same right of
citizenship accorded to men. I think women love their country as
much as men, and since women are not to-day property as they
were thought to be in days gone by, but thinking individuals, I
appeal to this House of Commons to take the first opportunity to
do all that can be done in this matter. Let it be taken up by the
League of Nations or the next Imperial Conference; let us do
anything that can be done in order to remove this injustice.*[16]

On April 9, 1927, during another debate on cadet training, Agnes asked
why the cadet vote had been increased from $400,000 to $500,000. She
argued that cadet training was clearly military, not physical training; that it
was teaching Canadian boys to become "killers of men." She said: "We
cannot find security by arming ourselves to the very limit. I do not believe
that preparedness for war will bring peace. What we carefully prepare for
we usually get. If we prepare for war we get war; if we prepare for peace
we shall get peace. . . . We may safely conclude that war settles nothing. It
causes other wars by arousing hatreds. It brings unemployment, poverty,
misery, crime and death . . . leads the youth to think of it as the one
method of settling international disputes. . . . Wars are now world-embrac-
ing, and civilization can stand few more of them. It is more than likely that
it would find it impossible to stand one more. . . ." She moved that the item
be reduced by $499,999, leaving one dollar for cadet training.

M.P. Brady disagreed with Agnes and said in part:

The hon. member for Southeast Grey is very strongly opposed to cadet training. . . . I do not hold that view myself. I believe that cadet training in this country is one of the best and one of the finest things that has ever been inaugurated in the Dominion of Canada. I believe it is a good thing for the boys to come under a certain amount of discipline and be taught to play the game and cooperate with others. To say a boy who is taught to march and counter-march and go through some of the simpler elements of drill in the schoolyard is having his mind filled with a desire to slaughter and that it makes him want to kill people is the most utter nonsense that ever was uttered by anybody in the world. To say that to teach a boy to shoot straight is to fill his mind with the idea of killing his fellowmen is colossal nonsense. We can all recollect the times in the past when the little boys wore a broad white collar about a foot wide, and a long flowing tie, with a little hat on the side of the head, and how pretty they were. How we loved those little fellows — little Lord Fauntleroys: We all admired and loved those little chaps, but where I differ, and where I think most members of this House differ, from the hon. member for Southeast Grey is that while it is alright for these little chaps to be little Lord Fauntleroys when they are six and perhaps eight years old, we do not want them to be little Lord Fauntleroys when they grow up to be men, and to have an extra cookie when they go to bed at night and have grandma sing lullabys to them to put them to sleep. We do not want a class of men in this country that you might call she-men.

To which Agnes replied:

I think it would be very much better for a lot of men, possibly for the hon. member who has the floor, if they could be called she-men. If that meant they had some of the attributes of women, it would be a very good thing for the men. I resent very deeply the hon. member's insult to women calling boys whom he wishes to discredit she-boys. Since when did the male become greater than the female? [17]

On February 29, 1928, an editorial writer of the *Ottawa Journal* said he wished more members "could speak with the wit, satire and good humour of Miss Agnes Macphail." The editorial referred to a speech which was "by long odds the best and most arresting that the House has had this year." While the writer did not agree with some of the subject matter,

the speech was an excellent one, passionate enough to show sincerity; witty beyond the capacity of most males in the House; satirical enough to delight a Lloyd George.

Miss Macphail has captured the best parliamentary manner. It is a manner, unfortunately not much prevalent here, but it is a manner that would go at Westminster. The old pompous rhetoric has gone out of date, and it is the master of the light touch and the deft stroke that is now supreme. Miss Macphail has developed

*the latter gift to an extraordinary and surprising degree, and
whether one agrees with her or not, one cannot but salute her for
her skill. That, indeed, is what Parliament did for her, as for forty
minutes Grit and Tory remained glued to their seats, alternatively
amused, irritated and chastised by the flash of her eloquence.*

The speech was made on Tuesday, February 28, 1928, during the debate
on the budget. The *Ottawa Journal* reserved its headline ("Miss Macphail
Most Critical Liberal Action") and lead paragraphs for Agnes Macphail.
("Miss Agnes Macphail had words of caustic criticism in the House yester-
day. As she rose to continue debate on the budget, she faced a well-filled
House which laughed and cheered as shaft after shaft went home.")

Hansard, February 28, 1928, recorded her words:

*We come again to a consideration of the budget brought down
by the Minister of Finance (Mr. J. A. Robb). In the opinion of the
members of the Liberal Party that budget is a good one and I am
sure they will support it. The Liberal-Progressive members, I am
sure, do not think it is a good budget, but they will support it.
The Liberals from Saskatchewan, coming as they do from that
part of this enlightened Dominion, cannot like the budget and yet
I am expecting to hear them say it is a good budget. The Conservatives think this is a good budget but they must declare it not to
be so and having said that, they will not be able to vote for it. I
think it a rich man's budget and I am in the splendid position of
saying that I do not like it and of voting in accordance with my
views. So also are those honorable members who sit around
me. . . . Agriculture is still the main business of the Canadian
people. The nation's prosperity depends on a bumper crop. It has
been well said that the agricultural returns are the barometer of
national prosperity. . . .*

*The roots of the tree of Canada's national life have been
injured. We have, for a young and rich country, a depleted and
impoverished agricultural industry. In this young country, agriculture has not held its own people, nor its power of place and
influence. I regret it, but it is true.*

*I do not think anyone in this House will care to deny that our
educational, religious, business and political policies have been
framed, not with rural needs in mind, but rather, whether consciously or unconsciously, directly antagonistic to those needs.
The result is clear to anybody who cares to look around, namely,
that our people are leaving the land in numbers that would worry
any government, even this one. It does not seem to go further than
worry with them, but still it worries them. . . .*

*It is quite true that many people who leave the land and come
to the cities give leadership to city enterprises and gain for
themselves a place of power and possibly of wealth; but again the
country is robbed of very much needed leadership and the places
in the country that have been vacated are being taken by citizens
of other lands. . . .*

*Country life develops thoughtful, wholesome and genuine
people, to a greater extent than any other life, and I think it is
true that in the last analysis the conscience of the nation lies in
the country. I think we can all bear testimony, if we care to, to
the fact that in cities and towns the conventions of life veneer
even the ways of our friends and it is in the country that we find
the beauty of simplicity and sometimes the bluntness of unaffected
candour. Country living makes for character and because of the
need of character in all national undertakings, and because of the
importance of agriculture in our national life, we see how disastrous the results must be if people continue to leave the land.
Aside from the economic consequences, it heralds the approach of
the time when the country will no longer furnish that leadership
in business and public life which has been so influential in shap-
ing the course of events.*

*The rural problem is a many-sided problem and I am not one
of those who think that governments are so important that they
altogether make the problem, or, to any great extent, solve it. I
know there are many other forces which operate. It would take
too long — and I never wanted to speak for forty minutes until I
could not speak any longer — to go into all the phases of this
question, but I should like to mention one thing that I think has
done much to aggravate our rural problem and that is our educational system. It is true that the whole educational trend is towards the city. Our educational system in Canada has acted
simply as a "gangway" to life in urban centres . . . too many
people are rushed into city enterprises; we have an abundance of
people hunting for white-collar jobs and too few people who are
willing to do the very much nobler and better work of nation-
building in the open spaces. I am glad that I have not had too
much of that kind of education to prevent me thinking for myself,
but we have an educational system that actually stuffs children
with facts and creates in them a reverence for things as they are,
and this is a great disaster to our children, because it hinders
them in creating institutions to meet changed conditions. . . .*

*Until lately the fact that the farmer produced goods but did not
market them added greatly to the rural problem. He was not a
business man. Now the farmer is becoming a business man, and
as a keen business man he is not going to put up with the slip-
shod methods that obtain, particularly in this House I
thought it would be worthwhile putting on Hansard this sentence
of Professor Macklin of Wisconsin University: "The industry that
neglects to assume the responsibility of marketing its own products arrives last in the race for the consumer's dollar — like the
runt pig."*

*The farmer is ceasing to be the runt pig and he is learning to
market his own products. He is not going to be last in the race
for the consumer's dollar, and he is going to demand educational
systems that will meet his needs. I should like to know why some*

> *fellow with a fossilized brain sitting in some office in some gov-*
> *ernment service should direct the kind of education which the*
> *children of farmers are to have, and I hope the day may speedily*
> *come when that will not be the case.*

Agnes went on to review for the "edification" of the House "a history of the political life of Canada as it related to farmers just before and since 1896."

Prior to 1896 Canadian farmers were, to a large extent, Liberals because they believed the Liberal party "was opposed to special privileges and high tariffs." In 1897, however, Sir Wilfrid Laurier's protectionist policy "betrayed" Liberalism and all it had stood for "from the days of Wm. Lyon Mackenzie." "From that time on [the Liberals] never did regain the confidence of the low tariff farmers . . . and [the betrayal] was really one of the causes of the revolt which brought in the 65 Independents in 1921."

She told of the trials the farm group endured from 1921 to 1925 and of the legislative program they forced the government to adopt in 1926. "We got a reduction in the tariff — the only real reduction the Liberal party has ever been guilty of; we got rural credits; we got old age pensions — not as good as it might have been, but certainly something worthwhile; we got the Hudson Bay railway. In fact we got many things, and this legislative program captured the imagination of the people, with the result that the electorate sent back the Liberal government as you see it today. And they sent back the independent group that sits in this quarter of the House."

She ended by upbraiding the government for the "false friendship" they had shown the new groups from 1921 on and for discouraging progressive thought in Canada. [18]

Toronto's *Saturday Night* referred to this speech as the most eloquent she had ever given and said she had developed into "one of the most forceful voices in the party, the most effective tormenter of the government and so the special object of Liberal resentment." It said she had obviously "punctured" Mr. Dunning's [19] skin because he spent a good part of his forty minutes "talking rather violently about her." Mr. Hepburn of Elgin also tried to "destroy her by a closer approach to personalities than is usually resorted to in the House. But she is easily a match for both, and gives a little better than she receives." [20]

A reporter from the *Detroit News* described Agnes as a "snappy person, very snappy." He had expected a "wizened old maid" and was startled when he saw her.

"Here," he said, "was a very personable young woman, trim of figure, quite good looking, modishly gowned, with big blue eyes that look squarely into yours as she speaks. [Most said her eyes were dark brown or hazel. Consensus is that they were brown.] She has all the poise and confidence of a duchess. She speaks English like an American and certainly knows her grammar. As a public speaker she easily outranks 75 per cent of the members of the Commons. When she speaks, the English language is in the hands of a friend, although she is not averse to a bit of slang which she handles adroitly."

The reporter wanted to hear her speak in the House and Agnes said, "The first time I get a chance I'll rip into the boys." She kept her promise the next day. The House was debating bringing back titles for Canadians. Five minutes before the House adjourned "there came the clear tones of a woman: 'Mr. Speaker. It is five minutes to 6, but five minutes will be quite enough to permit me to express my utter disgust with the proposal to bring back titles to this country. Surely we have in Canada enough fuss and feathers and grandeur and nonsense without having senseless, meaningless titles dumped on us.'"

There was more of the same, reported the paper, and "the Liberals and Conservatives sat silent, although the Prime Minister watched her intently. He evidently was interested, as anyone would be."

Agnes told the *News* that the Progressives didn't have as much power as they had when the King government was dependent on them for its existence. "Then we could demand reforms. Now, all we can do is to set the pace. . . ."

The reporter had heard that Agnes "had rather cut their Excellencies (the governor-general and the Viscountess Willingdon) . . . that you gave them a curt nod instead of a curtsey."

"'It wasn't quite that bad,' she said with a laugh. 'But I did make it pretty snappy. I'm not much for bowing and scraping. Why should I curtsey to any woman any more than she should curtsey to me? All this bowing stuff, all this gold braid and pomp and ceremony and grandeur are just — what is the word you Yankees use?'"

The reporter suggested "damned rot," and Agnes agreed it was an appropriate description.

She asked the reporter what he thought of Calvin Coolidge, President of the United States. "'He's from Massachusetts,' said the reporter weakly, not knowing what else to say.

'I don't care a whoop where he's from. But how about him? I spent three minutes with him in Washington and when I reached the street I wanted to scream, 'How does he get away with it?' He didn't appear to have an idea.'" [21]

Later that day the reporter met Agnes at a vice-regal ball given by Lord and Lady Willingdon at Government House. He said that Agnes wore an evening gown "that certainly did not come from the back concessions that form her bailiwick. Her blue eyes are smiling and her face flushed with excitement and the vigor of the dancing." They danced and the reporter ended his story [which Agnes labelled "mostly rot"]: "Agnes Macphail, M.P., is interesting, very interesting." [22]

In an age which glorified war in poetry, prose and song, Agnes was very much out of step.

"Patriotism is not dying for one's country," she said, "it is living for one's country and for humanity. Perhaps that is not as romantic but it is better." [23]

On March 26, 1928, she moved for the establishment of a Peace Department to work for peace and international understanding. She said in part:

> We have not in Canada, and indeed not to any extent anywhere in the world, studied constructively the art of making peace or the technique of peace. I think the technique of war has been studied by some of the most astute minds in all countries. . . . No one can doubt that in Canada the institution of war is a most respected one which the "best people" like very much. . . . I view this condition with alarm.
>
> I do not however question the patriotism of those people . . . who believe that that is the way to be a patriotic citizen. . . . I simply question their wisdom. . . . On the other hand, often in the past in

*this house, the patriotism of people like myself and those who think
with me has been questioned. . . . One might ask, what is patriotism?
Surely it is loyalty to a group; but sometimes we forget that we owe
loyalty to many groups. We cannot have too much loyalty. . . . But
we can have too much loyalty to one group, forgetting the other
groups to which we also belong. We are more and more coming to
know that every one of us belongs to that group which is known as
humanity, and that we do owe a very great loyalty to that largest
group of all — humanity. . . .*

*It is worthy of note, too, that patriotism is not an innate thing; it
is cultivated, and it will be just what we train it to be. If we train the
children and the young people of this country to view patriotism as a
very much bigger thing than we have thought of it in the past, then
within one generation, if we set about it with decision and a desire to
win, we shall have a new patriotism, which, while not making light of
the love of our own country, will expand to cover the needs of all
countries. . . .*

*Canada is young . . . and youth always looks to the future. In
looking to the future, and not to the present, we must all realize that
we need to build the security of the world on something more stable
than military preparedness. We have had since the end of the great
war a very great many memorials to the brave who gave their lives
in the service of their country during that awful conflict. My own
personal opinion is that many of the memorials which are supposed
to lead us to think of the service and love and devotion of those who
died simply glorify the institution of war. I think that the formation of
a peace department would be a fitting commemoration of the devotion and sacrifice of the 60,000 Canadians who died. . . .*

*We have at the front of this building a tower which is called a
peace tower. I was greatly interested in going through it and looking
over it carefully, and my conclusion was that it is a very exquisite
piece of work, but that it is misnamed. No one who looks over it
carefully can call it a peace chamber. It so clearly, one might almost
say so brazenly, though beautifully, glorifies the institution of war.
That sort of thing will never lead the young men and young women
of Canada to think of new methods. It will simply lead them to think
of the glory of the old. . . .*

*I do not wish dogmatically to lay down what a department of
peace might do, but I hope I shall not tire the House too much by
offering a few suggestions as to the work of such a de-partment. . . .*

*A department of peace should be twofold in character. First, it
should have general supervision of an extensive program for peace
throughout Canada. Secondly, it should cultivate friendly relations
with other countries by promoting our knowledge of other people
with regard to their cultural, moral and social achievements. This
would be very interesting to Canadians, and we have very much to
learn along this line. Then, too, it should encourage the work of
international institutions, including the League of Nations, and make
known their work to our people, so that we would be made ac-*

quainted with all the machinery that has been set up in any part of the world for finding new methods of settling international difficulties. I think that such a department should also study the causes of war, and by frank discussion present evidence revealing the wastefulness and ineffectiveness of war. It might also make clear to our people some of our own mannerisms that offend the sensibilities of other nations. I do think we have a British superiority complex which must be very offensive to other nations, and cannot be making any contribution to the harmony of the world. . . . The department could also prepare a list of speakers, who, while not employed by the government, could, through the department, be made available for addressing public meetings. . . . Our government departments issue booklets, pamphlets, posters and films, and there seems to be no great reason why a department of peace could not use the same means to make known to the Canadian people the truths regarding peace and war.

And how little money it would cost the government to make a gift of books for the promotion of peace. These books could be issued to our public and school libraries. We have Rhodes scholarships in this country. We might establish peace scholarships on a somewhat similar plan, allotting a scholarship to each province. The Rhodes scholarships I think are confined to young men, but I would want these peace scholarships available to young women as well. The winners of these scholarships would go abroad each year to study along lines which would make them better world citizens and at the same time better citizens of Canada.

It has occurred to me — I do not claim any originality for the idea — that we might very well establish a yearly peace award for the best work done in the cause of peace. This award I suggest should be given by the government and might be confined to Canadians or be made open to the citizens of any country. The award would not be confined necessarily to the greatest contribution scholastically to the peace of the world, but to the best work to this end along any line.

We have a military college where young men are prepared to be warriors. Why not establish a college to train young men in promoting understandings throughout the world? This would be far better work and those engaged in it would become much better citizens, with all respect to the graduates from the military college. Then instead of making grants for the training of cadets in summer camps — and but for these grants the cadet movement would not continue for another five years — the government might use the money to much better purpose for the establishment of summer schools to promote the study of international friend-ship. . . . I should think that the work of this department would be unlimited, adventurous and wholly positive rather than destructive as is military training at the present time. Such a department would call to the highest in us; it would call out our mental and spiritual attributes, challenging them, rather than the physical, which is on the lowest possible plane. . . .

In closing I would ask the government not to consider the matter *lightly, because it is not a trivial subject; it includes within itself all others and is the most important subject facing mankind to-day. If we do not find some new way there is nothing surer than that, if we keep on for another twenty-five years as we have been doing since 1918, we shall have another war whether we like it or not. Nothing can prevent it if we keep preparing for war.* [24]

Several members replied to Agnes' speech. While all were in sympathy with the object of the resolution, most opposed the establishment of a separate Department of Peace. On March 28 she withdrew the motion but not before she castigated her opponents. She said she had been almost alarmed on Monday when all parties had seemed to endorse almost everything in the resolution. She thought times had changed — "but I feel more at home today." She respected the views of others in the House but did not understand how they arrived at some of their conclusions:

The honorable member for St. Lawrence-St. George (Mr. Cahan) dragged in the Crimean War, perhaps unhappily. I believe it was Lord Salisbury of England who said long after the Crimean War that England had backed the wrong horse. I suppose a lot of people died because England backed the wrong horse, but if anyone had said so at the time there would have been a great hullabaloo; they would have been unpatriotic. The honorable member also said that on this subject women have different views from men; I hope to heaven he is right. That should be a good argument why the women of his province should be given the franchise. Half the people of Canada are women and there seems no good reason why the voice of women in regard to peace and war should not be expressed in the House, and also through the actions of the government. We do believe that women have a different point of view in regard to war; women place life on a higher plane than men have placed it in the past, because women have suffered more that life may be."

She told Prime Minister Mackenzie King that she had heard him make good speeches but that his recent one on peace was not one of them.

The statement of the government, through the Minister of National Defence and the Prime Minister is something like this — we want security, and we are trying to win it in two ways — through education, which we leave to all departments, and through military preparedness, which we carefully organize and put under the direction of one of the ablest men . . . in the cabinet. But the idea that security can be obtained by wiping out suspicion, fear and ignorance we leave to everybody, and what is everybody's business will be well done. That was the argument advanced by those gentlemen. . . . The Prime Minister is a sensible and clever man, and he knows as well as I do that what is left to all the departments will not be done by any. [25]

On January 24, 1929, the *Durham Review* reported a story of "historical" interest — a woman had been invited to debate at Hart House, the University of Toronto's athletic and social centre for male students. The woman, of course, was Agnes Macphail. The men had broken their inflexible "males only" rule because Miss Macphail was a member of the federal Parliament.

The motion for discussion — that female emancipation had not justified its promises — was to be moved by R. W. Finlayson, son of Honorable William Finlayson. Miss Macphail would have the moral support of the co-eds who would "be admitted to the gallery of the House for the first time in its history."

The *Alberta Labor News* reported:

> *Miss Macphail upheld and won her side of the debate . . .*
> [she] *scored a triumph for women — and brought new laurels to herself.*
>
> *In speaking to the argument that "a woman's place is in the home" Miss Macphail said: "I take it a woman's place is any place she wants to be." . . .*
>
> [She] *said that woman's emancipation had not yet been completed, will not be until the emancipation of all humanity is complete and that will not be until personal rights replace property rights as the basis of society.*
>
> *"I am not insensible to the high honor done me," said Miss Macphail. "The first speaker said that all women got out of politics is the chance to choose between two crooks. Well, she has had plenty of practice. In this whole debate you see clearly the superiority complex of the male."*

She recited a list of women's wrongs not yet righted. Women did not get equal pay for equal work. Nor did they get equal honor. In handing out political honors in England they made men dukes but did not make women duchesses. If a woman in Canada married an alien she lost her citizenship. A woman could not establish a legal domicile for a divorce. The supreme court of Canada had declared that women were not "persons." All the laws of all the countries were based on that theory.

> *Man had always done his best to suppress the superior type of woman who might rival him and refuse to obey him. "Through the ages man had chosen the kittenish, soft, clinging, pliable type which made it easy for him to hold the place his superiority complex told him he should have." Twisting the views of the founder of Christianity as St. Paul had done, the Christian religion had taught for long centuries of woman's slavery that "man was made for the glory of God, but woman for the glory of man."*
>
> *"How can the great mass of women be free," she asked, "when they have no economic independence? There are two classes of women whose absence from the home no one gets excited about. Those are charwomen and society women. It is when the middle-class women who are the mothers of our most intelligent citizens leave the home that an outcry is made."*

She said in conclusion of a speech that had more argument and just as much wit as the undergraduate funsters: "If there was a promise in woman's emancipation, it was that she would put human rights above property rights. Woman's effort along this line had been encouraging, for instance in child welfare, education and the movement for peace. With the current of public opinion all against woman, I am not ashamed of her record." [26]

Referring to the debate in her weekly letter to riding newspapers, Agnes said:

And then the Hart House debate! When the Warden of Hart House wired me to take part in the debate in Hart House, conducted in Parliamentary style. . . . I was glad to accept and I must say the men of Hart House, once they decided to do this awful thing of having a woman come to eat dinner and debate like a human being, did the business thoroughly and well. It was a delicious dinner and quite possibly cooked by women and served by girls — but it tasted none the less good on that account. The undergraduates didn't take the subject dealing with women's progress very seriously. They were witty and light and a bit contemptuous but they voted right and that helps a lot.

It was a real experience for me and added to the richness of life and I am grateful. [27]

A month after the debate, Parliament re-opened:

A typical February snowstorm ushered in the third session of the 16th Parliament. Snow had fallen steadily all night. The morning of February 27th found the snow piled high everywhere. The Capital City was in festive robes of white.

Everything went off well — the 19 guns included. Reviving an ancient custom, the Governor General drove from Rideau Hall to Parliament Hill in an open sleigh, accompanied by out-riders and received by a company of Governor General Foot Guards.

After a fitting word of thanksgiving for the King's progress to health the speech said a good deal about the good and abundant crops. They are always good crops the next February to people who did not grow them and who live comfortably. Prosperity was given much space. We are very prosperous; if you do not feel it, just take the Government's word for it. The speech did not make it quite clear whether our thanks for the prosperity was due to Providence or Government but the impression was left that the Government bulked largely in the cause. . . .

Usually several weeks are taken up by what is called the Address to His Excellency in reply to the Speech from the Throne. This year only seven members took part. In five hours it was over. The unexpected speed left us breathless. It was as though the threshing tractor went tearing up the road like the new Chevrolet. [28]

On February 19, 1929, during a debate on International Peace and the Kellogg-Briand Pact — the latter condemned war and agreed to peaceful settlement of international differences — Agnes congratulated Prime Minster

Mackenzie King on his "very excellent work" while in Paris to sign the pact. She praised M. Briand's speech, in which he called the pact, upheld by sixty-two nations, "a direct blow at the institution of war." She continued:

> *The people of the world want a reduction of armaments, they want to recognize the causes of war and intelligently strive to remove them. . . . The leader of the opposition this afternoon used these words, "educational obligations rest upon us." I thank him for those words. I hope to use them many times in the future. That is true; we must organize peace. . . .*
>
> *We might very well listen to the Right Honorable Stanley Baldwin, Prime Minister of Great Britain, who, addressing the League of Nations Society of Great Britain this year, said that all those who really desire peace should be missionaries of peace. I take it that he is a missionary of peace and that he is exceedingly desirous of the peace of the world. It is well for us at times to be idealists, not to be scoffers and doubters, not to be cynical, but to believe that all the people of the world, regardless of colour, regardless of the country in which they live, are fine people, and if we treat them as though they are, they will treat us in the same spirit. It is well for us sometimes to go to the hilltops, and when we do as individuals and in great moments as nations, we see a fairer world. The fairer world is no dream; it can be made a reality if each of us takes the matter seriously and works towards that end.*[29]

Her next few weekly letters to her riding comprised a variety of topics:

March 6, 1929

> *"There was a sound of revelry by night,*
> *And Canada's capital had gathered there,*
> *Her beauty and her chivalry, and bright*
> *The lamps shone o'er fair women and brave men."*[30]
>
> *That night was Wednesday, February 20th.*
> *Other nights we work until 11 p.m., but when the Cabinet Ministers' wives give a reception on our only free night, we quit work at 6 o'clock, get a bite to eat and from then to 9 o'clock we do our best to overcome nature's deficiencies and fit ourselves into the poetic description given above. We call a taxi — even if it is our last cent — it isn't good form to walk or take a street car — and grandly draw up to the members' entrance of the House of Commons.*
> *Although the reception begins at nine, it is frightfully embarrassing to be first and as everyone tries not to be, the whole affair is delayed a bit, but by 9:30 the crowd is passing in front of the Cabinet Ministers' wives, who stand in a semi-circle in the stately Hall of Fame, saying a kindly word of welcome to everyone. The wives of the cabinet ministers are a remarkably fine group of women. Two ministers haven't any wives — poor things.*
> *For some time the crowd mince about, speaking to friends and greeting new people, but soon the orchestra strikes up and those who enjoy dancing go to the railway committee room or dance in the corridors to the music supplied by the amplifiers. Such a gathering gives*

*one a chance to meet people as human beings, not as members of a
certain party or representatives of a certain country, but just folks.[31]*

April 18, 1929

*The uproar in the House of Commons on April 11th would have
done credit to a loyal town with the home team on ice. The long dreary
budget debate was finishing. And boys will be boys — though bald and
weighty. The gang spirit was evident; only the opportunity was necessary
to let loose party antagonism.*

*Dr. Manion of Fort William came to address the House. Dr. Manion
is a fiery, fluent and exceedingly rapid speaker who more than any other
man in the Conservative Party tends to rouse party animosity. The
Conservatives supported him with almost continuous applause; the
Liberals interrupted with growls, yelling and yapping. I have seen two
gangs of boys, each with a favorite fighting dog watching their struggle
for supremacy with much the same look on their faces. Dr. Manion
twitted the cabinet members with spending Easter in the United States
with low tariff talk and high tariff performance. On the matter of the
tariff, Dr. Manion stated that our government policy was made in
Washington, not Ottawa.*

*And now Pouliot [Jean-Francois Pouliot, Témiscouata], the aggres-
sive, unmanageable Frenchman arose. The waves of applause carried
him as the orchestra carries the soloist. The yowls and growls now
came from the Opposition.*

*A talkie-movie of the performance would be very enlightening to the
citizens of Canada. The scene defies description. Had a burlesque of
Parliament been well written and well played it could not have excelled
Thursday's performance.[32]*

April 25, 1929

Wednesday night, April 17, at 7:30 o'clock, I saw Dr. Edwards [the
Honorable J. W. Edwards, Conservative, Frontenac] *and Mrs. Edwards
in the dining room. The first news Thursday morning was of his passing; so suddenly does death come.*

*Dr. Edwards had been ill two days before; he left the hospital
against the advice of his doctor, thinking his faintness not due to his
heart. He was in the building all day Wednesday.*

*Practically the whole membership of the Commons and the Senate
attended the funeral service held before the body was taken to Kingston,
his home city.*

*Death is the common denominator; the great leveller. How vain is
the high places of man. Never was the lesson brought home to me so
clearly. The Prime Minister, Sir Robert Borden[33], Hon. R. B. Bennett,
Hon. Rodolphe Lemieux, the cabinet ministers, robbed of power of place
were, just as we plain people, awed and questioning in the presence of
the Grim Reaper. He was — he is not.[34]*

On March 19, 1929, Hansard related Agnes' reproval of the Conservatives for
claiming they had given the vote to women:

I sometimes think that Canada suffers greatly from an inferiority complex, but evidently it has not infected the Conservative party. I greatly enjoyed the speech of the hon. member for Vancouver Centre (Mr. Stevens). He always speaks clearly and well, but I am astounded that in this enlightened day he should claim credit for the Conservative party for giving the franchise to women. I do not know of anything more scandalous except the War Time Elections Act, of which it was a part, than the manner of granting the franchise to women in 1917. Does the hon. member for Vancouver Centre and his party not know that it was the starvation and the fighting and the going to jail and the forcible feeding suffered by suffragettes of Great Britain, and to a lesser extent of the United States, that gave the franchise to Canadian women?

Some hon. members: Oh, oh.

Miss Macphail: Hon. members do not show good sense in laughing at that. It is true; it is not a thing to be laughed at. The Conservative government — they called themselves the Union government — gave votes to women in 1917, but not to all women. That would be too risky, and I have noticed that the Conservative government and the Union government did not take many risks; in fact, governments, no matter what kind they are, do not take many risks, and so the Conservative government did not give votes to all women.

Mr. McGibbon: They gave them to those who were qualified.

Miss Macphail: The hon. member for Muskoka-Ontario (Mr. McGibbon) can make his own speech. They gave votes to women who they thought would vote for them at that particular time, and their guess was good. They gave votes to some women, not to all women, and not because they were intelligent, but because they had a husband or a brother or a son fighting at the front. Whether war time or not, it was a very stupid way of extending the franchise to women.

Mr. Hanson: You were not qualified, that is all.

Miss Macphail: If my hon. friend was, I have no apologies to offer because I was not. In 1921 for the first time, women voted, and I am very glad to say that 1921 brought me here. I am sorry that more did not come with me.

Again that March Agnes criticized the Conservatives more or less in passing as she rebuked both major parties for their stand against free trade. During the Budget Debate on March 19 she discussed Canadian prosperity and how farmers might share in it. She said that there was a degree of prosperity in Canada but it was "spotty" and farmers did not share in it. The government was offering two remedies, protection and immigration, and she agreed with neither.

"At the moment the Conservatives are advocating protection for agricultural products," she said. She referred to a speech by "the hon. member for South Wellington [Mr. Guthrie]" and said, "I gather from that speech that the honorable gentleman advocates in the main keeping our agricultural products at home; that is to say: Don't let the other fellow's products come in, but keep our own products in Canada. One might boil it down to this: Let us eat our own products and so make ourselves prosperous. I am not sure it would make us prosperous, but it would make us full."

She quoted Hansard, in which Guthrie said that in many respects the United States market was "the very best market in which to sell many of our farm products. . . ."

"If the hon. member was speaking officially for the Conservative Party, then that party was eighteen years too late in finding that out, for in 1911 that was the very thing that was advocated by people who still believe that the U.S. market is a very good outlet for a considerable proportion at least of our agricultural products. And if the Conservative Party actually thought that the U.S. was a good market for our farm products, when they went into power in 1911 they could have turned right about face and helped us to market our products there — that is, if it is really the farmer they want to help."

She considered the inaugural speech of Mr. Hoover, the newly elected President of the United States, "masterly." She thought it

> broadminded with one exception — that being the fact he had talked of a tariff for farm products.
>
> We must remember however, if we intend to be fair, that the United States offered us a market for our farm products and kept that offer open for a long time. We did not accept it, and it is their own business if they shut out our products; and we have no right at all to feel any resentment against them. Indeed, they must think we are very hard to please if neither thing they offered pleases us. I am not one of those who believe that the raising of the tariff will not injure agriculture in this country; I think it will. It will particularly injure the cattle and dairy people.
>
> The hon. member for South Wellington did not make clear to me how it is, if protection can operate to the benefit of the farmer, that the American farmer, who has been enjoying a large measure of protection for some time, is poorer, more discouraged and less able to help himself than the Canadian farmer, notwithstanding that he has access to one of the best home markets in the world. . . .
>
> The only other remedy I have heard proposed is immigration. . . . [The government's solution] for the agricultural problem was the tariff plus bringing in more farmers to produce more goods further to lower the prices we are getting for farm products. Isn't that brilliant? Only a government could do a thing so stupid; they were afraid they could not do it fast enough themselves to ruin agriculture and so they called to their assistance the railway companies and certain religious organizations. I hope that when the immigration estimates come up, every farmer in this House . . . will take the stand that he is not going to be so dull as to sit still and see the people's money spent to bring in more farmers to compete in an already under-paid field.

She concluded that the way out

> lies with the farmers themselves rather than with the government. They must as a group enter the marketing, financial and legislative fields. . . .

If the men who produce the milk which is made into cheese will make of themselves a co-operative unit; if they will study the needs of the market and the needs of the consumer they will get a better price. . . .

Why is it that the British Columbia apple can compete at a higher price with our Ontario apple right under our noses, when the British Columbia apple has not the flavour of the Ontario Spy or McIntosh? Of course we have been trained to think of an apple as a beautiful thing and we buy it on its looks, just as men pick their wives. That is why I have been so unlucky.

Mr. Ryckman: You have your chance yet.

Miss Macphail: There is no use building up false hopes. When a person buys graded apples he knows they will be uniform and attractively and conveniently boxed and he is willing to pay a higher price. Just as soon as the Ontario apple grower wants to get into the co-operative business he can command a higher price.[35]

Agnes with her Starr automobile, used in early campaigns

In April 1929, Agnes addressed a peace convention in Detroit. While there she was entertained by Henry Ford and on April 29 wrote to her riding giving her impressions of the "motor magnate" and his family:

I am rubbing my eyes, trying to find out whether or not I am awake or still dreaming.

Did I meet Henry and Mrs. Ford, eat supper with them, spend all afternoon at the Dearborn plant with Mr. Ford and his wholly delightful secretary, Mr. Campsall? Did I dance with them, see the great works, talk over many things, laugh and joke and enjoy them? Did I go back the same night to a dance given by the Fords? Did I pleasantly visit with Mrs. Ford, junior and senior? Did I watch the beautiful dancers do the Lancers, the Quadrille, the Waltz, or didn't I?

Yes, I must have, for here on my desk is the little book, "The story of Mary's Little Lamb" and on the fly leaf, "To Jean from Henry Ford." Jean is one of my little nieces who loves the story of "Mary had a little Lamb." She follows me about a lot, and I told her she was the little lamb, but she stoutly maintained she was not. She was Mary. When I told Mr. Ford the story, he said, "I will send Jean a book" — and here it is. [Jean Reany Huston still has the little book — "one of my most prized possessions."]

You see there was a real Mary, and a real lamb, that would have died a hundred years ago had not Mary nursed it, wrapped in a warm blanket by the fireplace all night long. No wonder the lamb loved Mary. It followed her to school "one day." Mr. and Mrs. Ford have had the school restored as it was then, and have caused this little book to be written.[36]

Just as I was getting all set to address the Women's International League of the United States, at the banquet in the Statler Hotel on the subject of "The Creation of the International Mind," I saw the Fords. I was as amazed as if His Majesty had casually dropped in. Yet it was natural enough. The Fords are interested in peace, so they came. They liked it and they stayed. Afterwards I was invited to a late supper with them, Mrs. John J. White of New York City and Mrs. Tussig of St. Louis. We all enjoyed it so much that we stayed till 12 o'clock. Mr. Ford asked us if we would like to see the Dearborn plant the next a.m. We could not go on Thursday, but I stayed over Friday to accept the very kind invitation. Mr. Ford said he would send a machine for us at 9 a.m. He did. We were whirled out of the city, passed the air port, and on to the engineer's experimental station, where we were met by Mr. Campsall, who ushered us to the very modest office occupied jointly by Mr. Ford and Secretary. Their desks are arranged so they face each other.

Mr. Ford's office has many proofs of his great devotion to his friend, Thomas A. Edison. A large portrait once presented by him to a college, and lately by the college to Mr. Ford, hangs upon the wall. On it in Mr. Edison's hand is written, "He wins, who hustles while he waits." I noticed a picture of Lincoln and several air pictures of the Ford plant. A bicycle ridden by Mr. Ford when he was working as chief engineer for somebody else has been refinished, and is now a decoration.

With Mr. Campsall we began wandering over the great building, seeing the men working on the blueprints, the cars with which they experimented, and a number of machines showing the evolution imprinted from the crude hand machine to the last bit of efficiency. These are collected to go in the museum now being built. Here Mr. Ford joined us. We did not see him or hear him coming. He is very slight, though not thin, and has an oddly energetic motion to his shoulders that reminds me of Vincent Massey.

We saw the last Model T car — the 15th million; the Ford, Ford drives; the first model of the new type and many more interesting things.

Mr. Ford asked if we were interested in old fashioned music and in the old dances, and when we assured him we were, he led us to the dancing auditorium and there to the music of a string orchestra we danced. The dancing professor was in attendance. For our pleasure, Mr. Ford had enough of the office staff brought in to form a quadrille and they danced for us beautifully. I have never seen more graceful motion.

And now Mr. Ford left us. We were shown over the great works by his secretary and a guide. The most gripping sight was the great stamping mills with the huge machines pounding out the heavy parts. The red metal glowed and rained showers of fire. The throbbing, roaring place seemed alive, the humans mere attendants. Above the tumult Mrs. Tussig shouted, "This is America."

In the assembling plant the most fascinating thing was "the line." The chassis is on a moving truck. The men are stationary and each one does something to the car-in-the-making as it passes. The last one gets in the car and drives it out on its own power. It is not heavy work but it is steady. I cannot think that human beings will be benefited by such machine action.

At the airport we saw the cement runways where the birds of the air take off. The field is lighted for night flying. The great hangars are crowded with all sorts of flying craft. We saw the Fokker plane, Josephine Ford in which Byrd flew over the North Pole. Also the big passenger planes with their comfortable cabins and many privately-owned planes. Edsel Ford is specially interested in aeroplanes. Mr. Edsel Ford is a handsome, slight man. He looks remarkably young. He has pleasant manners and is approachable and keen.

Mrs. Henry Ford is short, a dark-complexioned, natural and lovable woman. She was well but plainly dressed, once in a black dinner dress and again in a red chiffon with red satin slippers. Mrs. Edsel wore at the dance a simple ivory satin dress and slippers, with sun tan stockings, but no jewelry. She looks a mere girl and is very pretty.

The dance was very informal. The people were very friendly. We had to leave early to catch the train, so the efficient Mr. Campsall saw that "the boys" served us with delicious hot chocolate, sandwiches and cake. The Fords — all four — came to the door with us and Mr. Campsall to the car. Never have I received more gracious and more abundant hospitality. I shall treasure the experience.

*Henry Ford is very likeable. One is attracted by him, not because
of his wealth, nor wholly because he is a mechanical genius and an
organizer par excellence, but because he is so human, so alive. One
is always conscious of his controlled forcefulness. He has clung to
the fundamental things in life — wealth has not spoiled him. The
satisfying simple things, a happy home life, the beauty of nature,
sweet music, old friends, "the works," these are his interests. He has
a natural easy manner, direct, but exceedingly courteous. He is a
gentleman in the best sense of that fine word.*

*Mr. A. S. Watson, son of James Watson, Normanby, treated me to a
long drive. We saw the International Bridge, Belle Isle, the Fisher Bldg.,
the Boulevard, etc. Many former Southeast Grey friends telephoned or
came to see me. It was, in every way a most delightful visit.* [37]

Refreshed by her "delightful visit" to Detroit, Agnes rose in the House on
May 7 to debate a woman's right to establish a legal domicile in divorce cases.
J. J. Ward of Dauphin, Manitoba, had moved an amendment which would
replace most of the original bill, namely:

*A wife deserted by, and living separate and apart from her husband,
shall be deemed to retain the domicile of her husband at the time she
was so deserted until she has acquired a domicile of her own choice
in Canada and may acquire such domicile for herself in Canada as
though she were a femme sole when such desertion was continued for
a period of two years, and on acquiring such domicile in Canada
may commence an action for divorce where so domiciled praying that
her marriage may be dissolved on any grounds that entitle her to
such divorce in any court having jurisdiction to grant a divorce a
vinculo matrimonii* [from the bond of marriage].

According to Hansard, Agnes commented:

*I cannot think any hon. member of this house will oppose the bill as
amended, because it involves human rights. Although anxious that it
should be in good legal form, I am not so much interested in the
legal aspects of the matter as I am in the human rights of the case. A
woman has just as much right as a man to be able to establish a
legal domicile of her own where she can take action, and it is only
because we still have a hang-over from the dark ages that this action
must be taken today. While I am not really particularly interested in
the involved legal argument of the hon. member for St. Lawrence-St.
George I want to see the bill passed in such form that it will enable
a woman to establish a legal domicile of her own, and until she can
do that she is indeed not a "person," as the supreme court decided
some time ago. I feel that everyone will agree with the principle of
the bill and will be anxious that women may be afforded the same
privileges which men have enjoyed for a long time. There is no
reason why men should have a corner on all the good things in life.*

*Mr. Lapointe: Does my hon. friend claim that there should be two
domiciles in a marriage union, one for the husband and one for the wife?*

Miss Macphail: Certainly; are there not two people?

Mr. Lapointe: That does not sound like the dark ages; it sounds like the period before the dark ages. It is against the natural law.

Miss Macphail: That natural law stuff covers a lot of special privileges. Will the Minister of Justice, who gets so righteously indignant about two domiciles, say that if we should have only one it should be the domicile of the wife?

Mr. Lapointe: I would have no objection. If the hon. member had been here the other day she would have heard me say that I care not whether it is the domicile of the husband or of the wife, but so long as there is a marital bond there must be only one domicile. That is the principle of British and International law.

Mr. Brown: Following out that argument, then, I think it might be well contended that the woman should have equal rights with her husband in the one domicile.

Mr. Lapointe: I think my hon. friend should abolish matrimony altogether; let us all be equal and free.

Miss Macphail: Even that would not be as bad as some of the things we have now.

Mr. Lapointe: Free love and free everything.

Mr. Ladner: On the argument presented by the Minister of Justice I would like to ask whether, in the case of a man who has been iniquitous in every sense of the word as far as his marital relations have been concerned and who moved off to unknown parts, he thinks the domicile should walk with the man and leave the poor woman stranded without any rights in regard to her future life or with regard to her children?

Mr. Lapointe: I am informed that in such cases the court always goes a long way to decide that the last domicile persists. If a man goes all around the world surely he would not benefit or profit by such vagrancy.

Mr. Bennett: Then the domicile of origin commences.

Mr. Lapointe: Yes, and I am told that this is usually accepted by the courts.

Miss Macphail: If that is true why is it that the legal profession has passed legal resolutions on this subject asking that these changes be made?

Mr. Lapointe: The "legal profession" is a very wide expression; I do not think all the members of the legal profession have endorsed such resolutions.[38]

In her next letters Agnes reported on the progress of the Bill.

May 9, 1929

I have been watching for some time a Bill sponsored by J. J. Ward of Dauphin, Manitoba, asking that women be given the right to establish a legal domicile in their own right. As it is, she cannot establish a legal domicile apart from her husband. It is just part of the old business of thinking the woman as something less than a person. Rumor has it that Mr. Lapointe, Minister of Justice, was against the Bill. He said it was just opening the door; I suppose he fears it would let women completely out of the enclosure which has surrounded her during the centuries. Mr. Ward, who is a Progressive Liberal, dropped the Bill. Next year if he is not willing to take it up, someone who is must do it. Many of the legal profession are very anxious that this Bill should go through. They have the utmost difficulty serving their women clients because of this stupidity.[39]

May 16, 1929

Mr. Ward, M.P. for Dauphin, Manitoba, did not drop the Bill dealing with the right of married women to establish domicile. He brought it up again on Tuesday night when public bills were reached. Mr. Lapointe was unalterably opposed to it. Mr. Cahan of Montreal greatly feared legal complications but sympathy for the Bill was shown by all parties and groups. It would easily have gone through had not the hour for private bills expired too soon. It will come up again. Mr. Lapointe and I rather lost our tempers over it. Because a law was in operation in 1855 is to me no good reason why we should still be using it if conditions have changed in the meantime. And who will deny that the whole position of women has changed in the last 75 years.

Mr. Bennett's speech was so clear, and for once so concise, that quoting it gives the whole principles of the Bill:

> *I am perfectly certain, unless we do this [pass the Bill] the very injury which the Minister of Justice desires to avoid, will continue, namely, we shall have people leaving Canada, going to the United States, setting up fictitious domiciles and securing a divorce with all the consequences incident thereto, and all the uncertainties as to the legitimacy of the offspring. That is a very serious matter.*

> *Mr. Lapointe: I would rather have the U.S. assume the responsibility than ourselves.*

> *Mr. Bennett: The Minister of Justice and I differ in that regard. I would rather be a party to this legislation to give legality to the situation than become a party to the scandals that we know exist in regard to it. I am in favor of giving her that right to acquire a domicile in order that her status, which is that of a single person, with respect to contracts, obligations, property and everything that concerns her existence as a citizen may be the same for the purpose of a domicile for the purpose of securing a divorce."* [40]

In her June 13th letter Agnes reported that the Bill had passed, but the matter came up again the following year.

Agnes' fame as a speaker spread throughout Canada and the United States as she lectured with Chautauqua, the Belo Lecture Foundation and Harold R. Peat, Incorporated. She was a remarkable ambassador for Canada and at the same time thoroughly enjoyed the famous people she met. Through it all she never forgot the people at home, writing to them faithfully, sharing her experiences and broadening their horizons as she did her own.

She spent much of the summer of 1929 lecturing in the states of Illinois, Missouri, Nebraska and Iowa, finishing in New York City.

July 16, 1929

Our routing a few days ago sent us through Springfield, Illinois. We stopped over to visit Lincoln's tomb. The taxi driver didn't know where it was. "Truly a prophet hath honor save in his own country." With little difficulty we found the park in the centre of which is the tomb — the base is really a building filled with books, magazines and pictures of Lincoln. At the back is the vault with the casket. A wreath had been recently placed by Herbert Hoover.

We saw a letter written in October, 1860, by a little twelve-year-old girl — Grace Bedell — to Lincoln. Grace was an ardent Republican. A campaign was on. A picture of Lincoln endorsed by a split rail fence was sent around; one came to the Bedell home and Grace was upset by the teasing of her brothers and playmates over the homely features of her hero, so she wrote and suggested that he grow whiskers and promised if he would, she would do her best to get her two Democratic brothers to vote for him. She added, "I think the fence is really pretty." If he were too busy to write to her, Grace asked that he get his little girl to do it for him.

Abe Lincoln was in the throes of a general election for the Presidency of the United States, but he answered that letter by hand on October 19, 1860, beginning, "Your very agreeable letter of the 15th received" — he said he had no little girl so would have to answer her himself, that he had never worn a whisker and people might think it silly affectation if he did, but thanked her for her kind interest in him. Later he visited her town, asked for her and kissed her with thousands of people looking on — to her very great confusion — but he did grow the whiskers and improved his looks thereby.

Lincoln has been one of my ideals so the Springfield visit meant much to me.

For a week now I have been in the wheat and corn of Illinois and Missouri, speaking each day on "Uncle Sam and Jack Canuck." Many, perhaps most, of the people in my audience know little of Canada. Some have visited Canada, but their general idea about our country is pretty hazy. They give me a free hand to discuss trade, prohibition or anything I like. The farm audiences want to know more about the wheat pool, the farm organization, the national railway, etc. The people are so friendly. I like them and they have a free and easy manner in shops, trains, everywhere — men go in their shirtsleeves, it is so hot.

Corn is the principal crop — oats second. The corn that will ripen is now so tall the horses' backs just show above it, but the silage corn is only a few inches high. The land around Princeton and Bloomington, Illinois, sells for from $200 to $300 an acre; the farmers are heavily in debt to the mortgage loan companies and the banks.

We had breakfast yesterday in the City of St. Louis. Big cities and this heat are a poor combination. Today we are in Jefferson City, the capital city of Missouri, the home of Thomas Jefferson, third president of the United States. My room faces the grounds of the Governor's Mansion. This morning we visited the capital, a beautiful white building fashioned after the Federal Capital at Washington. It stands on the banks of the Missouri, the grounds going to the water's edge. The House of Representatives or Lower House has 150 members, the Senate or Upper House has 34. There is one woman in the Lower House.

Honey dew melons, blackberries and cream, hot corn bread, fried chicken and iced tea fortify me against the heat and constant travelling. More anon.[4]

August 1, 1929

Today I visited the town of Hannibal, Missouri; its chief distinction lies in the fact that there once lived Mark Twain, the great humorist, in one of its plain two-storey houses, crowded close to the sidewalk. From the time he was four until he was 24 he grew up in this humble home. His famous corn cob pipe and flannel coat are there and one of his favorite chairs and the desk. The coat and the chair belong to a later and more prosperous time. The queer little typewriter on which he did most of his writing has a place of honor. How little the citizens of that town knew that in their midst was living one of the greatest personages of his time.

The place is taken care of by a kindly but wholly illiterate woman who, when showing me the picture of the cabin in which he was born, the Hannibal house, and then the palatial residence in the Eastern States where he died, said, "It shows how he 'clum' up."

A Statue of Tom Sawyer and Huckleberry Finn has been erected at the foot of Cardiff Hill. They stand together on a high base. "Huckleberry," the town drunkard's son, dressed in tattered clothes too large for him, a torn brimmed hat and one suspender. Tom wears a cap and clothes a shade better. He has a bundle slung over his back in true tramp fashion and has the distinction of having two suspenders. Both are in their bare feet and their faces are alive with the promise of adventure. The artist symbolized in bronze figures the joy and hope of care-free youth.

A drive of a mile took me to Riverside Park high on the banks of the Mississippi and here stood the statue of Mark Twain. The face of the figure gazes wistfully across the river and far away beyond to the wide world. Underneath on a simple tablet is inscribed this beautiful tribute: "His religion was humanity, and the whole world mourned for him when he died."

It is a piece of rare good luck that I should have the privilege of talking Canada and the value of our trade to the Republic in the four farm states of Illinois, Missouri, Nebraska and Iowa just now. In the big tents on the campus or on the high school grounds, good crowds gather. They are friendly, questioning crowds. These same tents in the past have heard the deep tones of Chief Justice Taft [42] and the silver tongue of William Jennings Bryan. [43] I feel all unworthy.

A Chief of the Sioux tribe, Red Fox, cooked a supper for us the other night. He built a fire and over it baked bacon and omelet and with that he served brown bread and milk. It was a fascinating picture to see the Chief in his buckskin vest and trousers, lavishly embroidered, bending over the fire, absorbed in his work. Behind him lay a quiet lake with woods fringing its other side and this against the sky made brilliant by the setting sun. [44]

August 8, 1929

Illinois: If these towns do not know that Canada is the best customer of U.S.A., having purchased from Uncle Sam last year well over $800,000,000 worth of goods, and that keeping in the good graces of "best customers" is a good business principle, it just isn't my fault.

It is noticeable that no one here has goitre, yet these states are as far from the sea as we are. In our own Maritime Provinces the disease is most uncommon. I think it is quite time that we in Grey County organize to rid ourselves of this disease. It is a problem that affects almost every home and I believe we could solve it by united effort. The following which appeared in the Peoria Illinois Star of July 26th may be of interest: "Goitre, that dread and disfiguring disease, is diminishing in this country because it was generally due to a lack of iodine in the diet and now iodine is available to everyone." [45]

(At a Holdfast United Farm Women of Ontario Club meeting in June, 1930, the Flesherton Advance reported that "several packages of goitre preventative tablets were given out." Agnes was at the meeting and was no doubt responsible for the tablets. She was also responsible for having iodine added to salt in the first place, said a recent report in the *Dundalk Herald*.)

August 15, 1929

New York City: From a comfortable room on the 17th storey of the Pennsylvania Hotel the roar of the great city comes but faintly to my ears.

What a city! There shouldn't be many automobile accidents; the traffic moves too slowly to kill the jay walkers. I took a taxi to Exchange Place. I thought we would never arrive but all things end and so did the ride. The return trip cost 3.40 and the driver drove off with the four dollars. I find to get change back, one needs to use "Toronto Police" methods. Moral: have the exact change next time.

The Manager of the Canadian Bank of Commerce here says things are booming. Business in the central West States is below par. To get to the Canadian Bank of Commerce on Exchange

Place one passes through the money market of the world . . .
blocks and blocks of banks, exchanges, money houses of one kind
and another. Most countries in the world are represented. The
streets are narrow and pinned with traffic.

The young men go hatless — the older men carry theirs; the
ladies are wearing summer things but the shops are showing fall
styles. Brown and green seem to be the favorite colors. An effort
is being made to get the skirts longer — skirts and dresses are
longer in places, with the use of the uneven hemline dipping
longer in the back. I was only in one shop — Lane Bryant on the
Avenue. I do not think things were cheaper than in Toronto —
rather, more expensive if anything. [46]

Chapter V
At the League of Nations
1929

In her letter of August 15, 1929, Agnes told how she became a delegate to the League of Nations:

> Some time ago the Federal Government asked me if I would go as one of the Canadian delegation to the Assembly of the League of Nations. I talked it over with the UFO executive in South East Grey and while the majority did not object, I felt it would impair my standing as an Independent in the House of Commons and refused the invitation.
>
> On July 30 I received a letter from Mr. Mackenzie King dated Ottawa, July 25, which read in part as follows: "As you are already aware the Government would be pleased to have you act as one of the delegates to the forthcoming Assembly which is bound to be of marked interest and importance. In view of the desire of the Government to have the women represented on the delegation we believe that as the one woman representative in the House of Commons there is special fitness in your undertaking this duty at the present time."
>
> I wired my appreciation of his kindness but said that I could not accept. The same day I wrote to say that unless a Conservative was also appointed I would not go. I pointed out that the splendid work done by Sir George Foster in the cause of peace entitled him to the appointment. I wrote the letter to justify the stand I took and in support of a speech on parliamentary rather than governmental representation at the League which I made last session and not with any thought that the suggestion would be acted on.
>
> To my great surprise I received in Clarinda, Iowa, a wire from Right Honorable W. L. Mackenzie King, dated August 7, which reads:

> Cabinet today have appointed Dandurand, Euler and Elliott delegates to this year's Assembly of the League of Nations. Also the following as alternate delegates: Hon. Phillippe Roy, Malcolm McLean, M.P., Sask, Hon. Sir George Foster and yourself. Department of External Affairs is communicating with you further by letter.

> Signed W. L. Mackenzie King

> I shall do my best to represent Canadian women worthily. A letter from Mrs. J. A. Wilson, President of the National Council of Women, wishing me success in the mission and approving of my going, made me very happy.
>
> ·At 12:01 a.m. [August 16] the Mauretania sails. She is to arrive at Cherbourg on August 21. I go direct to Prague for a week. I will write from there.[1]

The *Flesherton Advance* reported that Agnes spent several days with her parents before leaving for Europe. On September 4 the paper carried the first account of her trip. The letter was dated August 20, 1929, and it read in part:

Today we land at Plymouth. Five days at sea has been a new and pleasant experience for me.

"All visitors ashore" was called in New York at 11:30 p.m. on August 15th and at one minute after midnight the heavy ropes were pulled on deck and the "Mauretania" for 23 years the fastest ocean liner, was on her way. . . .

The ship is 731 feet long, 89 feet wide at the widest and when loaded has a capacity, including crew, of 2,500 persons. This is a slack season travelling east so the passenger list is small. The "Mauretania" has first, second and third class accommodations.

On Sunday, service was held in the first class lounge for the whole of us — including crew, but the rest of the time each class is expected to keep to their own quarters. Brotherhood of man on Sundays — "money-hood" of man the rest of the time.

First class single costs $300. Second class $167 to Cherbourg. I do not know the third class rates. I'm travelling second. I have a four-berth cabin to myself. It is very comfortable with hot and cold water on tap, chair, couch, bed, clothes press, etc. The Library, Lounge, Smoking Room and Dining Room are quite sizeable and they are comfortably and tastefully furnished.

Most passengers spend their time pacing the deck or reclining on the deck chairs — cosily wrapped in a heavy rug, if the air is cool. An ocean trip would be just the thing to "set up" an invalid. Five meals are served — the three meals we are used to plus hot beef tea and biscuit at 10 in the morning, and tea, bread and butter and cakes at 4 in the afternoon — that is if one is on deck. Each night I find a plate of fresh assorted fruit in my cabin.

A Carnival dinner one night livened things up a bit — the decorations were gay — everyone dressed up and wore paper caps placed at each plate, and were a little more friendly than usual. The ship's officers tried to give us a dance but few danced. The crowd is a bit dull. I needed the rest so much that I am enjoying it — perhaps the others are the same.

My deck chair is one of a group of five. A Scotchman, now in business in New York, going to join his family for a holiday at home; a business woman from Detroit on a six weeks holiday, and two New England educationists going to a conference at Cambridge University.

An oil man from Oklahoma and his delightful young wife are on their way to the oil fields in Southern Russia. A retired professional man who speaks many languages and his Spanish wife are world-tramping. A number of Englishmen who have had positions in the USA are going home. One of them dresses in evening togs for dinner and wears a monocle, but more of him later. A party of Southern Europeans, who have gotten on well, are on a visit to their homeland — and so it goes.

The monotony might have been too much but for the thrill of a romance. A lady fair and two young men — the game captivates us. It is not yet played out so I cannot end it with "and they lived happily ever after." The lady has a German name and figure, a French face and manner, and an American wardrobe. He of the monocle — by name of Randall — courted the lady. His deck chair was next to hers; his place in the dining room was remote but this detail was soon remedied by an obliging steward — things seemed to be going swimmingly. They danced, played cards and drank wine — but alas! a dashing dark American, one generation removed from a southern clime, comes on the scene. With much ado he draws a chair, not his, but no matter, to the lady's side; talks Randall out, kisses the lady's hand in salutation and farewell; has his place in the dining room changed from a distant table to the other side of the young lady, and seems at the moment to have more than an even break. My money is on Randall who looks distinguished, monocle and all, though at the moment a bit melancholy. . . .

A morning paper the Daily Mail, Atlantic edition, is delivered to our cabin every morning. This, with hairdressers, barbers, and a stenographer on board makes us feel very near land.

The sea has been fascinating with its changing colors. Blue, almost to black, foaming fleecy white, and the indescribably sea green delight the eye. The moonlight on the sea is all the poets and artists have said, and the sunlight sparkling on the water is scarcely less lovely.

The sea has been smooth each day. In the Gulf Stream we suffered from heat; the water was hotter than the air, which the deck steward told me was unusual. . . .

Our rapid and pleasant crossing recalls the stories I have heard the pioneers tell of six weeks on the sea without comforts. How lucky we are, and how thankless! [2]

The next letter was sent from Prague, where she attended a meeting of the Women's International League for Peace before going on to Geneva.

Central and southern Europe is a seething mass of unrest. The Ukrainians and Poles are at each other's throats. Macedonia, carved up and given to three surrounding countries, is torn in spirit. The Bulgars and the Serbs are killing each other on the frontier. The danger spot of Europe should read the danger spots of Europe, any one of which holds the possibilities of future war. Millions of people are now discontented minorities.

Blessed are we who live in the North American continent, and because of our happy position we owe leadership to the world.

I landed at Cherbourg, where tenders came to the ship's side. What hustle and bustle! Tickets and passports to be examined, luggage to be got on the tender, through the customs and on to the French train without once losing sight of it! The "red caps" wore blue jackets. They talk only French; we only English; everyone gesticulated wildly but finally we were on the French train, sharing a compartment with the Bishop of Panama and the President of the League of Nations Society of Chicago.

The French customs officials seemed fussy only about tobacco — they asked "See-gar? No? Seegar-ette? No?" Then dismissed us by an expressive gesture.

On a French dining car one cannot have a choice of food. The food is odd, but good and abundant. In France and in central Europe the water is not fit to drink. A person has to get on as best he can on mineral water which tastes like destruction, vile coffee, sloppy tea and wine. I am still thirsty — the thought of South East Grey water tantalizes me.

Paris is a wonder city. With some friends I visited the artists' quarters on the hill where streets and sidewalks are very narrow and paved with stones. The pictures are beautiful and very reasonably priced.

One delightful hour was spent in The Louvre with a good guide who spoke English, but only a few of the art treasures could be seen in that time. The Louvre was once the palace of the French kings, though the original castle has been altered and added to. It is an endless place, part museum and part art gallery. The rooms are furnished in Louis 14th and Louis 15th style and the pieces of furniture in them were once used by the kings, their wives or their mistresses, of whom there seems to have been a bewildering number. Their jewels are also displayed and famous pictures, which I found most interesting.

The shops are very fascinating but the prices were quite high. We stayed at the California Hotel and found the rates to be 140 francs a day, or $5.60. Taxis are very cheap and their drivers drive like mad. Not being able to speak French was a great handicap. To be comfortable in Europe one needs two and preferably three, languages — English, French and German.

The countryside in France, Germany and Czechoslovakia looks equally lovely; there is no waste land, and in the two latter countries there is a great deal of well-kept forest — even the twigs are picked up by girls and women, tied into neat bundles and used for firewood. The fields are very small; they are not fenced off from each other, and with the different crops it gives the country a curious checkerboard appearance. Hops are a leading crop in South Germany, and on the same ground some other crops, which looked like turnips.

Coming alone from Paris to Prague — called Praha by the natives of the city — I thought I would find no one who would understand English, but almost all the travellers on the first class train, called the Orient Express, were English or American. On the journey two custom officials examined our luggage and passport. Three languages, three kinds of money were used and three varieties of food served. How can Europe understand herself when she speaks with a dozen tongues?

Prague is a beautiful city; the cathedral, the castle, old home of kings, now occupied by the President of the republic and Minister of External Affairs are very beautiful. The cathedral is of Gothic architecture, the oldest in Central Europe. The Czechs trace their kings *back to 900 A.D. Most of them are buried under the church where the graves have become almost shrines. The new part was begun a hundred years ago and is not yet completed. In spite of the size of the building the seating capacity is not great.*

The Women's International League for Peace held the Congress in a resident school owned by the Czech Farmers' Co-operatives. It is a large and well-equipped building.

Women from 26 countries convened here for six days. They were a remarkable group; the most prominent of which was the international President Jane Addams of Chicago. It is hard to say wherein lies the remarkable power of this woman. She is devotedly loved and can hold together people who, without her, would see only disagreement and discord. She had studied world problems closely for years — but with all her knowledge she parades none; she is motherly, witty, wise.

Emmy Freundlich, member of the Australian Parliament, is an economic expert. She was the only woman government representative at the World Economic Conference. Women who are medical doctors, doctors of law, scientists, journalists, teachers, editors, etc. attended. An arresting figure is Mrs. Skeffington of Ireland, who has suffered imprisonment and forced feeding in Ireland's cause. Her husband was killed in the Easter rebellion while trying to reconcile opposing forces.

Six women M.P.s represented Great Britain, Austria, Denmark, Ukraine, Belgium and Canada, and just to give tone to the Congress we had a Countess from Denmark and a titled English woman.

Twelve women elected by the Congress form the International Executive, to which body I have been elected.

The Assembly of the League of Nations convenes this morning, with Sir George Foster and myself as part of the Canadian delegation.[3]

From Geneva, she wrote:

Mr. Ramsay McDonald, Prime Minister of Great Britain, had the British family in to dinner almost a week ago; all parts of the Commonwealth were represented.[4] It was a particularly happy event. Ishbel McDonald stood by her father and said pleasant words to the guests as they arrived. Miss McDonald is dark complexioned and wore a red lace dress. My dinner partner was Mr. Costello, Attorney General for the Irish Free State, and my left hand neighbor was Mr. Frank McDougall of Australia.

September 8, Canada entertained representatives of 50 nations to dinner. It affords a splendid opportunity to meet our neighbors in a world community. My dinner partner was from Australia. He has struggled along through life, carrying a name like this: Major General, the Honorable Sir Granville de Laune Ryrie, K.C., M.C., C.B., V.D. It seems an additional argument against titles. He was genial. His Excellence de Jonkheer F. Beelearts van Blockland, Doctor of Law, Minister of Foreign Affairs for Holland, sat on my left and conversed in an interesting manner in perfect English.

Today, Australia entertained to lunch. I was fortunate enough to sit beside Philip Noel Baker of Gt. Britain, who has written some of the best books on the League and Disarmament. Professor Baker is Under Secretary of State for Foreign Affairs. These social gatherings, tho' they add very greatly to the duties of the delegates, serve a real purpose. At them one has connected conversation for an hour or two with one or two individuals and comes away with a fair knowledge of their outlook on at least a few subjects. . . .

Peace has its heroes who suffer and work unceasingly to make peace permanent. One of these is Dr. Stresemann[5], Minister of Foreign Affairs for Germany. Though ill unto death, knowing that but a short time is left him, he works on. Through the hard weeks at The Hague he stuck to his post, though sometimes so ill that he would hardly leave the room alive. At home his work is rendered more difficult by the opposition of the nationalists who do not like his conciliatory policy and methods, but he represents the progressive opinion in Germany, which is increasing every year. He is at once an inspiration and a challenge; his words are wise and his courage puts our inactivity to shame. Stresemann, Briand[6] [France] and McDonald [Britain] are the big figures. McDonald, too, shows plainly the struggle he has made to serve humanity well. He has an arresting face in which strength, tenderness and sadness are blended. Briand is popular; his oratory is of a high order; he used no notes and speaks in an intimate way, and in his flights of fancy he carries his audience with him. His deep interest in the League keeps him in the Assembly through dull speeches and tiring translations. The subject matter of his address was good, particularly the closing passage: "Peace rests on this. When children shall be taught love of country alongside a proper appreciation of other peoples; when they have been taught to search in mankind for that which unites rather than that which divides men, then peace shall be among nations."

Briand is far and away the orator of the Assembly, but for practical and concrete suggestions on disarmament, financial security, eliminating the causes of war, McDonald, Henderson[7] and Graham of Great Britain hold the palm. . . .

On Sunday I went up into the Alps to see the Monastery founded by St. Bernard hundreds of years ago, from which he rescued distressed travellers in the mountain passes. To get there we had to pass through a part of France, then back into Switzerland again, and after we had made the stiff climb by motor and arrived at the monastery, we walked about a mile which brought us into Italy. All of which means we passed through the hands of three sets of Customs officials going and the same number coming back.

The St. Bernard Hospice is 8,110 feet above sea level; only a little grass and moss grows there; it is the highest all-the-year-round residence in Europe. As we climbed, the deepest impression I received was the terrific labor expended on the little mountain farms which were terraced almost to the top. In many places walls had to be rebuilt to retain the few rods of earth which is called a farm. We passed through several mountain villages; the struggle for existence is written deep on every adult face. The women look prematurely old; I cannot forget their faces. Coming down from the mountain in the evening, the glory of the setting sun creates a picture of surpassing beauty. The little farms terraced up the mountain's sides, the crude slate-roofed houses clustered in villages, the crags, the waterfalls and the precipices looked so lovely that one forgot the toil and moil of mountain life and revelled in nature's beauty.[8]

A week later another article appeared:

Miss Macphail at League of Nations in Geneva

Geneva has become the Capital of the World. Fittingly it flies the flags of all nations in honor of the Assembly of the League of Nations. The whole place is astir for this great event which occurs each year on the first Monday in September.

The League of Nations has survived the first troubled years of its existence and now each year becomes more permanent and the interest of the public in it increases as the attendance of 200 able newspaper representatives shows.

The same eagerness noticeable in Ottawa at the Opening of Parliament was manifest last Monday at 11 o'clock when the Assembly was called together. The arrangement is parliamentary in character; the place of meeting is the Reformation Hall where John Knox and Calvin once fought the battles of religious freedom. In size it is a great hall. On the floor are the representatives of 53 nations. The arrangement is in alphabetical order which gives Canada a seat but one from the front. On a raised platform sit the President, the Secretary General of the League, chosen by the Assembly, translators, experts from the Secretariat, etc., and on a lower platform is the speakers' rostrum with amplifiers arranged in front. Two galleries run around three sides of the room, the lower for the press, the other for the international public. Tickets of admission are very much sought after; greater accommodation would be helpful to the progress of world peace.

One would be cold indeed not to be deeply touched when the nations of the world file in, row on row, with McDonald, Briand, Stresemann and Nansen[9] and other distinguished men, leading their respective countries. When the nationals of 53 countries mingle together in good fellowship, prejudices are broken down, friendships founded on understanding are built up, the truth of the words of Lord Cecil: "The world is one; humanity is one family" is brought home. Conflicts become more difficult; judicial methods of settling disputes become possible and natural.

The work of the first day was purely formal. The Chairman of the six committees were elected and we heard addresses from the retiring and incoming Presidents. I am so happy to say that Sir George Foster and I have been appointed to the Disarmament Committee. For the first time a woman is on this committee. Usually the women have been shunted to Committee Five which deals with Social Service.[10]

An article two weeks later read:

League of Nations Problems Discussed by Miss Macphail

After ten days in the vile air of the crowded and badly ventilated Assembly Hall, we began our work on the Third Committee, which meets in the Glass Room of the Secretariat. It is a beautiful room, jutting out at right angles from the main building; three sides are of glass. At first, gazing on the spreading green trees and the calm waters of Lake Geneva, I was deceived into thinking we were breathing the pure air of out of doors. But a week of work in that room has convinced me that tho' one can see through glass one cannot breathe through it. People in glass houses should not throw stones is an adage familiar to us all, and that may be the reason why the gentlemen on the committee take such pains to be exceedingly polite to one another. One has a feeling at times that a little plain speaking might clear the atmosphere.

The discussion has centred around radio control. All concede that in times of stress the League needs a broadcasting station and the problem of maintaining it through normal times might be taken care of by a private company or the Swiss government. The feeling was that the League should be in control of the station all the time.

For many days we discussed prevention of war through financial assistance, the plan to work out something like this: in case of dispute between two countries being carried to an open rupture, the Council by unanimous decision would say who the aggressor was. The nation attacked, under this plan, could at once borrow money, backed first by that nation, second by all nations that had signed this agreement, and third by certain strong financial powers. It was finally referred to the standing committee on security and arbitration and will come up next year. We are just beginning the debate on disarmament. Great Britain, France and Germany are quite clearly the leading powers on the Committee. . . .

My dinner partner at the Indian dinner was Prince Verveldyn of Siam, and a handsome, charming prince he is. He said he attended Oxford with Vincent Massey and was very interested on hearing of his work in Washington. It was a small party, not more than 20 people, which made it much more pleasant and less confusing. The Indian and Siamese delegates speak perfect English and that, in this Tower of Babel, is a great relief to me.

The Chinese dance was last night, and was a very enjoyable affair, in spite of the terribly oppressive heat. There were some lovely costumes especially those of the Japanese ladies present.

This mountainous country of Switzerland is an appropriate place to hold the League of Nations; for long centuries it has been a free country, democratically governed by an alert and well informed people. Yet it would have been better still for the nations to have purchased territory and on it built the first world city. This would have left the League of Nations absolutely free of interference from any one in its domestic affairs. Such things as the bad ventilation of the Assembly Hall and the desire of the Swiss Gov't to own the broadcasting station illustrate the need of a separate community.

Members of Parliament in the many countries who have not been delegates to the Assembly, will find it exceedingly difficult to understand why the expense of the delegates run so high. In this hotel de la Paix, a very ordinary room without bath but with telephone and running water, costs $7 a day without meals. Rooms with bath cost from ten to twenty-two dollars a day, with meals, telephone, service by the desk extra. In a world city a fair rate could have been set and would have had the tendency to interest nations and individuals in the League to a greater degree.

The beautiful dahlias of Geneva are now in full bloom. I visited the other morning a little square in the old part of town where executions used to take place in olden days, and which is now the flower market. The roses, asters, delphiniums, with which we are familiar were all there and also those exotic dahlias in so many beautiful colors and great jars of flaming orange flowers that reminded me in shape and color of Japanese lanterns.[11]

And finally:

Miss Macphail Glad to Be Back in Canada

A storm caught us before we found our sea legs, resulting in sending almost all the passengers to bed. It began the first night out. I found I couldn't get up the next morning; after repeated attempts I called the stewardess to ask what was the matter. "It is a nasty sea, Madame," she said. It felt nasty enough — I couldn't stand up to have a look at it.

A few days later when it was still far from calm, I saw the sea from the Captain's bridge. It was magnificent, with the waves breaking time and again over the bow and once leaping to the bridge. The "Duchess of Bedford" in her 15 months on the ocean had not before been so tested by storm, but she is a gallant ship and justified the pride of her skipper Captain Sibbons.

We saw an iceberg looking like a white mountain and the ship came close enough to feel its cooling influence.

Leaving Geneva was not all joy. We were anxious to get back to Canada but our friends in the Canadian office had been so kind we did not like leaving them. Colonel and Madame Vanier, D'arcy McGreer and Dr. Riddell were at the train to wish us a pleasant journey. Everything that our own countrymen could do for us they had done; their expert knowledge had been freely given us and I fear their leisure hours also. Little wonder we parted with them regretfully.

Wellington Whittaker of Artemesia met me in Paris.[12] He married a Parisian girl some years ago and has since lived in gay Paree. I had only four hours but we made the best of them. It was good to have a talk with a friend of other days. He was most interested in hearing home news; his interest in the neighbors, in the affairs of Grey Co. and in Canadian conditions generally showed that Mr.

Whittaker has not allowed the years that brought him success in a far city to wean him from the love of the land of his birth.

We visited the Chamber of Deputies and the Senate. They are in quite different parts of the city. Both buildings are enriched and beautified by famous tapestries, pieces of sculpture and paintings; both Chambers are semi-circular in form, resembling in many ways the House of Representatives and the Senate of the United States. . . .

Mrs. Whittaker joined us for lunch and all too soon the "Golden Arrow" as the train for Calais is called — was ready. The crossing from Calais to Dover was very pleasant — the Channel was calm. The white cliffs of Dover, familiar to every school child, were soon seen and a fast train carried us to London. The English country looked so like some parts of Ontario, that we each exclaimed over its familiar appearance. Flocks of sheep and herds of good cattle were grazing in the rather parched fields. England has been needing rain for a long time.

The hustle and bustle in the Victoria Station defies description. A Canadian National Railway agent met us and swiftly got us and our luggage into taxis. One piece of mine was found to be missing but the Canadian National located it in Paris and sent it to me by aeroplane the next day.

It was my great good fortune to be the guest of Dr. Hilda Clark, the granddaughter of John Bright. In her narrow little car, which nosed its way through the thickest traffic I saw as much of London as could be seen in one day. Due to the kindness of the Under Secretary of Foreign Affairs, we were shown through the Parliament Buildings by the Secretary to the Speaker. The Houses of Parliament seen from across the Thames are strikingly beautiful. Westminster looks every inch the "Mother of Parliament" and one's heart grows warm with the sense of a noble heritage. The stately and extensive pile of buildings of rich late Gothic architecture contain 1110 rooms, one of which is called Westminster Hall and was once a part of the Palace of the Anglo-Saxon kings. It was enlarged in 1398 by Richard 2nd. In this hall Charles 2nd stood to hear the sentence that cost him his head.

The Speaker's official residence within the buildings consists of over 50 rooms and in these the official entertaining is done.

The House of Lords is very colorful. It is often called the "Gilded Chamber." The most interesting thing to me was the sort of round soft lounge on which the Speaker of the Lords sits. It is called the "Woolsack" and originated as a token of respect to the greatest item in the export trade of England — wool. The Chamber has splendid stained glass windows with portraits of the Kings and Queens of England and in the niches between them are the statues of the barons who compelled John to sign the Magna Charta.

The Commons is much too small for the 615 members. They cannot all get in at once; many of them use the galleries. The seats for the members are long — very long — holding easily twelve members. The Government sits on the right of the speaker; the Opposition on the left. Only Cabinet ministers and ex-Cabinet ministers occupy the front seats above the gangway. I often wondered what the gangway was. It is the wide aisle dividing the long row of seats. Those who are of an independent turn of mind sit below the gangway. A member must speak from the floor, and he must have his feet on the red carpet which extends a few inches beyond the bench. This habit originated in the days when a rapier was carried by every honorable gentleman, which, in heated debate, was often thrust at his opponent with the intention of running him through, but if the member's feet were on the red carpet, he couldn't reach far enough across to do any harm.

William Ewart Gladstone[13] had a great habit of pounding a box which stood on the clerk's table just in front of the seat. The marks made by the ring he wore, are still there.

Statues of great leaders, including Pitt,[14] Peel,[15] Gladstone, Bright have been placed at long intervals along the great corridors. Never before was I so interested in seeing buildings. One understands our own Parliament better after seeing the one on which it was modelled.

Hyde Park with its soap-box orators; its Rotten Row where fashionable London rides; Buckingham Palace; Downing Street and Fleet Street and Canada House on Trafalgar Square had great interest for me. The time was so short I could only see a little but enough to feel the lure of London.

The train ride to Liverpool was slow and tiresome. The ship left almost immediately after. . . . Truly the best part of getting away is getting home again.[16]

Agnes made a favorable impression in Geneva. The *Beaver* said: "In eight years Canada's only woman Member of Parliament has advanced from country school teacher to equal place with premiers and foreign ministers in the greatest international assembly of all time, the League of Nations. . . . Yesterday's Sharon teacher and today's daughter of a country auctioneer has become one of the famous women of the world, though millions of her fellow Canadians haven't discovered her fame." The paper said that in sending Agnes Macphail to represent Canada at the League Assembly it had asserted unmistakably that her advocacy of peace was very valuable to Canada.

"When she tells Parliament about this first adventure into the higher regions of international politics where no Canadian woman and not fifty women in the world's history have appeared, she will be as eagerly heard as she was in Toronto when three hundred friends of Peace lunched in her honor and sat at her feet. How long will it be before Agnes Macphail's inherent, tested distinction is fully recognized in her native country?"[17]

The *London News* reported that British M.P. Mrs. Hamilton had returned from Geneva and was "particularly impressed by the great ability, knowledge and understanding of women delegates and most particularly of Miss Agnes Macphail, Canada's only woman M.P. . . . Agnes Macphail is the personification of strength and silence. She speaks little, but when she does, weighs her words carefully and is always interesting; whether she speaks at all or not, invariably she gets things done. In her is combined a vigorous intellect and a strong sense of humor."[18]

The *New Outlook*, official organ of the United Church of Canada, paid tribute to the world leaders in Geneva and concluded:

> *But to Miss Agnes Macphail of Canada, has been assigned the plum*
> *in feminist eyes. She is serving on the Disarmament Commission*
> *which has hitherto been regarded as a masculine preserve. "I wish,"*
> *she told me, "that I was better prepared. I only knew that I was to*
> *serve just before I sailed." That she will make the best use of her*
> *opportunity I am convinced: and if I lived in her constituency she*
> *could depend on my vote. She strikes me as a fine type of woman in*
> *public life, enjoying it, but out first and foremost for the causes she*
> *has at heart: human enough to appreciate popularity, but quite*
> *prepared to do without it and champion alone, if need be, a policy in*
> *which she believes.* [19]

In some quarters, however, her achievements were hardly acknowledged.
When she spoke in Toronto on her return, publicity for the speech was touched
"gingerly, very gingerly," said the *Beaver.*

> *It was true, and should have been obvious that the first public ap-*
> *pearance of Canada's first woman delegate to the League of Nations,*
> *also the first woman to sit on the Disarmament Commission, was a*
> *real political event; and that as she was truly an official ambassador,*
> *it deserved large notice on the pages where political significances are*
> *customarily displayed.*
>
> *The newspaper which, every day of its saintly life, proclaims itself*
> *the one national newspaper, reported the Macphail deliverance on*
> *international affairs of the first magnitude on the one page of the*
> *paper to which readers interested in politics do not turn. It also put*
> *in the headline as THE feature of a statesmanlike address, the purely*
> *incidental Macphail criticism of the abundance of summer heat and*
> *the absence of ventilation in the Hall of the Reformation where the*
> *League Assembly sits.* [20]

Chapter VI
Changing Times
1930

Since the Great War Canada had enjoyed expanding trade and was fifth among exporting countries in the world. However, new protectionist policies in Europe started a decline in Canadian exports and left Canada with a surplus of wheat and manufactured goods. In October, 1929, the New York stock market crashed; many people lost their life savings and many more were thrown out of work. The crash marked the start of an era of world-wide depression and unemployment.

Agnes wrote an article for *Chatelaine Magazine* rebutting one by Mederic Martin in which he "proposed the novel idea of curing unemployment by herding women back into the home and keeping them there." He advised an international conference to decide how to accomplish this. Agnes suggested the conference be held in a museum and told Martin that his ideas were based on the

> *indefensible theory that women's rights and independence and happiness as individuals are secondary things and need not be put first in our economic planning. It is true that for a long time this attitude prevailed in the world, and women's lives were arranged in relation to the economy rather than the economy being adjusted to respect the fundamental human rights of women. But it is now too late in the day for Mederic Martin to take the position that women should be deprived of the sacred human right of self-expression to help solve an economic problem. . . . I cannot close without challenging any opinion which is based on an assumption that woman has not the same right to develop her true self as has man. Woman's place in the modern working world cannot just be considered in terms of economics, but of her mental happiness, which is a vital and fundamental need of every individual — man or woman. To countless thousands a career is life; it is the doing of the thing you want most to do. To propose that women as a sex should be regimented into one groove, no matter how widely varied their ambitions and talents, herded back into the home for economic reasons, without a thought of their individual spiritual destinies, betrays such a superficiality of thought and such a crudity of spirit that it simply staggers one.[1]*

On January 17, 1930, Dougald Macphail, the father who in many ways had been Agnes' role model, died in Ceylon at the age of sixty-five. It was from him she got her love of the soil, her talent in debate and her fiery temper. In fact much of the *Durham Review*'s description of Dougald could apply with equal accuracy to Agnes. It said:

> *His knowledge of values: his quick weighing of men: his understanding of human nature and his ready wit made him an outstanding auctioneer. . . . His personality was vivid and attractive and though*

quick to anger, he was also quick to forgive. His outlook was broad, his insight keen, which made him a good counsellor to those who sought his advice, and always he was a good neighbor.

He made his first sale in 1897 and in the following 28 years conducted 1,162 sales in Grey County. His success in this line, more than anything else, may be attributed to his integrity and honor. He never went back on a farmer and we carry in mind some of the stormiest days of past winters. A sale would be billed for one day in Normanby Township, the following day in Artemesia and through drifted roads and rough weather he was there. It was the exception when February and March would not be fully taken up and the Review made the dates for him. At that time it was a common remark how any man, even of Mr. Macphail's vigor . . . stood it so well. His passing marks another link with a well-known family of Proton Township who helped in the tilling of her lands and in adding to Canada's prosperity. . . .

Dougald Macphail was born in 1864 in the Township of Proton three and a half miles west of Hopeville, and was the eldest of eleven children of Alexander Macphail and his wife, Jean Jack. . . .

Forty one years ago he married Henrietta Campbell, also one of a pioneer Proton family, who with three daughters to-day, mourn his passing. They are Agnes C. Macphail, M.P., at home; Mrs. W. M. Reany, Toronto, and Mrs. Hugh Bailey, Shrigley, near Dundalk. . . .

The late Mr. Macphail was a member of Priceville Presbyterian Church and the service was held in McKinnon Hall there on Sunday last, Reverend Mr. Stewart officiating, interment taking place to McNeil's Cemetery, Priceville. [2]

Prime Minister Mackenzie King sent Agnes a letter:

You have, indeed my deepest sympathy in the overwhelming bereavement you have sustained in the loss of your dear father. Only those who have experienced a like loss can know what it means. Our parents mean so very much to us, a mother to her son, a father to his daughter most especially, and I imagine you are experiencing at this moment the strangest of all the many experiences of life, when suddenly you begin to find yourself looking back upon the influences that have been greatest and the affections that have been strongest in life, and seeming to be out in the front line with no one ahead whose presence there hitherto has meant more perhaps, than all else in the world besides.

I was indeed sorry when I learned of your recent illness. Long before this, I had meant to write you, and especially to thank you for the most kind letter which you sent to me on your return from the League of all you have been called upon to endure. You will just have to be doubly careful now, and for a time consider yourself first, if that is possible for you to do. Without health we can accomplish little. Even I have learned that at times of great exhaustion.

There is so little one can say in the presence of great sorrow but you know, I think, the thoughts I would most wish to send you at this time. I am glad your father was spared to witness the great part you have taken in the affairs of your country, and to experience that greatest of joys in a parent's heart, the knowledge that his life through his child has meant much to this world.

I am looking forward to seeing you again when Parliament reassembles. Meanwhile please believe you will be often in my thoughts.

C. Ramage, publisher of the *Durham Review*, wrote:

No one, I am sure you know, followed your career with more interest than did he. . . . I learned to respect your father for sterling qualities many years ago and have in mind my last interview with him in my office where he showed a good grasp of public questions you were advocating, and his pride in you was manifest.

R. R. Edwards Markdale, Dougald Macphail's clerk, said:

Many an evening during bygone years we rode together after sales, he filling the arduous duties of auctioneer and I trying to keep up with the work as clerk.

I learned to esteem him most highly, not only for his ability and efficiency, but far more for his manliness, honor and power to make and retain friendships. He was one of "Nature's noblemen."

Catherine Motherwell wrote from Ottawa:

I can imagine with what joy and pleasure you would look forward to your father's welcome to you when you returned to the home nest after your various excursions into the world — some of which would prove soul satisfying and some the opposite, but always could you bank on a fond father's pride and confidence in you — the very glint in his eyes as he met you saying as plainly as possible, "Well done my child. I am tremendously proud of you." And now — well the dear father has been transplanted and somehow the world seems very empty.

Dear Miss Macphail, I have some conception of how you felt. My mind travels back to the beginning of this century when I was trying to fill a "man's" position in our missionary work in the west, and whether I was worthy of it or not, my aged father thought my work was "simply wonderful" and looked upon me with such pride that at times I felt very uncomfortable for fear it would be noticeable to others; then he was suddenly cut off, and oh the feeling of loneliness as I stood for the last time by his open casket. No one left any more (my mother had died some years before) to magnify the ordinary actions of a very ordinary woman trying to make good in the world, or to look upon her feeble efforts with a fond, foolish pride — and life seemed desolate indeed.

I have never had the pleasure or honor of meeting your parents (I understand your mother is still living) but I can easily imagine the parents of such a clever daughter would be interesting to say the least, and as the three of you drew up of a winter's night around your little fireside, the contact would be affectionately intimate. And now there is the break! [3]

Agnes was now almost forty years old. She had many friends and admirers. Among the latter was Preston Elliott, a Member of Parliament from eastern Ontario and a member of the Ginger Group. He had visited her home in Ceylon, attended her father's funeral and courted her for some time. She enjoyed his company and valued his friendship but eventually turned down his proposal of marriage. There were too many problems and inevitable conflicts involved in marrying another parliamentarian. She had no intention of ending her career and her deep commitment to South East Grey. She was a free spirit and wanted to remain that way. Elliott never married and died in his sleep in 1939 after an illness of only three days — "a shock to all his friends," wrote Agnes.

Another parliamentarian who fell in love with Agnes was Robert Gardiner, a member from Medicine Hat, Alberta. He arrived in Ottawa the same year as Agnes. A member of the United Farmers of Alberta, and later its president, he, too, was a member of the Ginger Group. He and Agnes had much in common. She seriously considered marriage with Gardiner but again decided against it. Gardiner was upset and, like Elliott, never married. He was defeated in 1935 and retired to Excel, Alberta. Agnes called on him during a western trip but Gardiner was ill and would not see her. When he died in 1945 he left $7,000 — most of his estate — to her.

Robert Gardiner, M.P., president of the United
Farmers of Alberta

Elliott and Gardner were not her only suitors. Agnes said she left a few letters and valentines[4] in her files so that people would know she had admirers, for it was typical of the times for people to assume that an unmarried woman was not that way by choice.

A letter from a *Montreal Star* reporter, dated March, 1936, says that he was glad Agnes was coming to Montreal as he was "uncommonly hungry" for her company. He would go to hear her speak and "spend as much of Sunday with you as desire or propriety may permit. I have nothing but contempt for an economic order that keeps me in such astringency that I cannot go to see the Girl I love, in spite of all the perils and dangers of your absence."[5]

Another letter, dated February, 1938, said he was thrilled to turn a page of the *San Francisco Chronicle* "and find you looking at me . . . never a day passes that I do not think of you and wish that conversations were not so hard to come at. That is the devil of falling for a woman with a career."[6]

Over the years she made many close friends in Parliament, not just in her own group, but in every party. For years she made a ritual of afternoon tea with Sam Jacobs, Liberal member from Montreal. In the Macphail files in the National Archives is a note from him on House of Commons stationery: "With all your faults will you have tea?"[7]

Another note, signed "J. C. E.," headed "House of Commons", reads, "Dear Agnes: To me you always look wonderful. But you look much more wonderful sitting and chatting to another wonderful lady than when you are sitting across the aisle from where you are now even with an awfully nice and clever man. When am I to have the pleasure of seeing you?"[8]

While she disliked R. B. Bennett's politics, she had a pleasant social relationship with him and they held hands frequently. Friends once heard him remark, "Why Agnes, you have nice ankles." When asked how he felt about her choosing him as the most distinguished looking man in Parliament he replied, "I always have respected Miss Macphail's intelligence and good judgment."

Dorothy Dennison[9] said, "I was told by one who knew her intimately that when she was in Ottawa she was very close to that arch-Tory, R. B. Bennett. That they agreed on nothing politically but as people they were so fond of each other that (I was told), he proposed marriage to her, but for one reason or another she refused him. Just think, she might have been Lady Agnes Bennett, wife of Lord Bennett as he eventually became."

In 1939 Agnes told a *Dundalk Herald* reporter that she had always liked men as "opponents and friends. . . . I have always got along fine with men. Why, when teaching school as a young girl in Bruce County I used to be criticized because I talked with them too much — usually about politics though."

Explaining why she never married, Agnes wrote:

> *I love children and I have always had dear men friends; it was a deep sorrow to me that I couldn't do all that I expect women to do, to be a wife and mother, but also an untrammelled active person finding outlet for her ability in the fields of learning, agriculture, industry, business, the arts or government. I was poor and had I married, the man would not have been rich or even comfortable in a financial sense. In addition, I have never enjoyed housework. I can do it if I must, but it gives me no sense of fulfillment. This I regret, but so it is.*

Deciding on such a matter can never be final; the whole question has to be threshed over again and again, according to the success of one's work, the attraction of one's men friends, the lure of children. [She told H. H. Hannam, President of the Canadian Federation of Agriculture, that she regretted more not having children than a husband.] *To have part of life can never be enough; one must have it all. That is what I want for women. There are some women who want only a husband, children and home. For them there is no problem. Keeping the home is enough. But for others it is not.*

One of the outstanding features of this age is the number of intelligent women who do not marry. Some old-fashioned and stupid people may say that they had no chance; any normal woman has had the chance, but for some reason she hasn't married the man she could have married. . . . But I have talked to hundreds of these fine, alert and very capable women in business, the professions and the arts, and their reason was the same as mine; the person could not be subjected.

Newspapers constantly drew attention to her single state, and generally ignored the marital status of Mackenzie King and R. B. Bennett. One headline read: "Progressives Have No Love for Grits or Tories, Dramatically Declares Miss Agnes Macphail, Does Agnes Know What Love Is?" Papers commented on an Ottawa wedding in March of 1928: "There was much laughter," said one, "when [Agnes] was handed the bride's bouquet." There were "dire predictions that the House would lose its lone lady member — her terse criticism and steadying influence." One paper said the movement to marry off Miss Macphail started in Parliament when in reply to Miss Macphail's criticism of Quebec's turning down votes for women, Premier Taschereau suggested her ability was wasted when spread among 244 members. She should concentrate on one man and he promised her a husband "if she would permit him to act as matrimonial agent."

Agnes got the message — her criticism of Quebec was not welcome. She soon learned to protect herself from attacks on her personal life. When a heckler yelled: "Why don't you get yourself a man?" she replied: "What guarantee have I he wouldn't turn out like you?" And in Parliament one day when a member taunted her with, "Doesn't the honorable member wish she were a man?" the House held its collective breath while Agnes re-arranged her pince-nez glasses. Looking over them, she asked reasonably: "No. Doesn't the honorable member wish he were?"

"It brought down the House," said Tommy Douglas [10] recalling the incident for James Palmer.

If the dissection of her private life bothered Agnes, it did not lessen her broad sympathy for men as well as women. In Parliament in March, 1930, she asked for justice for disabled soldiers:

I want to join with other honorable members in saying that I feel exceedingly sympathetic toward the men who were in the war. . . . All of us will, I am sure, agree that the soldiers who saw active service are breaking down much younger than men who did not see active service. Each of us has many applications from soldiers asking for pensions and in many cases they cannot prove that their present condition is due to the war. Attributability is a hard thing to prove, and we should so amend the law that if attributability can [not] be proved, at least the benefit of the doubt or a portion of it will go to the soldier. I have cases, as have all of us, where soldiers are totally disabled and yet where we are not able to secure pensions for them. I cannot understand why the onus of proof should rest upon the sick and discouraged man. He is possibly poor; he lives distant from any centre where he could get help to prepare a case; he does not quite know how to go about the matter and I do not think the onus of proof should be upon him. . . .

I do not take very seriously the argument that it will cost Canada a great deal because if Canada wants war she must pay for it. Surely we should not ask these men who fought the war to suffer financially as well as physically and mentally . . . and we, who did not suffer as they did, are the ones who should pay in order that they may live in comparative safety and comfort, so far as the security of their families is concerned.

I have in the riding of South East Grey two cases, which I suppose are typical and I will cite them briefly. One is the case of a man who was a minister but who was a private in the ranks. He was shell shocked, but feeling that other cases were much more serious than his, he did not report to the hospital and carried on. That man to-day is a complete wreck able to do no work at all. He did not apply for pension within the time set by law. He did not want to ask the country to bear any expense for him. He tried to carry on as a minister and moved out of the province of Ontario into the province of Nova Scotia. He has quite a sized family and now he cannot get even a mother's pension for that family because they have been out of the province for a period of seven years.

The other is a medical doctor from the same village. This man went overseas. He was in an ambulance corps close up to the front until he completely went to pieces and was sent to a nerve hospital in Great Britain. He remained there until the end of the war: he was taken home in a hospital ship: he was put into a hospital in Toronto and was discharged as an A-1 man. He is trying to carry on a general practice but he cannot do it. He is working a few days and in bed a few and he sometimes closes his office for a month at a time. The result is that his practice is going to pieces. He is not able to work in any other way and his family suffers.

I feel that these two cases are only typical of many others and I think the members of the Commons this year if we do nothing else . . . should at least see to it that we do something for the returned soldiers and that we do not ask these men to bear the misery and agony of not knowing where the meals are to come from for their children, of seeing their children grow up without the education that the ordinary people are able to give to theirs. I think some person said that this question should be taken out of party politics: I agree: and so should all other questions.[11]

In March Agnes again took up the case of equal rights for Western women at the time of divorce. Hansard, March 13, 1930, reported:

> *Miss Agnes C. Macphail: I am surprised and I think it would not be too strong a word to use if I said I was amazed — that the honorable member for Labelle (Mr. Bourassa) should ask this Parliament to turn backward. I have often thought that Parliament moved rather slowly in the right direction, but it is seldom that Parliament doubles back on the path it has already gone over, and that is in effect what the honorable member for Labelle is asking us to do — to undo what we finally accomplished in 1925, namely the putting of the women of the four western provinces on the same ground as men in regard to divorce.*
>
> *I feel quite sure that this House will defeat the bill. There is absolutely no doubt about that, but I do feel the honorable member from another province is taking a good deal of responsibility upon himself to introduce a bill which, if carried into effect, would take from the women of the four western provinces in Canada rights which they so lately and so hardly won. The honorable member for Winnipeg South Centre (Mr. Thorson) made the case so clear that anybody who today believes, as I believe, that progressive happiness rests upon equality between the sexes, could not possibly support the bill introduced by the honorable minister for Labelle. I believe, when I say that, that most members in this House will vote against the bill. There are a number of members in this House who time and time again have said how evil they think divorce is, and there have been possibly, not insinuations, but a feeling that those of us who want a divorce court in Ontario are in favor of divorce. Well, I will say this: divorce has increased and I believe will continue to increase, because as women win for themselves the right to earn a living; when they win for themselves the right not to endure that which no human being should be asked to endure, they are then in a position where they can apply for divorce if the grounds are there. And they will, because they see economic safety outside. Formerly that was not the case. And so divorce has increased, and has increased very largely because woman has become a person in the fullest sense of the word, a person who can support herself, and one who does not care to have anyone think of her as less than that. I would not for one moment support a bill that would seem to say that women are inferior to men, and I say that with some warmth.*

The Bourassa bill was rejected by a heavy majority, 114 to 58.

In May the House took up again the question of a deserted wife's right to acquire a separate domicile when seeking a divorce. In 1929 a bill had granted her "the right to acquire a separate domicile from that of her husband and it would have permitted her to go from province to province in order to acquire a separate domicile" for the purpose of commencing an action for divorce. Clearly this would still cause problems for the woman. A new Bill (31) stated that the home in which the couple were domiciled immediately prior to the desertion by the husband should be the domicile considered for the purpose of commencing an action for divorce. As W. J. Ward (Dauphin) said when he moved second reading of the bill: "I am sure the House will readily see how inconvenient, if not impossible, it would be for a woman of moderate or small means, working for her living and bringing up several small children, to travel from province to province in an effort to run down or catch up with the husband who a few years before deserted her."

> *Hon. Ernest Lapointe* [Minister of Justice]: *Under the British law and for that matter under the law of all nations, the domicile of the wife is the domicile of the husband. As long as the marriage lasts there is only one matrimonial domicile and surely everyone will admit that this is a good law. . . . The Honorable Member for South East Grey may not like that; nevertheless it is so.*
>
> *Miss Macphail: Well, I do not like it.*
>
> *Mr. Lapointe: I know my honorable friend does not like it, but I am afraid it cannot be changed this year.*

Lapointe said that if Ward's bill were adopted, a divorce granted under its provisions would not be recognized outside of Canada because it would be against the principles of international law. There could be only one real domicile. He quoted Lord Haldane: "Otherwise proceedings for dissolving the status of marriage might be carried through in two jurisdictions, possibly with different results." Lapointe continued:

> *My hon. friend said: we must have equality of the sexes. Equality is a pleasant word and discrimination, I agree, is unpleasant. Still, equality — and I think my hon. friend may agree with me on this — may mean reduction as well as addition. Would my hon. friend — and I will even ask the hon. member for Southeast Grey — would she want all statutes to be changed where inequality exists between the sexes? After all there are the physical laws against which nobody can contend and which we must recognize. Complete equality would be more detrimental than beneficial to women.*
>
> *Miss Macphail: Will the minister explain that more fully? I should like to have an instance of it.*
>
> *Mr. Lapointe: I will with the greatest pleasure. . . . There are in several provinces laws concerning labour for women, laws concerning minimum wages for women and not for men. Does my honorable friend desire equality on this?*
>
> *Miss Macphail: Certainly I do.*
>
> *Mr. Lapointe: But equality does not exist and this law was made for the protection not of men but of women.*
>
> *Miss Macphail: Implying that men have made women their inferiors.*
>
> *Mr. Lapointe: My honorable friend does not like the one I have mentioned; let me cite another. There are laws making it an offence and a crime for men not to support their wives. Does my honorable friend wish equality on that? Does she think it should be a crime for a wife not to support her husband?*
>
> *Miss Macphail: Yes, if all the laws and all the customs of civilization with regard to women were changed.*

*Mr. Lapointe: Exactly. My honorable friend is making up my case.
All the laws of civilization make the situation different and it cannot be
otherwise than different.*

Miss Macphail: Yes, it can.

Mr. Lapointe: Non-support laws?

*Miss Macphail: All the laws have been made by men for the protec-
tion of men, how can we change them but gradually.*

Mr. Lapointe continued that there were laws granting pensions to widows and
not to widowers and that military laws were not the same for women as for men.
"It would be cruel to women if those laws were changed to make them equal as
between men and women."

Agnes replied: "It would be much better."

Lapointe mentioned other laws which he thought favored women and said they
illustrated the fact "that it is impossible, because of natural conditions, that complete
equality should exist in regard to legislation as between sexes, and I do not think it
is desirable that the changes suggested should be made. We do not know where we
are going to land."

Miss Macphail: Terrible.

*Mr. Lapointe: My honorable friend says "terrible," but I would ask,
when there is a marriage law and both the law and custom have
decreed that the girl shall assume her husband's name, shall we change
that for the sake of equality?*

*Miss Macphail: I make the suggestion to the minister that the hus-
band take the wife's name.*

*Mr. Lapointe: That would perhaps be just as logical as many of the
proposals that are made. . . . I think that in the interests of the wife and
in the interests of woman it is well that these differences which have
existed since the world was created should be permitted to continue to
exist. . . .*

*Miss Macphail: I never can quite understand how a man of the
ability and charm of the Minister of Justice can be so antiquated when it
comes to an opinion on women. It is clear to me that he was born
about five hundred years too late. The thing we are discussing is this. A
man and a woman get married and establish a home, a domicile. They
may or may not have a family. The husband deserts the woman, clears
out for two years or longer. The wife wants a divorce, but according to
our law she must chase her husband over the face of Canada in order
to sue for divorce. . . . It is a humiliating thing. If domicile is a real
thing, it must be the home that was created by the marriage. The
husband deserts his wife and children, forsakes the home, and then the
Minister of Justice asks that the man alone shall retain the domicile. If
that is the law, it is a poor law, and let us change it. International law
may not be in accord with the principles of the bill, but we do not make
international law; we make Canadian law, and if we enact this bill into
law and other countries make similar laws, international law will come
into harmony with advanced thinking on this subject.*

*So I support most heartily the bill that has been introduced by the
honorable member for Dauphin. If the present law is based on injustice,*

and it clearly is, let us change it. All this bunk, if you will pardon the word, about equality between the sexes does not impress me very much. We are actually working towards equality, and clearly from the instances cited by the Minister of Justice tonight we have not yet got equality; woman is not yet a person, in spite of the judgment of the privy council that she is a person in regard to the senate at least. We need very many changes in our laws. We can make them only one at a time. This is our chance at this one, and we will make the most of it. [12]

The bill was read the second time and the Speaker decided they would have the third reading at the next sitting of the House.

A bright spot in the session had been an invitation from Prime Minister King to dine at Laurier House. She told her constituents that it had been

my good fortune to be the guest of the Prime Minister at dinner on Wednesday night. The party consisted of twelve and it took place at Laurier House. Laurier House has a real historic value. Dr. Doughty, the Archivist, was also a guest and he showed me a pen that Mr. Gladstone [Prime Minister of Great Britain four times in the late 1800's] *had presented to Mr. King when he and Mr. Doughty visited the great English Statesman shortly before his death. Mr. King very kindly showed me letters written by his grandfather when he was in prison in the United States; sad letters occasioned by the death of his mother. Each of the beautiful rooms contained objects of historic worth and interest.* [13]

Chapter VII
The Bennett Years
1930-1932

By mid-1930, wheat prices were so low that farmers could not make a profit; business was depressed and unemployment was a problem. Finance Minister Dunning reduced duties on British goods, hoping for reciprocal treatment. But the Opposition accused the government of not doing enough to relieve conditions and Prime Minister King called an election for Monday, July 28, the first July election since 1872. Four thousand bank mangers told the Financial Post that the Liberals would be returned with a "handsome majority," but in South East Grey they did not even field a candidate against Agnes Macphail.

The *Toronto Star* commented: "The withdrawal of the Liberal candidate in South East Grey is gratifying for although Miss Macphail has freely criticized one old party as the other, she has always been true to herself and to principles that are worthy of the able and vigorous advocacy in parliament she gave to them. Few members are as alert, well-informed and courageous as Miss Macphail and Parliament would be poorer without her." [1]

On July 10, her only opponent, Dr. L. G. Campbell, ran a large advertisement headed "Miss Macphail and Divorce," attacking her for supporting divorce courts in Ontario. He said these courts would "assuredly seriously interfere with the sanctity of the marriage vow, make for looser morals and in the end prove the most unfortunate piece of legislation ever passed through the House of Commons. But Miss Macphail voted for it and voted for it in direct opposition to the desires and feelings of the people of South East Grey who elected her. . . ." [2]

Agnes answered her opponent's "unfair criticism" at the candidate's nomination meeting held in Durham.

"Probably the largest crowd ever to attend a public gathering in Durham thronged the skating rink Monday afternoon," said the *Durham Review*, "when about 2500 people heard the nomination addresses of the South East Grey candidates, Miss Agnes C. Macphail (UFO) and Dr. L. G. Campbell (Conservative). . . ."

In her speech Agnes referred to the Campbell advertisement and said she "did not need a divorce for herself or anyone else." She quoted figures showing how divorce was increasing rapidly all over the world; in Ontario, from 20 in 1913 to 206 in 1929. (The number was 20,854 in 1985.)

> *I deplore the increase of divorce; I hold high the sacredness of the home and one reason why I voted for a divorce court in Ontario is that whatever chance the innocent party may have will be in a properly constituted court, for they haven't the chance of a dog in the Commons. Last year the number of divorce bills before Parliament was greater than all others together. While Senate was not overworked, the 15 members of the divorce committee were and they divided into two shifts, neither part hearing all the evidence. Later the shifts would meet and the bill would be*

recommended for Commons to pass. On one occasion, 60 of these bills were rushed through the Commons in two minutes.

Mr. Campbell had found great fault with her for voting for the bill, yet twenty-eight Conservatives had voted for the bill and only ten against. In a proper court many divorces would never go through and she would vote for it again, even if it meant her defeat.

She went on to talk about trade. Canada was in fifth place in the world as a trading nation and exported more per head than any other country. "Our destiny is on the high seas," she said. "If we don't buy from others, we cannot sell. United States is feeling the results of a high tariff barrier, with exports off 20% in three months and 21% of the population unemployed. Canadian conditions are not nearly so bad.

"In 1911 Canada had a grand chance to get a market for much of our surplus products but listened to a party [the Conservatives] whose slogan was 'No truck or trade with the Yankees' and lost that chance." We had to spend our surpluses somewhere and Britain was the best market. She strongly favored British preference, part of the Dunning budget, but not the high protectionist part.

Both in the argument and enthusiasm roused during the meeting, Miss Macphail had a decided advantage, said the *Review.*[3]

Four weeks before the election, the UFO held one of its popular picnics. The June 11th edition of the *Flesherton Advance* carried an advertisement for the much anticipated event:

UFO PICNIC
Bigger and better than ever

Bring the capacity to enjoy and
a basket lunch

will be held in
Lever's Grove, Flesherton
on the King's Highway
1 mile north of Flesherton
Tuesday, July 1st.
The popular Tom Hamilton Company
will entertain afternoon and evening.
Full line of Sports will be offered —
Softball tournament; Horseshoe tournament;
Football games; races.
Speakers: F. R. Oliver, M.P.P and Miss Agnes Macphail, M.P.
Haw's Pipe Band will be on hand and the Drury Orchestra, so
*   well liked 2 years ago, will furnish the dance music.*
Skirl of the pipes begins the day at 1 pm — Haw's Pipe Band.
Hear Agnes Macphail discuss Trends in Trade.
F. R. Oliver will speak on the ills of agriculture and the need
*   for cooperative marketing of farm products*
Grounds electrically lighted. Hot and cold water supplied.
Dancing platform enlarged.
Children under 12 free. Over 12 — 25¢ Adults 50¢.

It would have been hard to convince the 3,000 people who attended the picnic in the gaily decorated grove that their candidate could be in trouble in the coming election. But as election day approached the *Durham Review* warned that the Conservative party was "making strenuous endeavors to secure the Liberal vote" and "was spreading tales claiming wide-spread dissatisfaction with our present representative."

"However," said the *Review*,

> *the Liberals of South East Grey fully realize that the common enemy is the Tory party . . . and while a few Liberals may support Campbell in this election, the great majority will not be stampeded and are standing firmly behind Miss Macphail who comes out strongly in favor of Premier King's platform for greater Empire trade.*
>
> *In his address at Newmarket on Saturday, Premier King said: "Even Miss Agnes Macphail, when it comes to choosing between Liberal and Conservative policies, will vote with the Liberals in a majority of cases and as long as Miss Macphail continues to stand for democratic principles, I hope the Liberals of South East Grey will not run a candidate against her, but will give her every possible support where there is a Conservative in the field against her." [4]*

Farquhar Oliver, Agnes' protégé and friend

King's support did little for Agnes as he himself was battling for his political life. On July 28 he lost heavily as Bennett's Conservatives swept the country. Agnes survived with a greatly reduced majority.

"But," said the *Review*,

> *considering the Tory landslide in general and the determined effort made in this riding to oust Miss Macphail, she and her supporters are to be congratulated upon coming out on top with her present majority. With no speakers on her behalf but herself, F. R. Oliver, M.P.P., and two or three other local men, large gatherings were attracted to all meetings; while assisting Dr. Campbell on his platform were Hon. R. B. Bennett, Conservative leader, Hon. Mr. Price, Earl Rose of Dufferin-Simcoe, J. N. Perdue, the last candidate, and several others. Unfair and misleading attacks were made upon Miss Macphail through press advertisements and platforms and no expense was spared to bring about her defeat.*
>
> *From 7 pm on Monday night cars kept rolling into town and the streets became crowded. The UFO headquarters at the Town Hall was crowded to overflowing and many were unable to squeeze in. The Ritchie orchestra provided music and the South East Grey returns were read out, showing Miss Macphail elected by something over 300. About 10 o'clock the only lady M.P. arrived and she was accorded a rousing reception. Mr. Joe Crutchley acted as Chairman and called her to the platform. She heartily thanked all for their assistance in another great victory and while it would have been greater satisfaction to have the former large majority, still 300 was ample and even if the majority were 60 it would be just as effective for her work at Ottawa as if it were 6000.*
>
> *"I am not in politics for money," she stated. "I have not made any, but am giving my whole time and the best of my life and ability in your service and hope to represent you faithfully in the coming years."* [5]

Agnes was now appreciated far beyond her own riding, as shown by the many compliments paid her by the nation's press.

> *In the nine years she has sat in the seats of the mighty at Ottawa she has developed into an astute parliamentarian, well able to hold her own with the best of her fellow members.*
>
> *We have not always agreed with her views, notably those on military training, but we have always admired her sincerity, her alertness, her ability, her fearlessness and her independence. Few male members can equal her record in taking pains to be a faithful and efficient representative. Miss Macphail has come to occupy a prominent place in parliament, and her defeat, which seems a long way off, would be like the passing of an institution.* [6]

The *Labor Advocate* said Agnes was the sole survivor of the agrarian movement which had sent a "formidable number" of members to Parliament in 1921.

> *She entered public life a farm girl, a country schoolma'am, almost painfully conscious of her inexperience. She came as one*

*of the latest of the suffragettes; she was an embodied protest,
militant, aggressive. But this was only a passing state of
mind . . . she has learned that "it is better to fight for the good
than to rail at the ill."*

*Those who have met her realize that she is a great personality.
. . . She is more outspoken than ever before — if such a thing be
possible — in support of those reforms for which she always stood.
She is the clearest voice raised in our House of Commons on behalf
of the great cause of international peace. Her championship of the
public against all forms of privilege is as strong as ever. And it is
well known and admitted by all save blind partisans that she has had
a really effective part in bringing about some of the reforms that
have been made in her time, such as old age pensions and others.*

*Her personal success is one of the noteworthy facts of current
politics. The first and most remarkable is her conquest, or partial
conquest of the House of Commons itself. . . . She has overcome in
no small degree the prejudice of the men against women in
politics. . . . She is constantly in demand as a platform speaker
throughout Canada and in many parts of the United States.*[7]

Before leaving on another lecture tour of the United States Agnes wrote
home and said:

*The bitterness of the conflict from which we have just emerged is
showing clearly in the debates. Mr. Bennett with a fresh mandate
from the people and a strong following in the House and carrying in
his own person the most important portfolios, has developed a fine
Mussolinian manner. Mr. King, especially in his opening speech,
showed the depth of hurt from which he is suffering.*

*A new Parliament brings joy to those who come again, but sorrow
also for the absence of friends. It takes at least a session to shake
down into comfortable living. There is, too, sharp regret that policies
which one believes are detrimental to the welfare of the country are
winning. It is strange, but we learn little from the experience of
others. As an individual, as in a nation, we must suffer for ourselves.
We have swung into a period of ultra nationalism, but one day we
will know that Canada's destiny is closely linked with the other
nations of the world and that economic nationalism is for us a
disastrous policy. . . .*[8]

In 1928 she had told an audience in Windsor that when "the Creator put
raw materials into the earth, He did not intend that one nation should corner one
section, and another, another. He meant that all nations should have free access
to all the materials and that is the way it should be."[9]

In a second letter of 1930 she said that the past election had been "one of
the hardest things" she had ever gone through.

*I am not speaking of the physical strain. During that experience and
as a result of it, I came close to losing my belief in the intelligence
and goodness of human beings. But strange as it may seem, the one
thing that is now in a measure restoring my confidence in humanity*

— and I am sure the honorable gentleman will be surprised — is the Prime Minister himself. This can be said, that he apparently has the courage of his convictions and I like people who have decision and act with despatch. But I am entirely opposed to the policies he is advocating and while at the moment we are seeing in Canada as in other parts of the world, nationalism gone mad, it is not a policy that in the long run will be beneficial to Canada or to any other country that pursues it. We are giving to the manufacturers of Canada the right to the cost of production, plus a fair profit, when at the same time the agricultural industry . . . is not getting any such thing; when this year it is not even getting the cost of production, leaving out entirely a reasonable profit. Why should we guarantee to any one group . . . the cost of production plus a reasonable profit when agriculture which the Prime Minister himself admitted is the great basic industry, is not benefitting similarly?[10]

In late fall on her tour south she wrote happily of meeting such famous people as Mrs. Eleanor Roosevelt, Pierpont Morgan's daughter Ann and Indian author Tagore:

My journeying in the Northern States brought me to Vassar college for a week and there I heard Mrs. Franklin D. Roosevelt, wife of the Governor of New York State. She is a remarkable woman; besides performing her duties as hostess, she teaches two days a week and is in partnership with another woman manufacturing rare bits of furniture. Her subject dealt with education. She has several children, two girls in college. She pointed out the great difficulty deciding what their life work was to be since they go on to school without any practical experience in work of any kind. She is a great believer in work and apparently does not lose caste as a Governor's wife because of it. Her personality is pleasing.

I was on the campus of North Carolina Women's College for two days. One of the lecturers told me she never heard Canada mentioned on the campus before. The two days made up for it. I had five lectures on Canadian-American relations in the League of Nations as well as a dinner and a tea at which I met the students and part of the faculty.

An interesting experience was an afternoon in Cleveland which took the nature of a symposium on "Whither Womanhood." Miss Alice Foote McDougall, who has made such an outstanding success of business in New York, spoke on women in industry. Mrs. Felix Levy of Chicago spoke on women in the home and I on women in public life. The audience of 1299 was composed wholly of women.[11]

Two weeks later she wrote:

What a place New York is with its skyscrapers and traffic jams and hurrying, high-tension millions! Yet crossing on the ferry one night from Passaic, N.J. just after dark, it looked a fairy city with its towers and domes picked out in lights against the dusky sky. On another occasion looking down on it from the 30th floor of a hotel, it presented a picture of extreme beauty, but to live there and be jammed round year in and year out must be a harrowing experience. I was fortunate in being asked to lunch or dine with the women of Wall Street, an executive group of women called Zonta, the Women's International League for Peace and Freedom and the American Women's Association, the latter a group which met in a four million dollar building for which women raised the money. It is really a women's hotel and managed by women.

At this point I was introduced by Ann Morgan, daughter of Pierpont Morgan, an exceedingly able and likeable woman. I had not much time to see the shows but I did manage to see Eva Le Gallienne [12] as Juliet. It is said in New York that she is the best Juliet that New York has seen.

Talk about London fog; one can see it by going to Pittsburgh some muggy day when there is no wind to lift the smoke. The morning I arrived I couldn't see across the street. I was billeted in Pittsburgh in the home of a Virginian gentleman, Mr. and Mrs. Carrol Millar. I enjoyed hearing his prolonged drawl. They had lived eight years in Japan and several in London, England, so their outlook was international rather than national. They were close personal friends of Woodrow Wilson and a large signed photograph of him hung in the library. I was there on Armistice Day and was asked to speak over the radio. From the same station I spoke on a nationwide hook-up on the subject of "Since we got the vote." At the public meeting in Pittsburgh I met many Canadians.

The Foreign Policy Association of Columbus, Ohio, asked Mr. James MacDonald of New York and me to discuss for twenty-five minutes each "The Changing British Empire." It is a subject in which I am keenly interested and I happened to have with me a couple of books by Zimmern on it. I was anxious to be fair to Canada's part and so got in touch with the Department of External Affairs, Ottawa, and they most kindly sent me much material. I enjoyed this evening most of all and we had an hour of rapid-fire questions afterward. [13]

In December she was on her way home again:

Detroit is largely a one-industry city — automobiles and more automobiles form its principal export. In hard times people do not change their car, nor is it a time when he who never owned a motor purchases one. All this results in great unemployment. Everyone was talking hard times and I saw long queues of men at the employment agency and relief stations. Unemployment is an unhappy feature in all American cities this winter. It is estimated that in Philadelphia alone 125,000 bread winners will need assistance. In New York, the unemployed selling apples at 5 cents apiece are seen on almost every corner. In the great metropolis particularly the white collared worker is swelling the ranks of the jobless.

People everywhere are seeking the cause of the general distress. Is it caused by the tariffs they ask? They are not as sure as they were a few years ago that buying the home-made product is the whole solution. If they do that always, who is to buy the vast exportable surpluses? People are questioning whether we can allow the control to rest in the hands of the few, bringing them great wealth while to the masses uncertainty and unemployment result. I heard several people also question the wisdom of attempting to stick to the gold standard as a basis for money. I am inclined to agree with Richard De Brisay who writes the very excellent editorials in the Canadian Forum: "The new industrial revolution has brought us to a point where there is no longer enough money and credit in the world to enable us to consume the products of our machine-equipped labor."

War debts are by many people admitted to be a cause of the present depression but U.S. is still in a goodish way from being willing to cancel war debts. When Mr. C. L. Burton, president of the Robt. Simpson Co., discussed this subject in Milwaukee, he was met by stony silence.

My two days visit in St. Louis, Miss., was altogether enjoyable. I addressed the open Forum and the day following was the guest at luncheon of a group of Jewish women and in the afternoon of the same day, addressed the Mary Institute, which is the Girls' College of Washington University. After each address there was a period of questions and discussions which I enjoyed. In these audiences, as indeed in all I met, a warm friendship for Canada was clearly shown.

Though I was a stranger I was shown the greatest hospitality. Dr. and Mrs. Seelig, whose guest I was, entertained 12 of us to a Sunday evening supper featuring a turkey and all the fixings and the next night the committee of the Mary Institute treated me to a dinner in one of their fine hotels and afterward we went to the theatre to see "Topaz" a wicked little French play, wonderfully well done. . . .

Crossing the line from the Canadian side we were held up almost three quarters of an hour while customs officials went thru the cars with a "flashlight in one hand and a fine-tooth comb in the other" as one indignant man phrased it, looking for contraband, but knowing perfectly well they wouldn't find it. The search coming north is scarcely less amusing. It is not quite as bad as the farce enacted when entering France where, in my case at least, the bags were never opened. They simply asked me if I had any cigarettes and when I said no, he O.K.'d the bag.

For a long time I have associated Tagore[14] with high idealism, poetic expression and great wisdom. It was therefore an event to meet him. His speaking tour in the United States has been cancelled because of ill health, but he was sufficiently recovered to meet in an informal way, groups of people, and in the home of the well known Violet Oakley, artist, I met this great Indian personality. He was seated in an invalid chair and dressed in a flowing black robe. With his dark, dreamy eyes, beautifully proportioned head, long hair, beard, he was indeed an impressive figure. He looked a seer. He

*spoke perfect and beautifully modulated English. His artist hostess had
done pictures of him which were speaking likenesses. Tagore's pictures,
about which one reads, did not impress me at all. He does them with
ink. They may mean expression, as he claims, but they do not mean
beauty to me.*

*With the poet was Andrews, who this year published the life of
Gandhi [15]. The Farm and Labor group had entertained him when he was
in Ottawa a year ago. It was a pleasure to chat with him again. He was
an English missionary to India and there became convinced that Tagore
and Gandhi had attained greater spirituality than he, and for many
years he has been associated with these two wise men of the east.*

*On both sides of the international boundary line, women have ex-
pressed the desire for a conference to be devoted in the main to dis-
covering ways of attaining peace. The first steps have been taken and it
now appears certain that a four day school will be held the last week-
end in May in Toronto. We hope in one of the University Buildings. The
subject of the Conference is "The Economic Basis of Peace." We
greatly hope that Jane Addams [16] will be able to attend. This will be a
great opportunity for anyone who wishes to spend a week in study and
fellowship. [17]*

The Bennett years were preoccupied with the depression and while Agnes held
hands with the new leader she did not spare him her criticism. In her letter of
March 30, 1931, she told of the formal opening of Parliament with R. B. Bennett at
the helm:

*The first regular session of the 17th Parliament was opened despite
the absence of the Governor General with all pomp and circumstance.
Booming cannon, shining uniforms and beautiful gowns all played their
part. . . .*

*The Speech from the Throne lays the blame — or the major part of
the blame — for the present economic depression upon world causes
and in case that does not absorb all the responsibility, Mr. Duff [Rt.
Hon. Lyman P. Duff, of the Supreme Court] was caused to say: "My
Government has explored the origins of our difficulties and is firmly of
the belief that many of our problems do not arise out of world-wide
depression but are antecedent to it, and that domestic factors have also
largely determined the degree of economic distress from which this
country is suffering." Having thus saddled the responsibility of present
conditions upon the world and the Mackenzie King government, the
present Administration emerges wearing the white rose of a blameless
life. . . .*

*Mr. Bennett is looking remarkably fit. Hard work seems to have
agreed with him. When the House of Commons met for a few moments
after the formal opening in the Senate Chamber, Mr. Bennett moved, as
is the traditional right of the Commons, a Bill of our own before we
went on to consider the King's speech. The Bill is never heard of again;
it is simply a dummy to show the King we consider our own bill first if
we wish and dates back to the day when the King's business was not
always in harmony with the thought of Parliament. [18]*

R. B. Bennett, Prime Minister of Canada from 1930 to 1935

On March 16 in her reply to the Speech from the Throne Agnes pointed out her distaste for the arrogance displayed by the Conservatives. While she saw little difference between the Liberals and Conservatives in policy, there was

> *a great difference in manner. I trust that the present government is not a fair sample of Conservatives in power. It has been very amusing to me to note the added touch of arrogance of practically every member of the government and particularly of the leader, Rt. Hon. R. B. Bennett.* [Agnes said once that she "never knew a man who could be so right all the time. He is right when he introduces legislation and he is right when he withdraws it." She said she wished she could achieve his "glorious self-righteousness."] *They can go too far and they should remember that governments come and governments go but always the people and the people's representatives in the House remain. Courtesy and decent treatment should at all times be accorded.*
>
> *Forty minutes soon pass and I must proceed with what few remarks I wish to make. We are living in a day of high pressure salesmanship, of which we saw a very fine sample last summer when the Conservative party was out to sell to the farmer of Canada a gold brick, the gold brick of protection for agriculture, and the sale was made. The farmer bit. The farmer in Canada, like ourselves in the House of Commons, had heard the Conservative party during the depression of 1920 to 1924 tell again and again and again, eloquently and well, how they could cure the depression if they were*

only in power. They had the remedy; they knew how to cure the disease. So the farmer, feeling that another depression was upon him thought: Well, these fellows say they know how to cure it; let us see if they will. So he bought the gold brick of protection for agriculture and since then he has been wondering why, just as many another one has wondered when the well-dressed salesman left. The remedy proposed is such a simple one; it was and is: Keep out all goods that might enter our country to come into competition with our goods, but sell our surplus goods upon the world's markets. It is an exceedingly simple remedy: Refuse to buy but sell.

She said Prime Minister Bennett had gone to the Imperial Conference to secure a market for Canadian wheat, but failed. She interrupted her speech

to thank from the bottom of my heart the Prime Minister for appointing the Hon. Howard Ferguson as minister plenipotentiary to the Court of St. James. It is rather hard on the Court of St. James, but it is a great relief to the Province of Ontario. When I read in the papers day after day Mr. Ferguson's speeches and saw his pictures and accounts of his career, and how proud that Canada should be that he had gone to London, and so on and so on, I said to myself: Has sincerity and honesty wholly departed from our province? I at least am thankful that he has gone, but I am sorry to see that a man of his particular type — not stripe — should be appointed minister plenipotentiary representing Canada in Great Britain.

(How much her opinion of Ferguson was colored by his public reproval of her for writing the "unpatriotic" letter on the Opium Wars, might be debated.)

Regarding unemployment, she said,

it seems quite evident that new methods will have to be found, for the old methods are no longer any good. One whom, I suppose, we would call a Conservative, the Right Hon. Winston Spencer Churchill, said that quite clearly in one of his Oxford lectures. I am quoting now from Toronto Saturday Night of January 31, 1931. He said:

> *The root problem of modern world economics is the strange disparity between the consuming and producing power. Have all our triumphs of research and organization bequeathed us only a new punishment — the curse of plenty?*

I think the "curse of plenty" is a particularly fine phrase. Churchill suggested that Britishers should create what he called a "sub-parliament," or at least a committee of experts who should investigate all ways — even radical ways — of solving the problem. . . . It seems to me that is a suggestion which this government might very well consider.

She advised the government to start a school where people could be trained in the management of co-operative enterprises. "That is something which will mean more than growing two blades of grass where one grew before, when you can sell neither." [19]

On April 21 she further criticized the Prime Minister in the House:

I listened with amazement to the Prime Minister of Canada speaking this afternoon. I wondered could it be just one year ago that we heard the unemployment debate in this house, a debate in which the government of that day showed a complete lack of understanding of conditions in the country. At that time the right hon. gentleman who is now Prime Minister was the leader of the opposition, and he and his colleagues told the house, and in many instances told very well, what the conditions were. Then we went through an election last July. We heard the moaning of the then opposition from coast to coast. The conditions were terrible. They were such that only God's anointed could save the country. There is no use in the Prime Minister now getting up as he did today and assuming the air of lecturing this house, particularly this corner of the house. I think the Prime Minister will find as time goes on that the speech which he made this afternoon was an exceedingly unwise one, and one which he will bitterly regret.

Some hon. members: Oh, oh.

Miss Macphail: He may not — he ought. The conditions since the unemployment debate last session and since the election held in July last year have not improved. On the contrary they have steadily become worse. Had the Prime Minister risen in his place today in the house and admitted that such was the case and that present conditions required the best efforts of every hon. member of the house he would have won the hearts of hon. members, because even this house has a heart. However he did not do that; he would not admit that serious conditions prevail, conditions with which all working people are familiar. It might do the Prime Minister some good if he went out and became acquainted with the facts. I think it is most unfortunate and ridiculous that the Prime Minister has not seen fit to admit the present condition in Canada. I would think that during the next two or three weeks editorials in our newspapers would make the blunder abundantly clear, even to the ministry who now grace the treasury benches.

During the Easter vacation I happened to be out west. . . . I was not surprised to read in the newspapers about the riot in Winnipeg. When I was in that city walking along Portage Avenue and Main Street I saw badly dressed men with nothing to do just milling around, moving up and down. . . . They walked one way and then the other. By law they are required to keep moving and that is the way they do it. I am not blaming the Prime Minister for the unemployment and stress, but I am blaming him for not admitting that such a condition exists. . . . It is true that the farmers are not unemployed; they are unpaid. They have plenty of work to do. There has been talk about new wealth which was created in Western Canada. Where did it go? It went to provide profits to the people who benefitted from the tariff. It went to provide bankers with their large dividends. Honorable members laugh! It may sound amusing, but it really is not a matter to be treated lightly. The wealth of Western Canada has gone to provide bankers with dividends, to build

*fine office buildings such as we see in Toronto, Montreal, Regina and
Calgary. It has gone to provide a better living for other classes in
Canada. When the farmer had paid out all these profits he had
nothing left for himself.*[20]

Agnes never changed her opinion of the Conservatives. In 1935 she spoke to
members of Toronto's Canadian Club and drew laughter when she discussed the
Conservative Party. "They are dominating. They assume a very superior attitude.
They have thought themselves to have a corner on superiority and it is long
known that they have a corner on patriotism. To be a real patriot one must be a
Tory. But lately they have gone a step further and have tried to get a corner on
godliness. I give you two examples: The Prime Minister recently said to a
meeting of Young Conservatives: 'God has been very good to me.' As the
second proof, I offer Denton Massey.[21] I must have been mistaken when I used
to go to Bible Class and read that 'whom the Lord loveth he chasteneth.' But
perhaps he will at that."

In the summer of 1931 a scandal involving the previous Liberal government was
revealed. Agnes told her constituents about the "Beauharnois Scandal" and gave
her reaction to it in her usual straightforward manner:

*By far the most discouraging aspect of this session was the
Beauharnois revelation. The whole story is a long one, but a group
of financiers wanted to develop the power of the St. Lawrence River
at the Soulanges section of the portion of it that lay between Lake St.
Francis and Lake St. Louis. Before they could proceed they had to
buy out the "rights" of the Robert estate; they also had to obtain an
Order in Council from the Dominion government giving them the
right to divert the water of the St. Lawrence from one lake to the
other. They needed also to sell bonds to the public and like any other
business they wanted to be sure of a market for their product when
they had it ready to sell.*

*The moving spirit in the scheme was R. O. Sweezey, an engineer
by profession. With Mr. Sweezey were associated many men, among
them Senator W. L. McDougald and R. A. C. Henry who became
Deputy Minister of Railways. There were several companies at one
time and another, but the main one was the Beauharnois Light, Heat
and Power Co. Apparently an obstruction was placed in their way by
a "fake" company called the Sterling Industrial Corp., the leading
figure in it being Senator McDougald and Mr. Henry. They (the
Sterling Industrial Corporation) had asked the Government for the
right to divert the waters of the St. Lawrence, but had not been given
it; they had no right whatever, yet Mr. Sweezey paid them over a
million dollars for their supposed rights. He also, either personally,
or as head of the company, roughly donated $800,000 to the Liberal
campaign funds and $125,000 to John Aird, Jr. of Toronto, who, Mr.
Sweezey says, suggested that they make a contribution to the Ontario
Conservative party because they would probably be having a lot of
dealings with the Ontario people and "gratefulness was always
regarded as an important factor in dealing with democratic governments." But Mr. Aird now says he received the money for himself in*

payment for advice he gave Mr. Sweezey, the nature of which he has forgotten. It is worth noting that it was from the Ontario Gov't. that the Beauharnois Co. secured the contract for a long term sale of electric energy which enabled them to sell their bonds.

Mr. Sweezey's company secured the Order in Council from the Gov't., but by it the amount of water they could divert from the St. Lawrence was limited to 40,000 cubic feet per second. In spite of that they had secured the whole flow of the river. Besides paying fabulous sums to lawyers, to individual politicians and to various other people, the Company has done very nicely for itself. In the words of the House of Commons committee: "As the situation now stands the promoters of the Beauharnois project, involving the exploitation of a great natural resource, have been able to secure to themselves a return of all money advanced to them, or any of them, a profit of $2,189,000 in cash and one million class A common shares, which, if saleable at the market quotation would at one time have been worth $17,000,000 and at today's quotation of $4 a share would be worth $4,000,000. This cash profit was paid out of monies borrowed by the Beauharnois Power Corporation Limited by the sale of bonds.

Mackenzie King's speech on the Beauharnois Power project was weak in the extreme. It was extremely lengthy. For hours he laboured to show that the government of which he was the head, passed the Order in Council giving Beauharnois 40,000 cubic feet per second of the St. Lawrence water in good faith. Nobody for a moment thought otherwise. Even opposition newspapers and the opposition party did not believe he knew at the time the Privy Council order was being passed that Senators in his confidence had received large sums of money on the understanding that their influence would be used to secure the order. He did not, it seemed to me, cut himself loose from the dubious method of obtaining campaign funds, nor did he make any constructive suggestions as to how the mess was to be cleaned up. He asked for a Royal Commission to further investigate the sources of campaign funds; he did show deep sorrow over the treatment accorded him by Senator McDougald, and that he deeply regretted the whole affair, no one could doubt who heard him. He was, he said, in the valley of humiliation. We live in too fast an age for anyone to listen contentedly to speeches 3 1/2 hours long, and terse speaking was never more required than on that occasion.

Mr. Bennett's reply to Mr. King was clever and in a measure, constructive. His attack of the Leader of the Opposition reminded one of Meighen. He said he would ask Parliament to cancel the Order in Council and that Beauharnois would be put under new management. When pressed as to who the new management would be, he stated "three bankers." Who they are, or from what banks, is unknown. The Order in Council has been canceled and legislation transferring the management passed. The persistent rumour is that the project will pass into the hands of Sir Herbert Holt.

My reaction to the whole situation I expressed in the House is as follows: I feel there should be a law — whether provincial or federal

*does not matter to me — to force those who so exploit our great
natural resources to disgorge their dishonest gains, or else go to jail
like any ordinary Canadian citizen would have to do if found guilty
of petty thievery. Why not? If a hungry person takes a loaf of bread
or a bag of potatoes, or some other thing of practically no monetary
value, he is sent to jail. So why should not people who have taken
wealth that certainly did not belong to them, whether they have given
it to somebody else or retained it does not matter — why, I ask,
should not such people be brought within the criminal code? We are
passing through very difficult and very hard times, and there is
nothing quite so nauseating to the people of Canada, nothing that
rouses a rebellious spirit so strongly as the fact that when they are
striving to remain honest and cheerful and hardworking, at the same
time they see a bunch of rogues making off with wealth that really
belongs to the nation. Unless something definite is done to curb these
so-called financiers and the senators who got some of the money
through their supposed political value, then as a former teacher and
as a woman, I would ask: What are we going to teach the children
of Canada? What is the use of saying to the boys and girls in our
public schools, we must have high ideals; we must look up to our
public men and have confidence in them, if such men are to be
allowed to remain in the Parliament of Canada? Here are three
Senators who appear before the Beauharnois committee and I suppose they will continue to bear the prefix "honorable?" If there is to
be any respect for the Senate — and there is precious little now —
we ought to rid the Senate of their presence and we should not be
afraid or ashamed to say so.* [22]

In the spring of 1932 Agnes wrote of meeting Winston Churchill; explained why
she missed voting on a salary cut; and told of the discovery of radium in
Canada:

*The Prime Minister entertained at lunch in honor of the Right Honor-
able Winston Churchill. Due to his kindness, all members of the
House of Commons and the Senate were given the privilege of
meeting this very well known and distinguished, courageous Britisher.
Not only has he been an adventurer in the political life of Great
Britain, but he is by many declared to be the best writer of English
prose living today. It is amazing how he found time in his crowded
and busy life to write the many books which today grace our libraries. We were all most anxious to see him. Mr. Bennett and Mr.
Churchill received at the entrance to the dining room and since my
place at table was advantageous, I had a fine opportunity of observ-
ing the distinguished visitor.*

*Even at lunch the terrific drive and energy of Winston Churchill
was quite apparent. He ate his hearty lunch with evident enjoyment
and talked to the Prime Minister throughout. When the meal was
coming to an end, he took from his pocket a bit of paper and began
thinking out his speech, making slowly and carefully a few notes.*

When the Prime Minister was introducing him, describing his activities and praising him very much, he smiled as though amused. His speech was short and beautifully phrased. He said what I have often thought is so true, that being a Member of Parliament was a great opportunity for continuing one's education. He stressed the benefit that comes from the fellowship of the members of the House and the opportunity that membership brings of meeting people from all over the world. The serious part of his speech dealt with the coming Imperial Economic Conference; he feels that it affords a great opportunity to each part of the Empire to find common economic ground with all other parts of the Empire. He apparently expects much from the conference. Personally, I cannot see how the result can be good unless each part of the Empire is willing to buy from the others as well as sell to them.

The facial resemblance between Mr. Churchill and Mr. Bennett is remarkable. They must surely look out on life through the same window since the character lines on their faces are almost identical, though Mr. Churchill is a much shorter and less robust-looking man and although but 57 looks older than the Prime Minister who is 62. [23]

April 7, 1932

Speaking of missing votes, I hear I am accused of deliberately dodging the vote on the 10% cut on salaries. That vote came early in the day on which the Prime Minister entertained us to lunch to meet the Right Honorable Winston Spencer Churchill. I was the only woman present and that gathering was a large one, including Members of Parliament, Senators and press men. The Prime Minister had treated his guests to very excellent cigars and while the odour of one good cigar may be pleasant, the same can hardly be said of hundreds being smoked at the same time in a crowded room. While I am usually indifferent to cigar smoke, it, on this occasion gave me a severe headache. The luncheon came to an end just at 3 o'clock and I decided to go for a walk hoping the fresh air would clear the headache. I was gone exactly 30 minutes and when I came back the vote was over. There had been no indication that it would be the first thing on after the Orders of the Day. However I had said I would vote in favor of the 10% reduction and since the Government has a majority of 30, the fate of the measure was not affected by my absence. [24]

In the Senate the other day a most interesting story of the discovery of radium in Canada at Great Bear Lake — about 1000 miles north of Edmonton — was related by General McRae. He was urging the Government for a Radium Commission to take charge of the development of the radium field and the putting of this life-saving metal on the market at the lowest possible cost. Only 300 grammes of radium for medicinal purposes are available in the whole world. It is used in the treatment of cancer. Ninety-five per cent of all radium is found in the Belgian Congo. The wholesale price of it is $50,000 a gramme, retail $70,000. General McRae quoted a Philadelphia

*authority for the statement that 960 grammes would be needed in the
United States if all cancer cases there were to be treated with
radium.*

*At Great Bear Lake there are three veins of radium running out
1400 feet and a fourth vein is indicated. General McRae believes that
a carload a day of ore could be mined and should that be the case,
in a year the Great Bear Lake deposits could produce 1800
grammes. The Department of Mines of the Federal Government
estimate that it would cost $10,000 a gramme but the General be-
lieves it could be done for a little in excess of $5000.* [25]

On October 20, 1932, the *Eastern Chronicle* of New Glasgow, Nova Scotia
commented on a speech that Agnes made in the House:

*We publish Miss Macphail's speech [Hansard, Oct. 13] and invite our
readers' attention to it. Miss Macphail is not a Grit, nor a Tory. She
is an Independent, if that be possible. At best, she comes as near to it
as anyone ever did in the Canadian Parliament. Her speech is the
best delivered so far in this session of the House of Commons. That
statement being made with the knowledge that the Liberal, Conservative and Progressive leaders have all made speeches and they were
able. The only lady member of the House crowded more meat into
her forty-minute limit than the leaders of the great parties did in their
speeches extending over hours.*

*"Mr. Speaker, my eleven years' experience in the House of Com-
mons led me to believe that the present leader of the opposition (Mr.
King) who for many years was leader of the government, was the
greatest master in Canada of phrasemaking. I thought that at any
time he could carry off the palm for the bringing together of beautiful
if sometimes meaningless words. However, after reading the second
to last paragraph in the speech from the throne, I feel he must give
place to the present Prime Minister (R. B. Bennett). We find such
expressions as the following: 'retrenchment and constructive development,' 'enviable financial position of this country,' and 'the integrity
of industry.' That, more than any other expression challenges my
admiration; I should never have thought of it. When one thinks of the
watered stock of industry and the callousness with which industrial
leaders turn out their employees; when one considers the tariff
concessions given year after year and time after time, and adds to
that excise protection — a new name for tariffs — and then makes
the addition of dumping duties, we come to an understanding of what
is termed 'the integrity of industry.'*

*"Then we find the expression 'the resourcefulness of agriculture.'
I understand that very well. The expression really means that the
farmer stops taking the daily paper, has his telephone removed from
the house, does without a new winter overcoat, and has his children
do without a much needed tonsil operation. The farmer's wife does
not get her new hat or new shoes; they are not able to take the little
trip they had planned — oh, yes, I understand that.*

"And then the last expression — 'enabled us to take quick and

*profitable advantage of improved conditions.' That is good. Then
there is one other I should not like to miss, namely his reference to
'approaching prosperity.' Of course, if it is on the road anywhere, I
suppose it is approaching — unless it is running the other way. That,
too, might be possible. The paragraph to which I have referred is
such a gem that, really, we ought to see that it goes into every home
in Canada. It is too bad that the king's representative had to say it,
but it is really rich — in fact, it is the best I have heard in eleven
years. . . .*

*"Now I should like to refer to the Prime Minister's speech. . . .
He has said that his government stands for sound money. In that connection his words are as follows:*

> *There is only one thing that can be said about this government
> with respect to its monetary policy, and that is this: We will
> stand for sound money.*

*I believe if he had taken the word 'sound' out, his statement would
have been equally accurate. I think it is apparent that the Prime
Minister and the government — if one must add the qualification —
do stand for money. I believe he stands for high interest rates, for
deflation, for the payment of debts with dear money — debts which
were contracted with money which was worth about half what it is
now, and at a time when commodities were worth about twice their
present value. The government and the Prime Minister stand for
money, because the terrific taxation in this country does not bear
very heavily upon the moneyed classes, but bears most heavily upon
the backs of the masses.*

*"In contrast to the position taken by the Prime Minister, either
that he stands for sound money or for money, I want to say quite
frankly that I stand for the people. I stand for those farmers who this
year have worked and were not only underpaid, but, as a matter of
fact, were not paid at all. I believe it is not inaccurate to say that
there is not a farmer in the province of Ontario who this year can
earn his taxes from the proceeds of the land he has cultivated. True,
he might pay them from accumulated capital, or by selling off some
of his young stock which he should not have to sell, and the selling
of which impoverishes him for the next year. He might pay his taxes
by doing without things that he needs, or by borrowing. I repeat
however, it is not inaccurate to say that there is not a farmer in
Ontario who this year will pay his taxes from the earnings of his
land. I am very proud to stand for that type of person.*

*"In the class I include not only the farmers, but also the unem-
ployed. Those people constitute a disinherited class, and it is a very
large class in Canada. One does not need to quote figures, but we
may have noticed that the leader of the opposition said there were
500,000 unemployed; probably 700,000 would be closer to the
number. There is in Canada this great disinherited class which in
these fall months must face the winter with fear. Some one must
stand for them. I think a great many hon. members in this House are*

seeking to serve them. I believe we are all sympathetic. I think the Prime Minister is sympathetic — but unfortunately, sympathy is not enough. We must stand for a money policy, and a general national policy which will bring this disinherited class into its inheritance again, a policy which will make of them people like ourselves who are not fearful that they will not get something to eat or have a house to live in, or clothes to wear.

"So the Prime Minister is exceedingly welcome to his statement that he stands for a sound monetary policy if by that expression he means the monetary policy he has been pursuing. Then later in his address, he stated that there were people going around the country — he referred to them as soap box orators, communists and socialists — who will endeavour to arouse the passions and prejudices of the people and who will carry to them tales of new nostrums and remedies that will cure all the economic evils of the day. I say to the Prime Minister that I suspect I am one of the soap box orators to whom he has referred. I have no apologies to make, but would say, to quiet the fears of the Prime Minister, that I did not stir the prejudices or passions of the people. He has done that already. Does he not know that the kind of speech he made the other day is the very thing that does stir the prejudices and passions of the Canadian people. We picture the Prime Minister in his absolute, assured and complete comfort this winter holding out to the unemployed the one hope that if they emerge from the present crisis, they will be better people, and that they will be strengthened by the fires of adversity. . . .

"I doubt whether in recent Canadian history the people have turned so unanimously to one man for help as they turned to the Prime Minister just two years ago. They have been listening all these months for something which, to them, might have the ring of reality, but they have been disappointed — just this talk about the fires of adversity. I hope he will not hear what the people are going to think of it. Surely he does not know the suffering of the Canadian people, the mind of the Canadian people today. And failing to hear from the Prime Minister, the things which the people feel that he ought to have said, things that need to be said, they have turned a listening ear to the leader of the opposition. All summer I myself have been waiting for him to say something that meant something.

"One thing I have heard in this long summer, however. The other day I noticed that he had undergone a conversion, a recent conversion to monetary reform, but it was so recent that he stumbled over the words. He does not use them glibly yet. That is why, to finish up with the soap box orators, the people are asking those of us who are saying different things to go and say them, not because they think we are necessarily right but because at any rate we are saying something that fits their case and they are therefore willing to listen. I have no apologies to make; I am rather glad that we have something to say to the people to which they are ready to listen. We do not have to have a band to meet us at the station; we are not expensive *people to have. You can go into little halls where there is hardly enough light to see by, but fortunately crowded with people who want to hear something different from what hon. gentlemen have been telling them. You do not have to assure the people that you are one of them, because if you are one of them the fact is obvious and if you are not no amount of explanation will help you at all.*

"Personally I was relieved when the Prime Minister hit upon the word nostrum; I was fearful of what might happen if his indignation did not find adequate vent. I want to discuss for a moment sound money, or at any rate money, whether sound or unsound; you might call it elastic money or vanishing money or apparent money, but it does not seem to me that you can describe our money today as sound. The Prime Minister tells us that it is sound because we are going to discharge our contractual obligations. I do not think we are. I think of the people who contracted debts when commodity prices were twice what they are today, and perhaps three times in some instances, and then I think of sound money in the language of the Prime Minister, which requires these farmers and others as well to pay back the debts which they contracted with money that is worth two or three times as much as the money they got when they borrowed it. There is nothing sound about that money. It is absolutely unsound.

"We have a fixed yard measure, a fixed bushel measure; but the dollar is not fixed; that is what is wrong with it. I think, therefore, that the money we have is unsound money. Most people realize that it is unsound. For instance, the dollar in 1919 would buy less than half a bushel of wheat; in 1929 it could buy a bushel and in 1931 three bushels, and a few weeks ago it could buy almost four bushels. Surely that is not sound money. Wheat is wheat and does not get bigger or smaller; it is just the same kind of wheat and a bushel is always a bushel. So that the only thing that was unsound in the whole transaction was the dollar by which unfortunately we have to measure our wheat and potatoes, our eggs and butter, and our beef and pork, to pay our debts. If sound money, so-called, has developed the situation we have today, and is in part the cause of the army of 700,000 unemployed; if it is the cause of the extremely low commodity prices of all basic products, then surely it is not sound and it is quite time we did something about it.

"There is one other thing I meant to mention before and that is that great crowds of young people, men and women, are coming into life thinking they are prepared for it and finding no place at all. You cannot see freight trains, even if young men are not supposed to ride on them, that do not carry boys going from one place to another. You pick them up on the roads. I have been motoring most of the summer and have talked to a great number of these boys, just lads, most of them, with high school education, and they are really desperate; they are beginning to talk desperately. It will be a great comfort to them, I am sure, to hear that this trial they have gone through will improve their moral fibre. They will not be able to see it, I am *afraid. And if this money we have in Canada has anything at all to do with these armies of young people who have not been absorbed into the economic life of the country, then it cannot be called sound but simply unsound money.*

"It does seem to me that all the people with low prices for the commodities they produce, all the young people who are unable to find employment, and the whole army of unemployed, are sacrifices offered on the altar of sound money and they are being offered up as a sacrifice to the few, the very few, so that those few sleek fatted favourites of the god of gold may be specially cared for. Personally, I am going to do everything I can to see that this money system is ended so that those who are suffering from low commodity prices and the young people who cannot find a place in our economic life at the present time, as well as the army of unemployed in Canada, will obtain relief, let it do what it will to the favourites of the present system.

"Eight or nine years ago when the hon. member for Wetaskiwin (Mr. Irvine) stood up in this House and said that money should be issued in relation to goods and services, we all thought that he was more or less off the track. We all had the notion that our paper money must be issued in relation to gold. Personally I have come to the conclusion that the money we use internally need not and should not have any relation to gold. As a matter of fact it has not and we should forget all about it and base our paper money on goods and services. Moreover, it should be issued by the federal government and by the federal government alone, and in quantities sufficient to move goods and services and to raise prices to a point more on a level with the point at which our money was when we contracted our debts. If such money is what the Prime Minister would call unsound money, then I proudly and gladly stand for unsound money. . . .

"I do not think the chartered banks of Canada should have the right to issue money. . . . This same opinion is held by many people. I think Henry Ford states it in an interesting fashion when he says that money should be for the service and use of all the people and the right of making it should not be farmed out to private interests like sandwich booths at a picnic. I think that would probably prove more profitable than running a sandwich booth, but it is really the same idea. . . .

"The banks not only have the legal right to issue money, but they have the further privilege of issuing ninety-six per cent of all the money used in Canada. We are told that the banker's pen makes it sound money. Is that not interesting! The Dominion government should issue its own money and put it out in relation to goods and services to be used in the day to day expenditures of the government. This could be done in connection with the St. Lawrence waterway. I do not want to see this project carried out with money borrowed against which interest will be charged. Let the federal treasury issue new money and put it in circulation. If it were done in that way, we could advocate the completion of this project, but we cannot do so *when it means that further debt will be placed on the people to provide transportation facilities when what we lack is not transportation facilities but something to transport. . . .*

"Though we have 'sound money,' we are caught between the American gold dollar and the British paper pound. We are neither fish, fowl nor good red herring and yet we are paying the price both ways. . . .

"I wanted to take time, but I will not do so, to quote again from John Collingwood Reade, as he gives several ways in which we could get more money into circulation. One is by lessening the amount of gold behind each dollar, and the other, and the one I like myself, is simply by the federal government printing the money and putting it out into circulation in quantities that will raise the price level, and also putting us on a level with the British paper pound. May I say, since I have not much time to go into the matter, that the array of inviting markets which the Imperial conference has opened up to us but which we cannot enter because of exchange, reminds me of how the unemployed must feel when they walk past a window full of luscious food. They have an empty stomach and the merchant has the food, but as they have not any money they cannot get food into the stomach.

"The conference says you can sell hundreds of thousands of pounds of bacon, so many cattle and so many this and that in England; think of the wonderful things we have done for you! But the Prime Minister and the Minister of Finance know — and they must know because they are intelligent men or they would not be where they are — that the farmer cannot enter that market when the British paper pound is worth $3.80 and when we are losing twenty-five cents on every dollar's worth of produce that we send over there. . . . Will some Conservative farmer try sending his bacon, his apples, his cattle, at this time to the British market? The result will be very interesting. . . .

"For any responsible minister of the crown . . . to stand in his place and say here is a great market for the Canadian farmer, is sheer nonsense. If they want us to go on respecting them they had better admit this. There is nothing quite so provoking about a person as to be always right; that is the thing about the Prime Minister that infuriates me.

"May I quote from Lord Rothermere — and I hope I may have time to do so because the Prime Minister holds Lord Rothermere in such high regard that he met him in preference to meeting a delegation of four thousand farmers from two provinces, one-third of whom had been his ardent supporters, a delegation that was supported by the clergy of the province of Quebec and by a very large number of prominent citizens, not farmers from the province of Ontario.

"But the Prime Minister was so busy — and one does not wonder at that — that he could not meet them, and his Minister of Agriculture was so overcome with work that afternoon he could not come down for half an hour. However, Lord Rothermere was honoured by an interview which we were not honoured with, although we had

*tried to make the arrangement on the 24th of May and had made
about six contracts with the Prime Minister between that time and the
date of our coming. Lord Rothermere, when speaking of the exchange
situation said: 'Canada's being on the gold standard and having her
currency linked with that of the United States rather than with Great
Britain was leading to a "slow assassination of the Dominion's trade
and industry."'*

"*If he really got that through the Prime Minister's head, I do not
regret that he had the interview. He ends up by saying: 'Canada has
a great future within the empire, but she can have none as an ap-
pendage of America.'*

"*I agree wholly with Lord Rothermere on currency. The odd thing
about the Imperial conference which met here was that while they
devoted a great deal of time to trying to work out trade agreements,
most excellent trade agreements, if they could be used, they dismissed
the whole problem of exchange and money with a pious resolution, a
resolution which said that price levels should be raised, and they let
it go at that.*

"*An hon. member: And they expect Providence to do that.*

"*Miss Macphail: Yes, but since we were given intelligence I fancy
we shall be left to do it ourselves.*

"*I would say in closing that while there are many other problems and while I do not maintain that an issue of new money based
upon the resources of Canada would solve all our problems, I do
say that if the federal government with the machinery they have
could be induced to put a large issue of new money into circulation
without interest, it would do very much to raise the price of basic
commodities in this country and it would lower our money to the
level of the British pound sterling, thereby enabling us to enter and
make use of the market so aggressively displayed by the Prime
Minister yesterday."* [26]

In November she mentioned the election of Franklin Delano Roosevelt:

*The House of Commons showed keen interest in the result of the
American election. The large vote polled is encouraging and whether
the Democratic policy will be substantially different from the Republican policy or not, it is surely healthful that the party which has
been in power with only two breaks since the Civil War, is dislodged.
Such supremacy as the Republicans of the United States have had,
invariably results in a corrupt and powerful political machine.*

*One wonders will Roosevelt revive the idea of reciprocity? And if
freer trade between Canada and the United States results, what
commodities will it affect? Will our imperial trade agreements affect
our action in relations to United States? What will President
Roosevelt's attitude toward the gold standard, international debts and
disarmaments be? These are interesting questions which only time
will answer.*

*When I was in Poughkeepsie two years ago, I had the pleasure of
meeting Mrs. Franklin D. Roosevelt. She strikes one as being more*

typically English than American; she is intellectual and though the wife of the Governor of the State of New York, as she was then, she was a lecturer in a girl's college. She is a rather tall, slender woman, wholesome and approachable; I liked her very much.

At last the Prime Minister has caused new money to be printed — only 35 million dollars of it, it is true — but it is new money. Call it inflation, reflation, whatever suits the individual the better, the Prime Minister still calls it "sound money" and this time I agree with him. He calls it sound money because it was not issued through the banks: I call it sound because it is based on national wealth. We have begun to draw on our national credit. In this instance for the relief of the banks, only, it is true, but it is a beginning. . . .

I rejoice in it because it is the beginning of the dislodging of the Prime Minister from his reactionary and unreasonable stand in relation to the issuing of money against the natural resources of Canada in quantities sufficient to move goods and absorb services. [27]

And the next week, on a lighter note:

I did a broadcast from Windsor on Monday. It was the first time I ever enjoyed speaking over the air. The same night I addressed the League of Nations Society there. A brilliant young lawyer, Paul Martin [28], *is the President of the Society and it is, in fact, an open forum for the discussion of national and international questions. We were favored on Monday with a capacity audience. I thought it was a delightful evening until I saw my photograph in the Borders City Star. Talk about stopping a clock! That one would stop an express train doing 60 miles an hour!* [29]

Chapter VIII
Birth of the CCF
1933-1935

Nineteen-thirty-three was a year of serious portent for the world as Adolf Hitler succeeded Von Schleicher [1] as Chancellor of Germany and withdrew from the disarmament conference at Geneva and from the League of Nations.

The *Owen Sound Sun Times* reported that "Fred Waring's Pennsylvanians, the last prominent dance orchestra to capitulate to radio" would make its bow that night when the Old Gold program returned to the air over the Columbia Network.

In Toronto the *Star* had just sent reporter Gordon Sinclair on a seven-month tour of the Seven Seas. In January Agnes was off on another lecture tour to the Southern States.

It is difficult to get a mental rest — going to bed, even calling in a doctor does not guarantee it. While the body lies inactive the mind goes racing on.

With me a diverting "movie," an interesting book, a dance, a strange country or place is the best possible way of resting. Texas always seemed to promise change — new sights and sounds, and so recently I went to visit two cities, Dallas and Houston, in the largest state in the Union.

The weather was a bit disappointing, with St. Louis, Mo., providing almost exactly the same "brand" as Toronto. The trainmen encouraged me by saying that there would be no snow in Dallas, but there was, more than in many years. However, Houston, two hundred and fifty miles further south, made a coat unnecessary and steam heat in the hotel a misery. The delightful southern people were quite disturbed over the naughty pranks the weather played. They are weather proud and days that are not balmy are unusual. The poinsettia made the gardens a glory before the "freeze." "Sure enough, you all missed a sight," said one dear lady. But though I did miss the Christmas red flowers I saw narcissus blooming out of doors and a most effective table decoration in red and white, red candles in white holders at either side of a blood red glass bowl of white narcissus, all on a mirror. Speaking of the dinner table reminds me of the Texas yams and grapefruit which were very good — the southern cooking is all you hear "where every prospect pleases and only tea is vile."

Houston, a city of three hundred thousand, had become the cotton port of the South, and one of the greatest cotton ports in the world. At the moment more baled cotton is on the docks there than at any time in the past. A cotton authority told me that never before in any part of the world was there so much cotton ready for shipping. . . .

The tornado and tidal wave in 1900 caused a flight from Galveston, which until then, had been the port of the south. Real estate values fell. No action being taken by the city to re-establish confidence, resulted in trade turning from Galveston to the more enterprising city of Houston, which, although forty miles from the Gulf of Mexico, had a "bayou" or dry river bed up which the Gulf waters backed. This was deepened into a ship channel and a turning basin made. To-day the ocean liners come right to the city of Houston, giving it a cosmopolitan air.

Both the Houston and Dallas Forum audiences were deeply interested in the question of Canadian-American trade figures and were surprised to learn that Canadian imports from U.S.A. had dipped from nearly 900 millions in 1929 to not quite 300 millions in the year ending October 1932, while exports to U.S.A. dropped in the same period from 536 millions to 178. The value of the export of Canadian farm products, raw and processed, to U.S.A. between 1921 and 1932 ending with June, fell from 159 1/2 million dollars to 8 3/4 million dollars. Between these two dates came the Emergency Tariff, the Fordney-McCumber Tariff and our very high tariff relations. . . .

My three days in Dallas were a constant delight, in spite of a pickpocket gathering my $50. Often I have wondered how awful must be the sensation of not being sure one had enough money to pay for food and shelter, so after the $50 left I thought I would experiment and find out a little about it. With two cheques of considerable size drawn on a Texas bank in my pocketbook, I started back with what was left in cash. The first day a playwright from Dallas, whom I had met, asked me to tea and dinner; that helped. I handled my own luggage. The next day I ate one meal, breakfast for 20¢ — griddle cakes, syrup and coffee, walked instead of a taxi, shoved breakfast on until mid-forenoon and found a lot of down and outs were doing the same thing; slept in an upper berth (was working too hard to go without); read papers other people had finished with. I spent my last $1 bill to send a wire from St. Louis to Byron Young of Brigden, asking him to meet me in Windsor, in order to get me to an afternoon meeting there on time. It had to be a straight wire and not over ten words; never did I choose words so carefully. Finally I arrived in Detroit and took a taxi to the tunnel bus which brought me onto Canadian soil with just 54 cents, which I had carefully kept for a real breakfast. However Byron Young insisted on paying for the "sure enough" breakfast and I gave the 54 cents to the crippled children's fund. But that was all just playing. What must it be for those who grimly face want and hopelessness day after day. [2]

A writer for the *Montreal Herald* commented on the theft of her money. It was not really stealing, he said. The "light-fingered gentleman" had merely been practising what Agnes preached — applied socialism. The "dip" had obviously been impressed by Agnes' arguments that "wealth is excessive profits; that a surplus over one's immediate wants is sheer wickedness. . . . When he shifted that fifty dollars from Agnes' pocket to his own he confirmed all the leading principles of the CCF movement and made Agnes the chief object lesson of her own doctrines." [3]

Not all reporters were so caustic. In fact more and more praised her as a humanist, a fiery crusader for peace and for putting "human needs before profit."

The *Detroit Sunday Times* of January 8, 1933, said:

> *A passionate crusaderess on behalf of the "forgotten man" — and equally of the "forgotten woman" — Miss Macphail is probably best known for her militant anti-militarism. In Parliament, and upon the platforms of two continents and half a dozen countries, she has pleaded the cause of disarmament with fervour which few can equal. She stands equally firm against high tariffs and against what she views as the injustices of the capitalistic system.*

The *Montreal McGill Daily* of February 24, 1933, said that

> *Miss Macphail is a personality of dynamic attributes, motivated by highest principles of uncompromising integrity. For her there is one aspect to every issue — the moral aspect — and there is nothing to indicate that she has ever deviated in the least from a scrupulous constancy to that principle. In these times when public affairs are so completely dominated by unbridled group and private interest, it is encouraging to find that the womanhood of the country is represented by one whose every utterance proclaims independence, her sincerity and her nobility of purpose.*

Saturday Night commented that

> *recent events have brought the heroic and determined figure of Agnes Macphail closer to the spotlight of the swing-to-the-left movement about which people everywhere are talking. She has come to be recognized as a commanding personality in the movement. And now there are those who are wondering if she, rather than Mr. Woodsworth, is not the logical leader. Discussion is enlivened by her part the other day in carrying the United Farmers of Ontario over to the Co-Operative Commonwealth Federation [At a UFO Convention Agnes had persuaded the members to join the recently formed Co-operative Commonwealth Federation, the UFO retaining all its policies and privileges]. . . . But what mostly inspires speculation as to her place in the movement is the quality of the leadership she has been displaying as it compares with Mr. Woodsworth's leadership. Her handling of the demonstration of Ontario and Quebec farmers who descended on Ottawa several thousand strong last summer to tell the prime minister what course he should take and who, despite notification that the prime minister would not discuss the conference in public, were indignant at not seeing him, displayed generalship of no mean order. Those several thousand farmers listened to her when they wouldn't listen to others. They took her advice. She carried her successes with them into the South Huron by-election and is credited with having much to do with the failure of the government in that contest.*

The writer, E. C. Buchanan, concluded that "eyes are turning toward the woman crusader of the leftward movement. If Canada should go all out to the left in next election, might she be called upon to form a government? A woman prime minister of Canada, and only a few short years since the sex were given

A portrait of Agnes by Karsh

the vote! Well, there would be many who would feel more secure with her at the helm than with Mr. Woodsworth."[4]

For a long time certain people had tried to tie up democratic socialists like Agnes with Communism, and in February J. R. MacNicol (Toronto Northwest) went further and accused her of sedition.

"According to the *Mail and Empire* of February 13," said MacNicol, Agnes had said that "the CCF was trying to establish a new social order . . . the old one surely would have to be destroyed before a new one could take its place. . . . Canada has the least liberty of speech and action of any country."

Tired of such accusations, Agnes responded with spirit:

> *Mr. Speaker, it was my privilege a week ago tomorrow night to address a large congregation in Donlands Church which is near the McGregor School in East York. I was invited by the Reverend Mr. Irwin, the pastor of the church to give an address; I was introduced by Dr. Salem Bland.*
>
> *Some Honorable Members: Oh, oh!*
>
> *Miss Macphail: I said there that I respected my colleagues in the House, but I am afraid after the laughter at the mention of Dr. Bland's name, I shall have difficulty in doing so in future. As I said, I was introduced by Dr. Salem Bland. I made practically the same speech as I made the following afternoon at McGregor School. The school I may say was crowded. . . . The minister of Donlands Church, and the East York Workers' Association, almost all of whom were unemployed, could have selected their own member to address them. I did not ask them to invite me. Possibly their own member had better do some heart-searching to find out why he was not asked. I do not know why he was not.*
>
> *As regards the subject to which the Mail and Empire was referring when I was reported to have said that there was less freedom of speech in Canada than anywhere else, the question I was discussing was freedom of action of elected members in the House of Commons, and I said that in the British House of Commons there was much greater freedom and that when a cabinet minister was not pleased with the action of his government, and when the action taken by his government was contrary to his personal convictions and showed this by resigning from the cabinet, something that practically never happened in this country. I went on to say that what I believe constitutes one of the real difficulties of government in Canada is the slavish adherence in this house to parties . . . if the hon. member for Toronto Northwest (Mr. MacNicol), who has just spoken, means that in our speeches we must defend everything as it is, may I say that I do not intend to do so. It is a long time since I decided that the upper house was of very little use to Canada. The hon. member who has just resumed his seat may disagree with me. That is his business, but I do not propose he shall tell me what I shall think, and for the hon. member to try to link up, as he did quite definitely in his speech, those of us who go out to speak in school houses, churches and public halls, on the economic condition and the need of constitutional*

reform — radical and fundamental, but constitutional — with communists, that just brands him for the excellent Tory he is. We are not communists, and I may say that the heckling that we receive comes from the communists who hate the hon. member for Winnipeg North Centre [J. S. Woodsworth], *myself and others associated with us more than they do anybody else, because we, by striving to bring about reforms constitutionally, stand between the communists and the violence they desire. . . .*

I am Canadian born, and I love Canada as much as any member who sits on the government side. My record of service in this country is as clean as that of any member in any part of this house, and I do not propose any longer to sit here and allow people to put into our mouths things that we have never said and attribute to us motives that we have never had. This business of continually trying to tie us up with Moscow is ridiculous; it is nonsense. It is a regular trick of the Conservative party. I remember when the Liberals were in power how the Conservatives were always saying that the fiscal policy of the Liberal government was dictated from Washington. Now if the financial policy of this government is not dictated by Wall Street, New York, I should like to know who is dictating it. The Conservatives are always trying to tie up those opposed to them with dictation from some place outside of this country. I myself and the members of the United Farmers of Alberta and the Labour group in this House are Canadians. We are not tied up with Moscow, and never have been. We are taking no orders and no money from Moscow. May I say to the hon. member for Toronto Northwest that we are striving by constitutional methods, by the exercise of our intelligence, which thank God we possess —

Mr. MacNicol: You will never get any money from me if you advocate that kind of stuff.

Miss Macphail: I would not want your money.

Mr. MacNicol: Then why mention it?

Miss Macphail: I did not; I did not know the hon. member had any money. We are striving by the exercise of our intelligence to bring about by constitutional methods the very reforms that must come. You cannot stop reform. You can try. You can stupidly stand in the path of progress and do all you can to stop it, but all you can succeed in doing is to dam the thing back until it gets beyond control and then causes the very upheavals and difficulties which we all deplore and which none of us want. I hope we shall not again hear such statements as those made by the hon. member for Toronto Northwest. I have no objection to the government members and the Liberal members fighting us on the merits of any question, but to intimate as the last speaker did all through his speech, that we are closely associated with communists in this country is simply laughable, and may I add that I think the hon. member is not doing himself or his party any good. The people of Canada know that the Conservative party has no corner on Canadianism, that it has no corner on loyalty to this country, that it has no corner on a desire to serve even though it means sacrifice, and it is about time the Conservative party realized that. They have waved the flag and prostituted patriotism as no other group in Canada has ever done — we have heard it until we are sick of it — and when the flag won't do they take the Bible and wrap their policies in both, hoping the people will then stomach them, and it is sometimes all they can do. We have listened to altogether too much of that sort of thing.[5]

James Shaver Woodsworth, M.P., first leader of the CCF, with his daughter Grace

In her weekly letter of February 18, Agnes summarized MacNicol's accusations against the CCF and defended the party. She said his "careful attempt to tie the CCF up with Communism in Moscow made me for the first time forget the nervousness and embarrassment of speaking in the Commons."[6]

In another letter she defended CCF leader James Shaver Woodsworth:

What sort of background has this man? Was he as well born and reared as the Rt. Hon. R. B. Bennett or the Rt. Hon. Mackenzie King? He is charged with being a Communist, a radical, a red. It has been even hinted that he is in the pay of Moscow because he visited there a year ago. So also, of course, did Frederick Griffin, writer on the Star, and Professor King Gordon of McGill and Colonel Mackie, once Conservative member of the House of Commons. But somehow that seems to be different. By the die-hard Tories on both sides of the House, Mr. Woodsworth is considered a dangerous man. Dangerous to whom and to what?

James Shaver Woodsworth was born in York County on the farm of his maternal grandmother, which now forms the south half of the T. Eaton farms. His mother's people, Shaver, were United Empire Loyalists who settled at Ancaster, near Hamilton, after leaving comfortable homes in United States at the time of the Civil War, to maintain their British connection. His maternal grandmother drove from New York to Little York, then a town of less than 1000 people, in order that she might live under the British flag. As they came along they could find no accommodation in the inns as soon as it was known they were English. The wife of Brock was an intimate friend of Mr. Woodsworth's maternal grandmother. . . .

J. S. Woodsworth's father, James Woodsworth, was born in Toronto, educated in the University there, and as a Methodist minister went to Manitoba as superintendent of Missions. . . . The much reviled J. S. was at that time just a child. Later he attended Victoria college, University of Toronto, for one year and the University of Oxford, England, for one year. While in the Old Country he lived on the east side of London in a settlement house and worked among the very poor. This experience was a great awakening. His heart was torn by the degradation and suffering of his fellow men in the slums of London. On returning to Canada he went for a time into the mission field in Saskatchewan and Northern Ontario and then took the position of junior minister of Grace Church, Winnipeg, the leading Methodist Church of that city, a church at that time attended by some men who are now members of the House of Commons. Mr. Woodsworth's special work there was among the young people.

It was during this time that Mr. Woodsworth married Lucy Staples of Cavan, Ontario, a graduate of Toronto University. They spent a year in the Old Country and during that time visited Palestine. It was during the visit to this ancient land that Mr. Woodsworth decided he was not orthodox in his belief and he believed he was in honor bound to offer his resignation to the authorities of the Methodist Church which he did. The resignation was not accepted.

Feeling that the position of junior minister in a fashionable church did not offer him the opportunity he desired to help the poor, he left Grace Church, moved his little family from the fashionable south end of Winnipeg to the new and stark north end where he lived among the foreigners. Mr. Woodsworth was put in charge of All People's Mission by the Methodist Church, where he, with his fifteen or twenty paid workers, tried to teach the newcomers of Canada, adjusting them to an unknown life in a strange country. They visited the homes of the people, held meetings, made known the duties of citizenship, helped in every possible way to get them jobs and to improve their standard of living. After six years at this work, Mr. Woodsworth resigned in order to enter what seemed to him a larger field. He organized the Social Welfare League to promote interest in social problems, particularly immigration and as a lecturer with Canadian Clubs and church organizations, travelled from coast to coast. He conducted a three months' course in McGill University on social welfare and during [his] stay in Montreal, founded the Montreal Open Forum, where I speak tomorrow, a forum of opinion which is without doubt, the best in Canada, due largely to the untiring efforts of the Sec'y, William Fraser.

The war was now on and it was difficult to finance a voluntary organization. The three prairie governments — Manitoba, Sask. and Alberta set up a bureau of social research, with Mr. Woodsworth at the head. The governments wished him to investigate living conditions among the foreigners. At about this time he wrote the "Strangers within our gate," "My Neighbor," and "Studies in Rural Citizenship."

Then came conscription. Mr. Woodsworth was opposed to conscription and said so in a letter to the press. His resignation was asked for by the Government. The day after his resignation his father died. He had now several children and as he had spent most of his savings on welfare work, he was entering a trying period. The Methodist Church sent him to the Mission field on the west coast. The citizens of this little community had started a co-operative store which Mr. Woodsworth helped in every way he could and thus aroused the ire of the largest merchant in the place who conducted a lobby against him. The church, too, objected to his specific sermons and asked him to resign, not on a matter of theology, but because of his political opinions. And so he left the little church at the coast and the church as an institution at the same time.

For one year he worked as a long-shoreman in Vancouver, loading and unloading vessels. Mrs. Woodsworth was now teaching in a country school and most of the children were in school. Mrs. Woodsworth had the same adventurous spirit as her husband. She believed with Kirby Page that creative living demands that we "resolutely run the risks and joyously accept the consequences of following our ideals." They divided equally the small amount of money they possessed and Mr. Woodsworth started on a lecture tour from the west coast eastward, speaking at towns and cities en route. He arrived in Winnipeg when the strike was well on its way. The very day he arrived, Mr. Ivens — the Rev. Mr. Ivens by the way — was arrested. Mr. Woodsworth offered to take his place as editor of the Labour paper, assisted by Fred Dixon, M.L.A. They were very soon both arrested and held five days without bail. The arrest was made *because of quotations from the book of Isaiah. "They shall build houses and inhabit them; they shall plant vineyards and eat of the fruit of them . . . woe unto them that decree unrighteous decrees" came in conflict with the Criminal Code. So Mr. Woodsworth visited again the jails of Manitoba, his first visit having taken place when as a lecturer on penology he took a group of students to visit the institution.*

Mr. Woodsworth, after his five days spent in jail, lectured for a year over the country to defend the men who were on trial. Fred Dixon was acquitted and was elected to the Legislature by the largest majority ever known there. Three others were elected while they were confined to the prison and were taken on their release direct to the legislative buildings. Two of the three are still members of the Legislature and Mr. Woodsworth was elected to the Federal House for Winnipeg constituency in 1921, and has been re-elected in each contest since that time, in 1930 with a majority of 6,229.

Of the six Woodsworth children, three are graduates of universities. The eldest daughter Grace, won a scholarship in French, which gave her a year at the University of Paris. Charles, after his course in the University of Manitoba, spent a year in the London School of Economics and is now on one of the Winnipeg papers. Belva graduated from the Manitoba Agricultural college and is in charge of Domestic Sciences in one of the Vancouver schools. Ralph, the second son, is graduating in medicine, and the two younger boys are still in high school.

No one could visit the Woodsworth home without knowing they are a cultivated, socially-minded and gentle family. Evidence of their scholarship and love of the arts is all about. They have all worked hard and are working hard: nothing else could account for their progress. Each child did any sort of honorable work that offered, to help finance their education or that of another member of the family.

Now about the trip to Russia. Mr. and Mrs. Woodsworth went to Europe a little over a year ago where for a month J. S. worked as temporary collaborator at the League of Nations during the Assembly, for which he got remuneration. After travelling some time in Central Europe, using on the whole journey, third class accommodation and staying at most inexpensive places, the articles written on Russia paid Mr. Woodsworth's trip into that much discussed country.[7]

Still on the subject of the CCF, Agnes reported that

the Rt. Hon. Mackenzie King spoke for two hours on the Co-operative Commonwealth resolution, the first half of which time was devoted to his interpretation of what the C.C.F. stands for. Mr. King says it stands for public ownership of everything and even went so far as to argue that we were against voluntary co-operation and public ownership as it is now understood, as exemplified by the post office, hydro, etc. He was very careful to point out that he favored humanitarian legislation such as workmen's compensation, unemployment, invalidity or accident insurance, old age pensions, mothers' allowance and the like but that did not mean that he was socialistic. . . .

*The Co-operative Commonwealth Federation believes in voluntary
co-operation by both producers and consumers, favoring gov't help
by way of loans at very low rates of interest and the loaning of
experts by the Dept. of Agriculture when a new venture is getting
under way, or at any time that the unit in the country or city feels
that it needs expert help. We believe that finance should be national-
ized and that all great monopolies should be brought under gov't
supervision and public utilities publicly owned. We believe that social
services will be greatly extended as time goes on but we do not
believe in the elimination of private property unless it is of such an
overgrown nature that the rights of many individuals are being
ignored.*

(The CCF was founded in Calgary, Alberta, in 1932. At its first annual
convention in 1933 it issued the Regina Manifesto, the party's bible, which asked
for socialization of finance, social ownership of public utilities and certain welfare
measures. Agnes said she believed the manifesto was "the most wonderful
political document ever drawn up in Canada," and said if she could get the
money she would send a copy to every home in her riding. In 1961 the CCF
joined with the Canadian Labor Congress to form the New Democratic Party.)

In the same letter, Agnes said: "One hears all kinds of rumors in the
corridors and offices regarding re-distribution. To-day it was reported that the bill
would not go through at this session but would be laid over till next year. It
seems pretty certain that Grey and Bruce will be hewn up in such a way as to
make three constituencies out of the four. In all likelihood North Grey will be
extended a bit further south, which will make it necessary for South East Grey to
take on a part of Wellington, Dufferin or Bruce." [8]

While re-distribution did not seem to alarm Agnes, observers saw it as a
definite attempt to "dynamite her" and it helped to do just that, not in the next
election, but in the one which followed in 1940. Commented *Saturday Night*:

*It isn't necessary that one agree with the position she has taken on
any or all public issues to admire the woman who has four times
been accorded the public confidence of a majority of her constituents
over aggressive male opposition. Nor does one have to be a woman
to harbor this admiration. More important still is the fact that the
dignity and usefulness of Parliament most positively have not
suffered.*

*In these circumstances not only the people of South East Grey, not
only the women of Canada very generally, but most men who lay
claim to the spirit of sportsmanship, will keenly resent what has all
the earmarks of lack of sportsmanship. It doesn't matter an iota if
geographical and census charts prove to the hilt the wisdom and
sweet reasonableness of the contemplated step. What will stand out
like mumps on a skeleton will be the belief that, unable to beat Miss
Macphail in fair battle on her own ground, the steering committee on
redistribution plans to dynamite her.* [9]

That spring her weekly letters to the riding discussed such topics as President Roosevelt's inauguration and the departure of the United States from the
gold standard:

March 16, 1933

The inaugural ceremony, the speech of President Roosevelt and the compulsory bank holiday of the United States have commanded the attention of Canadians. The inaugural speech was, I thought, excellent. I liked particularly the way the President faced realities. He admitted that values had shrunken to fantastic levels, taxes risen, the ability of the people to pay fallen, that governments of all kinds were faced with serious curtailment of income, that the means of exchange were frozen in the currents of trade, farmers found no market for their produce, the savings of many years in thousands of families were gone, the unemployed grimly faced the problem of existence and greater numbers toiled with little return. "Only a foolish optimist can deny the dark realities of the moment, yet our distress comes from no failure of substance."

The President blamed severely the financial group who have "through their own stubbornness and incompetence failed to effect an exchange of mankind's goods." However when he states that "the money changers have fled from their high seats in the temple of our civilization" one feels that he is expressing a hope rather than a fact. When the President later stated "practices of the unscrupulous money changers stand indicted in the court of public opinion, rejected by the hearts and minds of men" he has stated the most hopeful aspect of the present uncomfortable situation. Surely citizens in the great Republic to the south of us, and in this country as well, will turn their minds to the setting up of a sounder financial system, one that works for the benefit of the great mass of the people and not for the few financial magnates who operate it.[10]

April 27, 1933

The big news of the week is the United States departure from the gold standard and her plans for controlled inflation. Senator Thomas of Oklahoma introduced a bill in the United States Senate which will grant to President Roosevelt all the power to extend currency and credit, decrease the gold value of the dollar and accept, if he wishes, silver in payment of war debts. . . .

The House of Commons had a very brief Easter recess. Thinking it would be longer, I consented to address the Rural Trustees section of the Ontario Educational Association in Convocation Hall on April 18th and the Women Teachers' Federation at their annual luncheon on the 19th. I enjoyed both audiences very much. It is noteworthy that practically all the speakers at the O.E.A. stressed the need of change, both in the economic and educational fields. . . . The life of the school should be closely related to the life of the community. This note was repeatedly sounded at the convention.

We are too prone to think that education stops when school days are over, whereas they should be but beginning. One can be always learning, by reading, conversation and discussion, by travel and by thinking. Mr. Stanley Baldwin of Great Britain says that he did much

*better at educating himself than others did at trying to educate him.
And we have all noticed how easy it is to acquire knowledge when
we particularly need it. The Hon. Charles Dunning was not in school
after he was 11 or 12 years of age, but he is an educated man and
could master the details of a Department very rapidly: so rapidly as
to cause general comment in the House. We need learning that we
may think straight. Confucius, about 500 years before the birth of
Christ, stated that learning without thought is labour wasted: thought
without learning, is perilous.[11]*

May 18, 1933

*I have always wanted to see the Niagara Peninsula in blossom
time, and this year I did and a beautiful sight it was. On Saturday I
motored down Lundy's Lane and over the plain below Queenston
Heights. The peach blossoms were at their very best. Later we
motored to Welland and then along the shore to Hamilton, passing
through the Whitby district. The season is earlier in the Niagara
locality than about Hamilton, but it is all wonderfully beautiful and
well worth going a long distance to see.[12]*

In 1933 Agnes was asked to speak to members of the graduating class of
Ottawa Ladies' College. During her talk she gave her four-point philosophy of life:

1. *Cut out non-essentials. Don't do things which are no use to you
   and give neither help nor joy to others. Don't belong to clubs that
   are no value to anybody and waste time and energy.*
2. *Be natural. Polish the natural but do not distort it. All great souls
   are natural and simple.*
3. *Do not rely completely on any other human being, however dear.
   We meet all life's greatest tests alone.*
4. *Live in the present. Yesterday is gone; tomorrow has not arrived;
   live today. Don't live for today but in today.*

"Life," she said, "is a great teacher, but so slowly do we learn, life is nearly
over before we have found out how to live. That is the best argument I know of
the need of a world beyond."

She urged the girls in deciding on a career to "follow what the unresting urge
suggests, yes, compels. We have many urges but one which persists should be
obeyed. It is the voice of instinct, of intuition, wiser far than reasoned conclusion.

"The greatest joy in life is deep satisfaction in work, a feeling of fulfillment
through it. The money payment is quite secondary if one's field is well chosen
and one is faithful in that field.

"One of the great tasks of the young is to keep their ideals whole and untar-
nished as they grapple with life and meet the disillusionment and cynicism of
those older."

In November, on her way home from Nova Scotia where she had spoken to
university students and to another large gathering in Halifax, she realized that she
was seriously ill.

*I consulted a specialist in Montreal and really intended to go back to
Montreal for the operation which he told me was necessary. But after*

*getting home I felt I wanted to stay near there and to be with the people
whom I had long known.*

*Emerson was right when he said, "Everything has its compensa-
tions." At any rate, an operation has. After the first four days of intense
suffering were over, I experienced a feeling of such great joy that it
could, I think, be called exultation. In my little room in the Markdale
Hospital I lay and watched the snow softly falling and was glad, glad to
be alive. For the first time in a long while I had no responsibilities, no
ambition and no worry. I couldn't read — I didn't even want to; living
was enough. Then, too, an illness reveals the great kindness of human
beings and causes one to know again that underneath the prejudices and
little meannesses which we all have there is a great well of good-will,
which in the dark days will not fail us. Last, but certainly not least,
there is the skill and devotion of doctors and nurses, which we possibly
too often take for granted. Taking it all in all, I can say the last weeks
spent in the Markdale Hospital are among the happiest of my life.*[13]

By mid-January, 1934, with the doctor's consent, Agnes headed south and
reported that

*South East Texas was having the warmest weather in their history and
on the first day of February people were motoring without coats and
electric fans were running in pullman cars. Motoring from Dallas to
Arlington I saw farmers working on the land and passed nurseries doing
a stirring business getting ready for eager gardeners . . .*

*The National Recovery Administration has many subsidiaries like the
CWA [Civic Works Administration] under which an effort is made to
give employment to the unemployed. It is interesting, too, that the
unemployed are not all lumped together, tinker, tailor, candle-stick
maker, and put to pick and shovel work, but an intelligent effort is made
to sort them out and put each group to work for which they are fitted.
For example, 2500 artists throughout the nation are painting murals and
pictures in public buildings. . . . The CWA is not however always
intelligent in its effort. In Detroit I saw dozens of men digging ditches
with pick and shovel which could have been done by a machine in a
few minutes; going back to hand work is not enough. A machine must
be made the servant of man and not his master. . . .*

*The weatherman put on a special show for me the morning I arrived
in Ottawa — 35 below zero and a brilliant sun. Parliament Hill was a
sight with the white snow piled high on the many drives leading in to
the beautiful Gothic structure, carried out in grey stone with white snow
with a cold and brilliant sun over all.*[14]

In 1934 Agnes openly championed a prisoner, Charles Baynes, who, unknown
to her, had been convicted of sodomy, indecent assault and gross indecency. Before
speaking in Parliament on his behalf she tried to get his files. It was learned later
they were deliberately kept from her by Minister of Justice Hugh Guthrie.

In Parliament on February 14 Guthrie reviewed Agnes' request for special
treatment for the prisoner and then read out his record. He said

*the member for South East Grey is a sympathetic member of the
House and it is all to her credit that she is so; but I am informed
that there are cases in which her sympathies rather get the better of
her. I received from her a somewhat alarming telegram in October
last . . . to the effect that a certain man then in Carlton County Gaol
was sentenced on October 13 to serve five years in Portsmouth
Penitentiary; that he had tuberculosis and such a sentence means
death. She states further: "I am interested that he be sent to
Burwash, Guelph or Mimico. I have known this man favorably for
four years. He is an ex-serviceman with a good record. Tuberculosis
due to army." In discussing that particular case today, the hon.
member for South East Grey said: "He is a man who has a fine
social outlook," and she spoke well of him. I am afraid he is not the
kind of man to be encouraged, though we have every sympathy for
him so far as his physical condition is concerned. . . .*

*From the medical reports I am inclined to think that he is not
such a serious case as my hon. friend the member for South East
Grey has been led to believe. But I am sorry to say that his criminal
record is a very bad one. His first conviction was for indecent assault
at Winnipeg. His second conviction was for a bestial crime which I
will not mention in this chamber for which he was sentenced to five
years in the British Columbia penitentiary. He was released on ticket
of leave to enlist in the Canadian expeditionary force, in which he
served, but before he went he was again convicted of indecent assault
and sentenced to 12 months.*

Guthrie listed several other offenses and ended: "That is the case. I do not
wish to make any comment more than to say that the tubercular condition
spoken of has not yet developed to a serious extent."[15]

Discredited in front of the House, Agnes was mortified. In a letter to the
prisoner's brother, Edward Baynes, she said that she had suffered a great deal
over the incident.

[Charles] *should have told me of his previous record in order that I
could protect myself as much as possible. I am the only woman in a
House of 245 members and it is particularly distasteful to me to be
attacked on this sexual matter.*

*I have read a good deal of the literature written concerning
inverts and I think our method of dealing with them is cruel and
useless. Had someone of knowledge and broad human sympathies
talked to your brother when he was a lad I have no doubt he could
have become a very useful member of society. He is no more to
blame for his condition than we are for ours and his family who sent
him here as a lad are very responsible for his condition today.*

*After Easter I am going to visit Kingston Penitentiary and will
make a point of seeing* [your brother] *and anything I can do for him
will be done.*[16]

Edward Baynes, a respected government employee in the British West Indies,
replied that he deeply regretted the suffering she had gone through owing to her
kindness to his brother. He said that his brother's sad record had caused his family

great sorrow. Their father had held a responsible government position but died at forty-four, leaving Charles (a lad of thirteen) and six other children. The mother was a sweet, gentle woman who had never been out of the Islands. None of the family had any idea of conditions in "big countries." Charles was the first of the family to leave the small islands for the big world. ". . . I don't suppose for one moment that my mother had any doubt that Charles would make good when he went to Canada over 30 years ago, being then about 18 years of age."

Edward said that Charles got along well from the start and was a bank manager before he was twenty-one years of age. He left the bank, got into bad company, "and from that day, some 26 years ago to the present time he has been more or less a source of anxiety and sorrow."

Edward agreed with Agnes that

> *the general method of dealing with people like Charles is cruel and useless. I suppose in a way the sexual impulse is the most powerful thing in the world, and these sad cases of perversion deserve to be treated with sympathy like cases of any other disease — for disease it certainly is. The sufferers are undoubtedly a source of danger to others, but so are persons suffering from certain other forms of disease, mental and otherwise, and imprisonment in an ordinary penitentiary scarcely seems appropriate if the idea is to cure the disease, and enable the patient to take his proper place in the world. I have never seen any literature on the subject, and therefore have no idea what the medical authorities think is the best form of treatment. . . .*
>
> *For over 30 years Charles has not known what home life is. If only he had stuck with the Bank and married and settled down how different everything might have been. . . . It is greatly to his credit that he served in the war. He suffered much in France — one must not forget that.* [17]

Agnes explained her position to her constituents and then said: "The government is gloating over the serious reflection cast upon me and it was told me by one whom I believe knew, that a pamphlet was being prepared for distribution setting forth my defence of this man with a very bad record. I think I have not gone through such anguish since the first Parliament I attended."

She ended by saying: "If one is to keep warm-hearted and helpful as life goes on, one is bound to make mistakes. I think it is inevitable and so, when such a time as this comes, one must be willing to pay the price in suffering." [18]

A year later Agnes was still upset by Guthrie's action. Hansard, April 4, 1935, describes the situation:

> *Mr. Guthrie: I am aware that the Honorable Member for South East Grey perhaps is actuated by some animosity against me. I hope she is not, as I feel none against her.*
> *Miss Macphail: I would not trouble myself to feel any animosity. When I came into the House last year about as well as the Honorable Member for Muskoka-Ontario Mr. McGibbon —*
> *Some Honorable Members: Take it back.*
> *Miss Macphail: No, I will not take it back. When I came into this House last year about as well as the Honorable Member of*

*Muskoka-Ontario was yesterday, the Minister of Justice came over to
my desk and shook hands with me in the guise of friendship. I
assumed that his feelings were genuine. He suggested the holding
over of a resolution which I had been discussing through a special
arrangement. I told him that I was not used to asking for special
privileges in the House but I assumed that his offer was made in all
kindness. The matter was held over and because of that I did something which afterwards turned out to be indefensible. The Minister of
Justice deliberately made it possible for me to do this. This was a
very miserable case, in fact so miserable that only one newspaper
reported it. The minister thought he was doing something which
would injure me, and this matter was spread on Hansard in the
greatest detail. I do not know whether the minister realizes what he
did last year. I had just recovered from one shock [the operation] two
months previously and it took me weeks and months to recover from
the other shock. People told me that this would not affect me in my
constituency but I replied that oddly enough I had not thought of
that. That was not what concerned me — it was the fact that a
minister in the guise of apparent friendship led me on to making a
statement which he knew I would not have made had I known the
facts. I followed up this matter and found that all the files in connection therewith had been in the office of the minister from January 25.
I did not arrive in the House until about February 18 or 19. I feel no
animosity to the Minister of Justice but he is the only person in
public life in Canada for whom I have not the respect I would like to
have.*

*Mr. Guthrie: Apparently I was not very far wrong in my original
statement. I am afraid the Honorable Member of South East Grey
has not a very warm and friendly feeling toward me.*

Miss Macphail: You are quite right.

In spite of the misery she suffered over the affair and in spite of government
opposition, Agnes continued to push for penitentiary reform. In Parliament on
July 3, 1934, she spoke during a debate on penitentiaries, gave her ideas on how
to improve the system and asked for an "impartial investigation":

*I think anybody who has followed penitentiary conditions in Canada
during the last three or four years must know that a great many, if
not all the changes which have been made in penitentiary administration have come as a result of the uprisings or riots, or whatever they
may be termed. . . .*

*I have now come to the conclusion that very often ministers of
justice are not aware of what is done. . . . I recall on one occasion
asking about shackling to the bars and the then minister Mr.
Lapointe said that the men were not shackled for any length of time;
that their hands were never shackled higher than their waists, when
the actual fact was they were shackled eight hours at a time to be let
down only at noon, and their hands were placed high above their
heads. . . .*

Let me now read to the House, in order to be perfectly fair, the changes which have taken place either very close to or since the time of the riots:

1. *No corporal punishment until after the evidence has been taken under oath and award approved by superintendent.*
2. *Shackling to cellgate abolished.*
3. *Standardization of a minimum period of exercise in the fresh air for convicts employed in shops or cells — half systematic and half free movement.*
4. *Increased visits of relatives. Letters by convicts increased from one to three letters a month, but only to close relatives which shuts off many.*
5. *Close cropping of hair abolished, except in the case of convicts who had previously escaped from a penal institution.*
6. *Introduction of compulsory education for teachable illiterate convicts, school to be carried on during working hours.*
7. *Silence rule broken — can talk cell to cell until 7 p.m.*

The reform of the convict should be the aim of penitentiary administration, and to simplify this work, the hardened, brutalized and dangerous prisoners, usually called incorrigibles, should serve an indeterminate sentence in one prison. . . .

My second recommendation is the appointment of a superintendent trained in penology. There should be no more political or military appointments. Then there should be a system of adequate training for officials and guards. . . . I would suggest also the classification and segregation of prisoners. . . . We should have too a medical officer with some training in psychiatry and a travelling medical superintendent with psychiatric specialty. There should be no mental defectives or mentally diseased in the penitentiaries — and there should be work with pay . . . as a bit of encouragement.

I submit that there should be properly supervised work by which the inmates are taught a trade from the beginning to the end of that trade. . . . Every inmate should be in school part of the time, school sessions being held morning, afternoon and evening, if necessary, to accomplish this. . . . There should be properly supervised physical recreation . . . [and] there should be non-compulsory church attendance but increased facilities for personal religious work for those who want it. . . .

Lastly, we shall never succeed in reclaiming prisoners until some assistance is given them on release; not necessarily monetary assistance, but aid through prisoners' welfare associations or a combination of voluntary and government bodies. . . . It is in the public interest to have an impartial investigation which in all probability will result in far-reaching recommendations that will change the spirit of our penitentiaries without necessarily lessening discipline.[19]

On April 4, 1935 riots and fires at Kingston Penitentiary again engaged Parliament. Agnes asked Minister of Justice Hugh Guthrie if he contemplated "having a thorough investigation made into the penitentiaries, goals and reformatories of Canada; an investigation into crime and its punishment."

This gave Guthrie the chance he wanted and he replied that first he wanted to deal with another matter. Agnes had charged that, during an interview with prisoner Alfred George Hall, penitentiary inspector J. D. Dawson had made derogatory remarks about her. First he had asked Hall if he knew Charles Baynes, the convict Agnes had defended in the House, and then referring to that defence Dawson said: "Aggie made a god-damned fool of herself in the House of Commons, but when we are finished with her she will never be able to lift up her head in the House again."

Guthrie said he had made a full inquiry and found there was no foundation to the charge. He believed that Agnes had been "misled by certain people who had been furnishing her with information." (According to Inspector Dawson's own evidence, he had been sent to Kingston Penitentiary to find out if Charles Baynes was the source of Agnes Macphail's knowledge of prison affairs.)

Guthrie continued: "My honorable friend is of a very sympathetic disposition and I fear that she has been imposed upon. We are all liable to imposition from time to time, and I believe that is what has happened in connection with the charges she makes against Inspector Dawson. Her informant was a prisoner until some time in February when he was released. She based a rather serious charge against a high officer of the penitentiary's staff on information supplied by this man Hall."

Agnes interrupted to say that when she visited the penitentiary on February 16 she knew nothing whatever of the case. She was shown around by Warden Allen, and she asked to see Charles Baynes, "the convict who had caused me so much suffering last year. In the presence of the warden this convict asked me if I knew that Inspector Dawson had attempted to induce him, first by cajolery and then by threats, to sign a certain statement to the effect that he had given me information in connection with the Lloyd case . . . away back in 1927 or 1928." Baynes, said Agnes, would not sign the statement because she had not given him any information on the case.

> I could not believe that an inspector of the penitentiaries in Ottawa would go to Kingston and attempt . . . to have a prisoner make a statement saying that he had supplied me with the information in connection with any case I had brought up. . . .
>
> Do honorable members wonder that in those circumstances I did want to know whether or not Inspector Dawson had gone to Kingston Penitentiary and had tried to get him to sign a statement indicating that he had furnished me with information regarding the Lloyd case. . . .
>
> I do not want the Minister of Justice to tie me up a second time with somebody with a long record — I do not know whether it is a case of sex perversion or embezzlement or both. I simply know that a man . . . came and offered to take an affidavit as to the truth of the statement he had made. So that you have two convicts and a guard whose name I have, and who has since been promoted, who all seem to know of these circumstances.
>
> It does not matter that the incident reflected on me but it does matter whether any member of this House can be put in the position in which I was placed by this sort of thing.

Guthrie replied that he agreed with her last statement but was satisfied that she had been imposed upon. Since Agnes would not accept Inspector Dawson's denial on his word of honor, she had to listen to what was known of this man Hall. He had a criminal record that went back to 1923 and was a "confidence man out and out." He had been convicted of theft and obtaining money by false pretenses, by fraud and writing worthless cheques.

That was the man, said Guthrie, who had launched the charge against Inspector Dawson. In Guthrie's opinion, Charles Baynes was looked upon as the "greatest liar we have ever had in the institution. . . . I wish the honorable member for South East Grey would not be led away with stories of this kind and by men of this character. These men are trying to excite her sympathy and probably her animosity against the penitentiary staff. They have laid clever plans for that purpose, and I sincerely hope she will place no dependence upon those stories."

Guthrie said that while he personally did not think it was necessary, he would launch an investigation if she desired it.

Miss Macphail: I shall be very glad to have an investigation into this matter. But this particular question is not what interests me most, although I am most anxious that it should be cleared up, and I shall be very happy to accept the suggestion of the minister. But what I want is an investigation by a royal commission into the whole penal system in Canada, which is a very much greater thing than anything said about me.

One must say this at any rate for Hall, he was not asking me for sympathy. He said, "I have a bad record." I did not even ask what it was. He said, "The record will be spread on Hansard, so do not defend me." He said, "I am making an affidavit and the affidavit I make is true, and if it is not true, let them put me back in penitentiary." There you are. The department headed by the minister will not have an investigation into the penal system in Canada. It is all very well to put these two cases on Hansard and make it look very bad for me, but what about a penal system marked by demonstrations and riots and fires from one end of the Dominion to the other.

She listed twelve disturbances in penitentiaries since April of 1932, including one at Stony Mountain where a guard had been killed, and another at Kingston where damage had amounted to $35,000.

"We have a penal system in Canada in which seventy-three per cent of the total prison population are recidivists — I am using the figures of the hierarchy so they ought to be correct. Twenty-eight per cent have been in penitentiary before and forty-five per cent in gaols and reformatories; in other words, three out of four return again. Irrespective of any other evidence, there is something radically wrong with a system that produces such a condition. Imprisonment is necessary, but in my opinion it should be made to serve a constructive purpose, and the moment it does not do so it is failing in its object."

Guthrie replied that "in regard to the question of a committee to investigate penitentiary matters . . . notwithstanding the criticism that has been heard from some quarters of this House, and notwithstanding the attitude taken by some newspapers in Canada, I am proud to say that Canadian penitentiaries today stand

higher than, or as high as, those of any other country in the world. . . ." He said
that they had introduced so many changes in the last three years that one would
hardly know it was the same system. He did not credit Agnes for these changes
but attributed them all to General Ormond. (Prisoners knew better. When Agnes
died they wrote a tribute to her in the *Kingston Penitentiary Telescope* saying
that conditions were "far better than they were in the 1930's when Agnes
Macphail set foot within the Old North Gate. The changes wrought within these
cold grey walls were her handiwork; to her must go our tribute.")

On April 4, the member for Hamilton (Mr. Bell) related his experience on
visiting Kingston Penitentiary. While he sympathized with Agnes' desire for
reform, he tried to tell her that she should not rely on prisoners' stories: "The
trouble is, I think, that, in spite of an earnest, sincere, sympathetic — "

"Cut out the cant," replied Agnes.

" — Trusting nature such as hers," continued Bell, "and, in view of her
interruption I may add her sweet femininity, one of her difficulties seems to be a
lack of appreciation of the bona fide of those with whom she may come in
contact under these conditions. . . ."

Agnes told Bell that she appreciated his earnest plea for penal reform and
said, "If out of all this some good may result, any suffering I have endured is as
nothing at all. [20]

Guthrie set up a Commission to investigate Agnes' slander charges but he
would not investigate Baynes' charge that Inspector Dawson had tried to pressure
him into making false statements. Nor would he provide Agnes with counsel. J.
S. McRuer, later Chief Justice of Ontario, took her case and would accept no
fee.

Judge E. J. Daly presided at the Commission. In spite of Inspector Dawson's
admission to Col. W. B. Megloughlin (warden of Kingston Penitentiary at the
time the accusations were made) that he, Dawson, had called Aggie a "god-
damned fool," and in spite of the fact that Harry Anderson, editor of the *Toronto
Globe*, overheard two guards say, "The boss wants to land Aggie so be careful
what you testify," Judge Daly dismissed the case.

Chapter IX
A Liberal Landslide
1935-1936

Business conditions improved slowly — so slowly that voters showed their dissatisfaction by overthrowing Conservative administrations in Nova Scotia, New Brunswick, Saskatchewan, British Columbia and Ontario. Bennett decided to appeal to the people and called an election for October, 1935. Experts predicted that there would be a Liberal landslide. They also predicted that the new boundaries in her riding would "scuttle" Miss Agnes Macphail, the UFO-Labor candidate.

Agnes had two opponents in the new Grey-Bruce riding — Dr. L. G. Campbell, Conservative, and Dr. W. A. Hall, Liberal.

In preparation for the nominating meeting which was to be held in Durham Town Hall, Agnes asked her young campaign manager, James Palmer, to go through her set of 1930-35 Hansards and mark with a piece of paper every speech she made in the House. Dr. Hall's speeches were to be marked with a different colored paper. She set the books on a table and drew them to the attention of the audience:

"You want to know what I did in Ottawa? Every slip of paper in those books represents a speech I made in Ottawa on your behalf. If you want to see how many Dr. Hall made, come up and count them for yourself." There were eighty-six slips for Agnes, none for Dr. Hall.

Dr. Hall was not at the meeting and Dr. Campbell spent his forty minutes eulogizing Prime Minister Bennett. "Called on for her three-minute rebuttal," recalled Palmer, "Agnes strode to the platform and said bluntly: 'You really want to know what the Prime Minister has done for you? Put your hands in your pockets, and find out.' She sat down. There was a stir in the crowded room and one of the reporters said: 'Well, Aggie's just won the election.'"

At a UFO-Labor meeting in Durham Town Hall "standing room was at a premium," said the *Durham Review*. "On the platform were Miss Macphail, Mrs. Gladys Cornfield Howey of Owen Sound, Mrs. D. J. McGowan of Ravenna, Mr. F. R. Oliver, M.P.P., Messrs. Wm. Jack and James Palmer, with Mr. Neil Norman as Chairman. Mr. Jack, Reeve of Proton, welcomed Agnes and said: 'The County of Grey should be proud of Miss Macphail for her record of the past 14 years.' Mrs. Howey said: 'Miss Macphail has a great love for the common people; has a natural gift of statesmanship and we can count on her to do the right thing at the right time. . . . She is an authority on economics, monetary systems and prisons and we are too close to her to see her gifts.'

"The final speaker, Miss Macphail," said the *Review*, "introduced her speech by acknowledging the debt of gratitude she owed to all who had helped in her campaign." She paid special tribute to James Palmer of Dundalk who had "driven her car into every poll in her large riding." (In Dundalk this line was greeted by a burst of laughter, as Palmer had recently backed her car into a wooden pole and dented its fender. Agnes thought so little of the incident that she did not know why the audience was laughing and waited impatiently for them to cease so she could continue her speech.) Palmer was regarded as her "advance agent," Agnes said. McMaster University had excused him from classes to help out in the campaign and she was very grateful to him.

She told her Durham audience there were four necessary qualifications for a parliamentarian — the instrument of voice, integrity, right attitude and ability. "If you don't want these points in a representative of Grey-Bruce, elect one of the other parties; vote Liberal and get inaction." [1]

At another meeting in Proton Township she said, "We are deathly tired of Mr. Bennett's government and of Mr. Bennett who thinks he has the only brain in the country." She said he had too much money to understand the problems of the common people. And speaking of King, she said, "He lacks the power to change his mind and is unable to make up his mind on vital problems at the right time." [2]

Agnes with her campaign manager, James Palmer

This time five of her meetings were devoted exclusively to women. She took pains to make these meetings special, with solos by soprano Marguerita Nuttall, [3] and piano selections from Chopin and Bach by Gladys Howey. [4]

"I attended the meeting she held in Dundalk and still remember the beautiful long gown she wore," said James Palmer. "It was deep purple velvet with full gold-coloured sleeves. The skirt swirled around — cut on the bias I guess you'd say. She 'put on the dog' for them. Dundalk was a Tory stronghold. But they all came to hear her."

Agnes also sent a special letter to the women in her riding pointing out that it was in their power to keep at least one woman in Parliament:

> *With the Vice-Regal salute which brought to an end the seventeenth Parliament of Canada still ringing in my ears, I feel that I want to say to you that this year the people of Grey-Bruce and myself must shoulder the responsibility of deciding whether or not there will continue to be a woman in the House of Commons, in the eventuality of no other woman being elected.*
>
> *While in no sense representing women as apart from men, I have approached public questions from a woman's point of view. Like you, I want an opportunity for young people to develop their capabilities and, having done that, to find a place where they can use them. Like you, I desire peace that men, women and children may, in security, live their lives. Like you, too, I most earnestly desire a higher standard of living for agricultural and urban producers and hope for better days for the submerged poor and suffering.*
>
> *It is just Fate that we are the group of people in all Canada who have the opportunity of either keeping or breaking faith with those far-sighted pioneers who from the eighteenth century down sought earnestly the right of women to share the burden and responsibility of public life with men, as women share home and industrial life. We happen to be the link that binds the past to the future. We can make it easier for the women who are yet to take their place in legislative and executive positions in Canada by holding the ground we have already won. The importance of this rises above all party and personal consideration.*
>
> *If you see the importance of my staying in the Commons I am assured of your understanding support.*

"During that campaign," recalled James Palmer,

> *I sometimes stayed overnight at the Macphail home. I would sleep on the couch in the living room. Sometimes Agnes, Marguerita Nuttall and Gladys Howey would come in late, after I'd gone to sleep. They would expect me to get up and have a cup of cocoa with them — which I would do of course.*
>
> *Generally Agnes would take a rest after lunch. She'd go to her room or to the garden. Newspapers and other material would be spread all over the place. I never saw her use her desk in the living room.*
>
> *She could be quite informal. Once she wanted something in town. She hopped in the car in her blue silk pajamas — topped by a*

*matching kimono — and went shopping in Flesherton. She thought
nothing of it but some people criticized her.*

*On election day [October 14] while I drove women to the polls,
Agnes babysat in various homes. Once we picked up an old woman.
She told us she was going to the poll. She and her husband had
agreed not to go as they would only cancel each other's vote. Her
husband went to the barn to do the chores. Later she went to take
him a glass of lemonade.*

"He was gone," she said. "And I knew where he went."

*She set out on the two or three mile walk to cast her vote for
Agnes. Thanks to our lift, she met him coming out the door! We had
a good laugh over that.*

On October 17, 1935, the *Durham Review* reported that the "lady member"
had been returned to her seat in the new riding of Grey-Bruce with an increased
majority. She "piled up a substantial majority over Dr. Hall of Walkerton, Liberal
— 1399 — and Dr. L. G. Campbell, Markdale, Conservative — 2091."

The Liberals formed the new government, and Mackenzie King was returned
for the third time as Prime Minister, "with the largest majority given to a
political leader since Confederation." The Liberals won 171 seats, the Conservatives thirty-nine, the CCF seven, and for the first time Social Credit, seventeen.
There was one Independent.

Nineteen-thirty-six saw the death of George V. His son, Edward VII, gave up his
throne to marry "the woman he loved," and George VI succeeded his brother to
the throne. A Canadian nurse, Dorothea Palmer, was arrested for distributing birth
control information, and the murder of a young policeman by a paroled convict
set the parole system back many years. The first session of the Eighteenth
Parliament sat from February 6 to June 23. Agnes toured Russia and the Scan-
dinavian countries with seven other Canadians that summer. They visited co-ops
and folk schools in Denmark, Sweden and Finland, and Agnes was greatly
impressed by their brand of democratic socialism.

In January she signed up with a new agency, Harold R. Peat, Incorporated,
of New York. Peat handled speaking engagements for such well known people
as Thomas Mann, Thornton Wilder and the Right Honorable Winston Churchill.

In an early letter to Peat she wrote:

*At last I am getting off this agreement and four photographs. They
were done by the best character photographer in Canada; he does
not set out to make one look beautiful when one is not, but rather to
portray character.[5] A couple of these look pretty fierce, but it is
"distinguished personalities" you handle, is it not? My age, in case
you could not tell from the photographs, is forty-five.*

*Thinking over the address on women, I wonder if a better title would
not be "Whither woman?" Now please do not ask me to outline the
address. I cannot possibly tell you now what I am going to say next
Fall; if I did there would be no spontaneity or life in the thing.*

*If you would care to submit two subjects, I would be quite agree-
able to do an entirely different one as well, such as "The Trend of
Canadian Development" or, as you suggested, "Canada's Future."
So often a group might want a speaker but not the particular subject*

we are dealing with since it is too similar to others treated. It might make your task of booking simpler if there were two subjects and it suits me quite as well. I think one keeps fresher by having a change of subjects in a period as long as five weeks.

You asked how many women stood for Parliament in the last election. There were fifteen women candidates, only two of whom were elected, Mrs. Black and myself. Mrs. Black [Yukon] followed her husband in the seat he vacated last season, so I am still the only woman to come in quite on my own. I was first elected in 1921 and re-elected in 1925, 1926, 1930 and 1935. I have held a legislative position in the Government longer than any other woman on the North American Continent. [6]

The *Toronto Star Weekly* commented editorially on Agnes' success at the polls. It said she was successful because she treated her constituents "like friends" and talked to them "like neighbours." It praised her weekly letters as "well-written, interesting and homey," and said that this was not political craftiness. "The fact is that she has a natural friendliness and an interest in human beings and a capacity to write entertainingly and chattily." [7]

She wrote to her constituents on February 1, 1936:

Before the session gets under way I want to tell you something of the four weeks I spent below the "Mason-Dixon Line." [8] *It was my good fortune to be guest at a New Year's Party in New Orleans given by the Dean of the Graduate School of the University. One hears much of the gaiety of New Orleans but words scarcely describe the complete abandonment of the people of all ages to the spirit of a New Year's Eve celebration.*

The night was fine and warm; the crowds of joyous people swarmed Canal Street, the very wide and principal avenue of that interesting old city. The crowds, wearing hats, blowing horns, walked or skipped as best expressed their mood. Early in the evening every eating place was crowded from the quite ordinary places to the renowned German and French restaurants where the food, waiters and music made one feel the atmosphere of Germany and France.

Our host being fond of German food and music, we dined at Kobe's. Happy with good foods and good wine, the crowds lustily sang German songs and danced to German music afterwards continuing the Carnival in the streets almost until dawn.

Three trainloads of Texans wearing ten gallon hats had come into New Orleans to support their football team in the New Year's Game in the Sugar Bowl where they were to battle against the Louisiana State Football eleven. This western accent added picturesqueness to the street scene on New Year's Eve.

A sugar bowl had always meant to me a bowl to hold sugar; but on the first day of January, 1936, I saw a sugar bowl with 40,000 cheering Texans and Louisianians watching with intense interest their best football teams contend for top place in the south west. It was a bowl of wet sugar since the leaden skies hanging low all morning began, when the first quarter was over, to rain and kept on steadily

— had I not been in the L.S.U. box I would have sought shelter but
the weather and the loss of the game seemed enough for the Presi-
dent to bear without having his guests walk out on him. I was suffi-
ciently interested in watching his family party to feel that the new
hat, gloves, etc. which I had to buy the next day were not an
extravagance. . . .

The country below the Mason-Dixon Line is in the United States
but scarcely of it. The South has a silent contempt for the North and
feels loyalty for, if not the South only, certainly for the South espe-
cially. This is shown by the motto inscribed in hand-wrought iron in
the entrance to the State Capitol of Texas — "For State Rights and
Our South Land." And again on a monument at the entrance to the
Capitol grounds where the names of the states which seceded from
the Union are inscribed with this statement: "Died for State Rights
Guaranteed under the Constitution. The people of the South, animated
by the spirit of 1778 to preserve their rights withdrew from the
Federal compact — the North resorted to coercion — the South
against overwhelming odds fought until exhausted." There is no
admission of defeat there. When a Southerner speaks of war he
means the Civil War — to him there was just one.

The Southerner is a charming person, not overly energetic but
intelligent, hospitable, gracious and very friendly towards Canada
and Great Britain. I was talking to a British student from Oxford,
Tony Greenwood, one of the Oxford Debating Team and he was
telling me that all through the South after the debates people would
come up to him to say that they were English or British and when he
would ask, "When did you come over," he would get on many
occasions the astonishing reply, "Five generations ago. . . ." [9]

In her letter of February 13, Agnes described the reaction of the House
when King George V died on January 20, 1936:

A full House gathered the day after the formal opening to pay loving
and sorrowful tribute to King George V. The Prime Minister and Mr.
Bennett reviewed the work of the late Monarch, both as a sovereign
and as a man, and expressed in the form of a resolution the genuine
sorrow which members of the House of Commons feel. Said resolu-
tion will be forwarded to Queen Mary. Mr. Woodsworth, Mr.
Blackmore [Leader of the Social Credit Group], and Mrs. [Martha
Louise] Black also made speeches of tribute and condolence. A
resolution expressing the loyalty and affection of Canadians was
passed and is being forwarded to King Edward VIII.

The opening was quite unlike any other I have seen. Papers in the
Capitol City carried the heading "Court Mourning Worn By Ladies
Adds to Colorful Note." And as an explanation of this curious
statement: "Black gowns form vivid contrast to uniforms of officers
and members of the diplomatic corps and the purple of the church
dignitaries."

If black mourning for women, why was scarlet and ermine mourn-
ing for the Judges of the Supreme Court? Why, too, was the gold-

encrusted Windsor uniform of the Prime Minister an adequate expression of grief of the first citizen? It was said the judges had "weeping cuffs" and I dare say they had, but from my position at the bar of the Senate, I could not see them.

Contrary to the opinions expressed by society writers I did not think the dominant note of dull black added to the dignity and beauty of the opening pageant. Many women were unable to attend because of the extra cost involved by the requirement of all-black clothes. Of the four young ladies who were to have been my guests, not one felt she could purchase a second costume for the occasion. The same problem evidently faced many women, or at any rate that is my explanation of the empty seats on the Floor and in the Galleries. . . .

Senator Cairine Wilson gave a small but very enjoyable tea party before the House opened, to which Mrs. Black and I were invited. We had a happy hour visiting before the fire in the beautiful drawing room. The Senator had had a birthday the day before and she had saved some of her birthday cake for the tea party. Charlotte Whitton, the recognized authority on child welfare and Winifred Ydd, the retiring President of the National Council of Women, were two of the interesting and congenial group. It is delightful for me to have Mrs. Black in the House and to find that her office is opposite mine.[10]

The private side of Agnes was often a surprise to people. William Eggleston said that he had never met a person who was so different in her public and private lives. In Parliament Agnes could be "bleak" and "severe," but outside the House there was another Agnes — "feminine, kind and affectionate." She loved singing and would "laugh uproariously at a good joke."

Family and friends were well acquainted with this side of her.

Agnes' sister, Gertha Reany, said "she was always big-hearted. She loved comfort and wanted every other person to be comfortable."

Muriel Kerr, an Ottawa teacher and good friend, said that Agnes often visited her apartment with other members of the Ginger Group. They would send out for a Chinese meal, which Agnes liked, go dancing, or just talk. They had "heaps of fun," said Kerr, "and Agnes was delightfully gay and full of laughter. . . . She was always ready to go. Would ring a doorbell four times in impatience, when another person would ring it once and wait. . . ."

Kerr sometimes went to political meetings where Agnes spoke. She says she recalls "most vividly the gnarled hands of the farmers as they leaned forward on the back of the seats ahead, listening to Agnes."

Letters reveal her generosity and genuine concern for others. When niece Jean Reany was ill, Agnes wrote to Jean's mother:

I sent Jean a dress today, the twelve year size. The next size looked too big, but if this fits too snugly send it back and I will change it. Don't tell the Baileys you got it because I did not get three. This is just a little treat to cheer Jean up while she has the measles. Do see that she doesn't go back to school too soon.

Jack Lawson died last night and I think I must go home for the funeral. I feel so sorry for his mother and father. He had three operations for an abscess in the inner sinus and two blood transfusions. They thought he was improving but he had not strength to come back. [11]

Agnes in the flower garden at her home in Ceylon

In a letter to an old school friend, Annie Briggs, she writes:

I was indeed surprised to get your letter, and also delighted. It seems a long time since we spent all our waking hours together. I remember so vividly a threshing at our place when your mother was helping my mother and all the Cooper and Macphail children were under foot, and your mother said "Shoot the kids." I remember yet how funny I thought it was.

Your Uncle Donald has built a fine house on the site of your old one, but the one we lived in was torn down last year.

It would be nice if I could tell you I had three children — I wouldn't really care whether it was two girls and a boy or the other way about. My sisters have three girls; Lily has twins, aged 11, and Gertha a girl, also 11. They are great youngsters and I enjoy them. Of course to tell you the truth, mother and I always heave a sigh of relief when they leave after a visit but we are glad as ever to see them when they come again.

Mother and I live in Ceylon, which is only a little better than a mile from the last farm we lived on. We live very comfortably, if simply. Mother has help and she enjoys her garden. She is no sort of a traveller, though last year we did take a little motor trip which she enjoyed, and she likes to go back to visit with the old friends in Proton.

Mrs. Shand is living but my Aunt Agnes, Mrs. Sandy McKechnie, died a year ago, and the men are all gone. My father died in 1930 at 65 years of age.

Lilly married a very fine man who runs several businesses but lives on the old farm eight miles east of Dundalk. I like the way they live very much; they have the pleasures of country life without depending on the land for a livelihood. Gertha lives in the town of Southampton on Lake Huron. Her husband is an engineer with the Canadian National Railways.

I often think of old No. 4 school where we all went. Some day I must make a decent presentation to it of books or pictures or both.

I will carefully keep your address. There is always the chance that I might come your way some day. I am so glad you wrote to me. [12]

The improvement of social conditions was always a first priority with Agnes. People knew that she was interested in their problems and her mail was full of pathetic stories. She helped many personally and tried to get more help through Parliament.

In February 1936, during a debate on retiring allowances, she asked for pensions for the blind and disabled:

The honorable member for Rosthern (W. A. Tucker) gave the Prime Minister today all the praise for the present old age pension bill. I was in the House in 1926 when an old age pension bill was passed, and if I understand the situation aright, the present and then member for Winnipeg North Centre [J. S. Woodsworth] really was the man who got old age pensions. At that time the government needed votes, and they paid a high price. . . .

I want to emphasize the great need of doing something for two groups of people, one the blind, and the other those who are incurable invalids . . . . I think that we as a Parliament and as a country ought to be ashamed to say that we cannot afford to take care of the blind when they need care. The same might well be said of those persons who are invalids, incurably ill and unable ever again to earn for themselves. Surely both the blind and those who are ill and suffering pain are bearing enough without being required to worry and fret for lack of the little consolation and comfort that they would have if their bread and butter and their shelter were secure for them . . . .

Everyone is worrying as to where the money is to come from with which to extend the idea of pensions. . . . I have always had a couple of ideas as to where money could be obtained. . . . In the estimates at page 24 you will find two items I should like to see struck out. One is an amount of $368,400 for the Royal Military College and the other is $150,000 for cadet services. You might be able to get something out of the non-permanent active militia also. Then there are a great many other things which could be done away with or reduced. There, however, are two concrete suggestions as to where money could be obtained, and that would be sufficient to extend pensions to those who are invalids at any rate, whether or not we went any further than that. [13]

On March 8 she made a plea for help for unemployed youth:

Mr. Speaker, though not a young man, I desire to speak on this subject. I should like to see Canada comprised entirely of young men and see how they would get on.

I should like to read some extracts from a letter I received only today which perfectly illustrates the need of the debate that is taking place tonight and of some action being taken in this regard. This letter is from a mother in an Ontario town. It is beautifully written, and she tells that her husband died suddenly. They had some life insurance, but he had used it to change his business. He had been a blacksmith; the automobile had come and ruined his business, so he had gone into some other way of making a living and shortly had died suddenly, leaving her nothing. She received mothers' allowance until the last of the children reached the age of sixteen. In this letter she tells me the story of the family, and I should like to quote from it enough to place the situation before the House. She says that her eldest son is twenty-three; he has a first class certificate but did not get a school and is working for $3 a week. Her eldest daughter is twenty-one; she is a stenographer in an insurance office, but the man who employs her is not busy. He has little to do, so he can give her work only three afternoons a week, and she is paid fifty cents an afternoon. The next son is learning to be an operator in a theatre and gets only $1 a week. She says that there is nothing else to do in this town because the two factories in it are closed. The next son is sixteen; he has a paper route and earns $1 a week. The mother continues:

"When I received the mothers' allowance cheque I could always manage. . . . I could keep their clothes clean and mended, cook vegetables and plain meals for them, but we cannot manage now. Lorne - . . . says he is going to leave home. Where can he go? . . . Ruth's boss says he wishes he had enough business to keep her every day. . . . I lie awake at nights. I worry so, sometimes I am sure I will lose my mind."

This woman lives in a very fine town. I do not know her, but I know the town and undoubtedly the member for that constituency would be interested in the letter, which I will pass on to him. What can be done for people like these? This woman is worse off now, with her children over sixteen, than she was before.

I am not going to make a long speech because I am not prepared to do so, but I do want to say something about the necessity of giving youth a chance. They do not want to be unduly helped; they dislike that more than anything else. They want a chance to live; they want a chance to work. They do not want to be pampered and babied and subsidized, but they must be given an opportunity to help themselves. A quotation appearing in an article I saw in the New York Times a week or so ago by Aubrey Williams, a director of the National Youth Administration of the United States, very well expressed just what I am sure we all feel. He said: "We must not let a single spark of that splendid fire go out, in the boredom, hopelessness and actual want that unemployment brings to those who meet it at the threshold of their active lives."

That is the task we face. We have not attended to it well, and it will cost as much in relief, in illness, in one or another of our institutions and in the care of our criminals as it would have cost to give youth an opportunity. We have spent the money but we have spent it in the wrong way. I think youth is particularly idealistic. They like heroic living. They want to live for an ideal, for something bigger than themselves. Unfortunately that is why war appeals to them; it is something in which they can drown themselves and they certainly made a good job of it the last time. They want now a social order under which they will have an opportunity to live. They want to live normal lives. I hear older people say, "Well, these are hard times, and they can just go without this, that, or the other thing." What we forget is that these people will never have youth again. They are trying to have some fun, and why not? They have a right to it. They are trying to find some place in life. They are trying to set up homes. I suppose there is no need to enumerate all the things they want to do; but they do want work; they do want idealism; they do want an opportunity to care for somebody or some thing; they do want the fellowship of their kind. Why should they not want these things, and how much less would we think of them if they did not? . . .

As soon as people get it through their heads that this is not a depression out of which some government with a large majority is going to bring them overnight, but a condition which we are never coming out of because the machine is displacing more people all the time, they are going to prepare for a longer period of youth, for a longer period of retirement at the end of life and for increasing opportunities at both ends and, indeed, in the middle.[14]

Young women were of special concern to Agnes, and in the House she said:

We hear much about single unemployed men, and a good deal has been done to take care of them, whether it has been well done or not, by way of camps, and now by transferring them to work on railway maintenance. This leads me to wonder what has become of single unemployed women. There must be a terrible unrevealed condition affecting single unemployed women. Often in listening to debates in this chamber I have thought that we have a pretty masculine society, and at no time am I so impressed with that condition as when we are dealing with unemployment. A great deal has been said and written in times past about the "weaker sex." If men are not capable of taking care of themselves during periods of stress and unemployment, does Parliament think women are more capable of taking care of themselves? If they are not, what provision has the government made, or what provision does it propose to make for single unemployed women?[15]

Chapter X
Prison Reform
1936-1937

Agnes' first letters in 1936 covered many topics: health care, voting rights, the unemployed.

March 12, 1936

Ex-service men will be glad to hear that the great difference which has existed between the treatment of officers and men in regard to hospital allowances is greatly diminished. A sick general or colonel is not to wallow in wealth while the sick private gets a pittance.

I just returned from Montreal where I spent a very enjoyable weekend as the guest of Miss Helen Francis-Wood, a delightful English woman. While there I addressed the Royal Empire Society and the Alliance for Women's Votes in Quebec. Both audiences were most considerate. It begins to look as though the franchise would soon be extended to the women of Quebec in the provincial field. They now can vote in federal elections.[1]

March 15, 1936

This week has been an encouraging one for me. At last the Royal Commission for a thorough investigation of penitentiaries and of scientific methods of treating lawbreakers has been appointed. The single unemployed men in camps are in the way of being given work with wages. A courageous member of the governing party made a "money" speech which exactly suited me, and the Press Women entertained the four women Parliamentarians — just think — four of us! (Cairine Wilson, Iva Fallis, Martha Louise Black and Agnes.)

I regard the Royal Commission as competent. The Chairman, Mr. Justice Archambault, a former Member of Parliament, has had extensive experience as Crown Prosecutor for the district of Montreal. Mr. Craig, K.C., is former Attorney General of Manitoba, a man highly regarded. The officialdom of these two members will be counteracted by the humanity of the third member of the Commission, Mr. Harry Anderson, until recently Editor in Chief of the Toronto Globe whose deep interest and wide study of penal matters is well known.

The reference which will determine the scope of the commission's work is very wide, allowing not only for investigation into the six penitentiaries of Canada, but a study of penology and such liberal experiments as are being tried.[2]

March 19, 1936

There was a time when the introduction of a resolution or bill having to do with human betterment as distinct from the economic and legal aspect of public policy, emptied the House. I remember when Henry Spencer, UFA, first discussed the need of a national health policy he could scarcely be heard for the talking of members who visited while this "unimportant" matter was being presented. But times have changed.

When Dr. Donnelly, Liberal, Saskatchewan, discussed pensions for the blind, he had an attentive House and an almost embarrassing number of speakers supporting his motion. Moreover, the resolution passed unanimously, followed by disappointment and anger when the Finance Minister stated he could not afford the half million dollars necessary. The members enjoyed Mr. Harry Leader's indignant protest, in which he pointed out that in the last years the travelling expenses of government members and officials was over 17 million dollars.

An interesting suggestion as to method of raising money for payment of pensions was made by Mr. Coldwell, CCF, Saskatchewan. He said in Sweden they had converted the manufacturing of tobacco, which had become a monopoly, into a government-owned enterprise and had ear-marked the revenue for old age pensions.[3]

March 27, 1936

I have had another birthday [her 46th] and what a birthday! No one could mind being a year older when the occasion brings such joy. Letters, wires and callers expressed good wishes all through the day. Mrs. Black came across the corridor to present me with a beautiful corsage of orchids and lily of the valley and a number of pictures of the flowers of the Yukon on which she is an authority. Mr. Telford, the member for North Grey, "The Old Guard" (Mr. Woodsworth, Heaps and MacInnis) sent roses and so many other friends expressed their good wishes in spring flowers that my office was like a lovely garden. It was a gala day, ending with a birthday dinner, cake and candles and all![4]

On April 12 an explosion trapped three men in Moose River, Nova Scotia. A Dr. Robertson and two men named Scadding and McGill were entombed ninety feet down. McGill died of a fractured skull. Scadding and Robertson made verbal wills through a one-way phone. Water, soup, chocolate and diluted brandy were dropped down a hose in the diamond drill hole. Water rose steadily in the mine and was eighteen feet from the men when they were rescued. Public interest was kept at a high pitch by a CRBC broadcast team which reported non-stop for sixty-nine hours until the two survivors were rescued on April 22. The topic formed part of her next letter.

April 25, 1936

It has been a week of drama. Hour by hour members followed the events at Moose River mine; sometimes, like all other Canadians, hopeful, and at others despairing, with the nervous strain finally broken by the rescue of the entrapped men from the old mine.

> *We thrill to the heroism of the miners who hourly risked their lives to save others. We know it is right that great effort should be made to save three lives, but why are we indifferent to wasting and rotting humanity buried in inactivity and hopelessness?*
>
> *The Drama Festival has been engaging the attention of Ottawa this week. A renowned playwright, Mr. Granville Barker of Great Britain, is the adjudicator and to him falls the difficult task of deciding which of the many plays presented from over Canada is the best played. I have not had the opportunity of attending any of the performances but have read with interest the daily comments of Mr. Granville Barker and today had the pleasure of meeting the cast of Vancouver players who presented "Waiting for Lefty."*
>
> *The play has to do with unemployed youth, the frustration and impoverishment of their lives. The Vancouver group are for the most part unemployed and had at the beginning no thought of entering the National Drama Festival, but the extraordinary popularity of the play in Vancouver and the opposition of the police of that city to the performance spurred them on. A tag day and the net receipts of the many presentations of the play in their home city made it financially possible for them to come to Ottawa. It is ironical that this radical play should be presented to a fashionable and official audience in the capital city after the police of Vancouver thought it unsafe for local consumption.[5]*

In 1936 Agnes was involved in the infamous case of Norman "Red" Ryan. Ryan, with nineteen convictions behind him, out of prison on a "ticket of leave," shot and killed a young Sarnia policeman, John Lewis, while trying to rob a liquor store. Ryan, too, was killed.

That Ryan possessed a diabolic charm is apparent from the number of influential people who were deceived by him. Father W. T. Kingsley, Roman Catholic chaplain of Kingston Penitentiary and priest of the nearby Church of the Good Thief, was convinced that he was reformed and worked for his release. Prime Minister R. B. Bennett visited him in prison in 1934 and was "greatly impressed" by him. A reporter who saw him when he was returned to Canada after a series of bank robberies in the United States wrote: "One wonders how so seemingly mild and gentlemanly an individual could have got himself into such a predicament." On his release Ryan socialized with an archbishop, attended hockey games with a magistrate, wrote a "Crime does not pay" series for the *Toronto Star* and acted as altar boy for Father Kingsley.

It would have been understandable if Agnes Macphail, too, had pressed for Ryan's release. However, she had not. James Palmer was in Ottawa at the time of the Ryan killing and was with her when an Alberta senator congratulated her for not supporting the appeal for Ryan's release, although she had been asked to do so.

She had met him twice, was impressed by his appearance and demeanour, thought he was reformed, yet had reservations, for she would not support the appeal for his release. People assumed that she had and reviled her through letters to her and the press.

I am writing just a short letter to let you know of my disapproval of your activities in pressing so hard for the parole of "Red Ryan." I feel that the onus of the loss of the life of the Sarnia constable rests directly on you and certain others who intruded their ideas, and defeated the cause of justice by interfering in something about which they had no knowledge.

I believe your future actions will be guided a great deal by this happening and though I feel sorry for you that things turned out the way they did, it may serve as a lesson for you to confine your activities to those things of which you have cognizance. [6]

Someone else wrote:

Do you realize, you wretched woman, how large a share of responsibility rests on you for the murder of that brave young officer at Sarnia, and the loss of husband and father of that little family?

And will you take to heart what the widow of the murdered Stonehouse has said at Markham about the responsibility of those who worked for the release of the cowardly brute and killer, with his long record of crime?

To do this you persistently attacked and maligned the former Minister of Justice, and all who had to do with the Penitentiary administration. For his share in the evil work, the late slush-editor of the Globe received a pre-arranged political award. Through you and the degraded and degrading Globe the public have had evidence of a new development in political depravity — the linking of crime and criminals with politics.

Go on coddling crooks and criminals if you must, but have the grace to keep off the Uplift platforms from now on, and find some other pretext than the Boy Scouts for the parade of your unwholesome opinions. As the Psalmist has said: "Thou givest thy mouth to evil." [7]

Agnes defended herself against such charges in Parliament:

I rise to a question of privilege. My attention has been called to a statement alleged to have been made — it is in quotations — by Premier Hepburn, appearing in the Ottawa Journal of June 2, at page 11, in which discussing compensation for the family of Constable John Lewis, who was slain by Norman "Red" Ryan in Sarnia on May 23, Mr. Hepburn, the Premier of Ontario, is reported to have said: "We are not involved in any way. He was let out of the penitentiary because he was the 'pet' of R. B. Bennett, Senator Mullins and Miss Agnes Macphail. We had nothing to do with paroling the man."

Some hon. members: Oh, oh.

Miss Macphail: I do not believe that anyone really thinks this is funny, for it undoubtedly had most unfortunate consequences, resulting as it did in the death of Constable John Lewis. I have borne a good deal of adverse criticism about my activities in relation to penitentiaries, and in this matter, I thought I ought to make it clear so far as I am concerned, I did not intercede on behalf of Norman

"Red" Ryan. I asked Mr. Gallagher, chief of remission service, whether he would go through the files and give me a statement, which I should like to put on Hansard. I have received from him the following letter, dated June 6, 1936:

> *Dear Madam:*
>
> *Complying with your request, I have had the departmental records very carefully examined to ascertain whether you had at any time intervened, or asked for clemency on behalf of Norman, or "Red" Ryan.*
>
> *As a result of our diligent search, I may definitely assure you that we have found no trace whatever of any communication from you in this case.*
>
> *Yours respectfully,*
> *M. F. Gallagher,*
> *Chief of Remission Service*

I have no desire to blame anyone or to say anything further; I simply want to make it perfectly clear to the house and the country that at no time did I intercede on behalf of Norman Ryan.[8]

She explained to General A. E. Ross why she had not supported the appeal for Ryan's release; wrote a compassionate letter to Father Kingsley and as always explained her position to her constituents.

> *I was so glad to get your letter of recent date. Yes, I felt I had to clear myself on the Red Ryan issue. Remission Officer Gallagher very strongly recommended against paroling Ryan, pointing out to Mr. Bennett and Mr. Guthrie that he had previously made similar promises of good behaviour and religious devotion, but had committed another robbery and again been incarcerated. I have no desire to blame them since I think they acted as they did in good faith, but I had borne enough at the hands of Guthrie. I am astonished at what you say about Ryan being on the receiving end of a reception given by Father Kingsley. That was very foolish.*
>
> *I had greatly hoped that the third Commissioner for the enquiry [the Archambault Commission on Penitentiaries] would have been appointed before now. Long ago Lapointe said he would name him in a few days. Before the House prorogues I will ask him again when the appointment is to be made. Anderson's death [H. Anderson, former editor of the Toronto Globe] was a discouragement from which we will not easily recover. There is nothing to do except keep on trying, I suppose.*[9]

Dear Father Kingsley:

> *I have been wanting to write to you ever since Norman Ryan returned to his life of crime. His tragedy would bring sorrow and great disappointment to you, to a greater degree than to the rest of us. I simply want to express my sympathy.*

Many of us were convinced that Ryan had reformed and I still believe that he had. I do not think that his good conduct for so long was hypocritical. The thing that is difficult to understand is the killing. In all his many exploits he had been very careful to avoid the taking of life. [It was learned later that he had killed another man just before the Lewis killing.] To me it only emphasizes the great need of studying the convicts in prison and the suiting of all punishment to the individual, with careful supervision after release. There are undoubtedly some people who should never come out of prison but even these should be allowed to live as well as is possible in prison, and not be irritated and hardened.

I only want to say again how much I appreciate your great work in Kingston. You are the one enlightening influence there and I do hope that you are not too discouraged at this time.[10]

In spite of such setbacks as the Ryan affair, the Royal Commission to investigate prisons was finally established and many people applauded.

An Ottawa woman, Bess Barker, wrote:

It may be true that "they also serve who only stand and wait." But usually "they" are standing and waiting for someone else to do something.

Nothing would have been done about our mediaeval penitential and punitive system if you had not done it. Not only have you started the reform machinery moving, but you have changed the attitude of the average person as to the personal responsibility towards those who are so foolish or so unfortunate as to outrage our standards of social behaviour.

You have done something which marks an end — and a beginning.

As a confirmed stander and waiter, I want to thank you for doing my share for me in this step towards civilization, and to tell you that I realize vaguely the cost to you in courage, patience and forbearance.

Also I want to assure you of my admiration for you, and my very great affection.[11]

A letter came also from Nellie McClung. A native, like Agnes, of Grey County, McClung was elected to the Alberta Legislature in July of 1921 at the age of forty-seven. A Liberal, she was already a well-known writer and feminist who later became involved in the fight to force the government to concede that women were "persons." Agnes was sixteen years younger than Nellie but had read the McClung books to her school children and found her a kindred soul.

When she finally met Nellie she wrote: "We have all read Nellie McClung's books. We have heard much of her wit, her warm-heartedness, her fine human qualities. Often when someone has been greatly praised, all our expectations are not fulfilled on meeting. But Nellie McClung was just what I wanted her to be, just what I expected her to be. Her presence in the sun room of the Pallaiser Hotel made speaking easier. Her warm sympathy could not but help. I liked her immensely, and oddly enough felt that I had known her always. She is a very understanding person."

Nellie shared Agnes' feeling of revulsion towards hanging and felt that if Agnes spoke against it she could change people's attitudes:

My dear Agnes:

You and I do not write often, but that's no indication of the state of our friendship, which has never languished, or grown pale. I read of you always with pride, and a real warming of the heart. I see you were in Dallas, Texas again, and what a welcome you got there. I am very fond of the southern people and could live with them quite happily. We have had two lovely visits to Texas, and were there in '34 when you came to Dallas. We were about 100 miles away at a place called Tyler, where Paul lived then. Now he is in Kerrville — 65 miles from San Antonio.

There is a man in Moose Jaw, a Mr. Arthur Davies, who has interested himself in the matter of our barbarous method of execution. It is not a pleasant subject, but I do think it is high time some one spoke out. Surely we are sufficiently civilized now, not to want to make people suffer for the "good of society." I will enclose Mr. Davies' leaflets and if you would speak of this, I believe public sentiment could easily be stirred to the place where a change would have to be made.

All goes well with us. The onion bed lies under a bed of kelp getting ready for next spring, this spring I mean for tomorrow is March 1st.

Mr. McClung sends his best wishes to you and sincere regard. I'd love to see you.[12]

Maurice Bodington, CFRB reporter, wrote enclosing an article on prison reform and said his father, Dr. George Bodington, "had taken over the British Columbia Asylum after a very sordid investigation and instituted some very interesting reforms there." He said that he himself had seen what could be accomplished "by the right handling of such problems." He wished her success and said he had to hasten to his job "of announcing Dr. so-and-so's horse medicine for listless cows."

Agnes replied:

I recall with pleasure meeting you at the Toronto Exhibition a year or so ago. I was interested in your beautiful voice before that, and more so afterwards, so your note which came at the beginning of the session enclosing an article from the Herald Tribune pleased me very much.

My interest in criminals and their reclamation is as great as ever but we certainly have had a run of bad luck. Archambault, the Chairman of the Royal Commission, having two legs broke both of them — I am sure if he had more they would have gone also. Harry Anderson, in whom we had settled our hopes, died and after that the editor of the London Free Press, who also recently departed this life, was to have been appointed on the Commission. I believe now McRuer, who gratuitously acted as Counsel for me on the minor investigation a year ago, is to be offered the third place. Much as I want him to accept it, one fears for him if he does. The Ryan business was bad; unthinking people use it as an argument for a do-nothing policy.

The House is expected to close today, at least we greatly hope it is, but we have been expecting it since last Friday. People with grievances are airing them just now.

Two very readable books on prisons, in which you might be inter-

*ested, are "We Who Are About To Die," by David Lamson, and
"The Sing Sing Doctor" by Squire. They give one a great insight into
what prisons do to people.*
    Thanks again, and good luck.[13]

She replied to a "fan" letter:

Dear Mrs. Smith:

> *I do appreciate your letter. It encourages me and helps me to know
> that a woman like yourself is following what I do and thinks that I have
> not done too bad a job. I have been and still am most anxious to make
> the way easier for the women who will come after me in public life —
> and may they come soon and in quantity[14]*

In 1937 Mackenzie King met Hitler and said he was "a simple sort of peasant" and "no threat to the world." The Hon. C. D. Howe, Minister of Transport, moved for the incorporation of a company to be known as Trans-Canada Air Lines, and the first regular flight was made on September 1. The second session of the Eighteenth Parliament ran from January 14 to April 10.

To a certain extent Agnes had outgrown her constituents. They noticed it in little things like asking for a finger bowl in a rural home or ignoring small courtesies, but even more in her interests which had broadened far beyond the boundaries of her riding.

She was used to meeting famous people, the service of good hotels. She wore expensive clothes and had her hair set becomingly. In a CBC interview, one-time secretary Lilla Bell said that Agnes had a natural curl in her hair and was the "last word in good grooming." She shopped for Agnes in the French Room of an Ottawa department store and brought home dresses from which she chose. "They were usually black — and dresses, not suits — tailored." She wore heavy silver jewellery and liked capes which she would take into the House to protect her from draughts.[15]

"She was a theatrical, dramatic figure in a cape," said Eugene Forsee, Director of the Labour Council. In a CBC interview he recalled a meeting where Agnes was to speak. At preliminary proceedings, women kept interrupting, insisting that a woman be appointed to a certain committee. When it was Agnes' turn to speak, she strode to the platform: "All I have to say is this: I'm sick and tired of this woman business. If I didn't get anything by merit, I didn't want it." Swirling her cape around her, she "stomped" off without giving her speech.[16]

Each year she entertained dozens of people in the parliamentary dining room, helped support the Ceylon home, donated scholarships and prizes, contributed to endless worthy causes and bought numerous gifts for relatives and friends. Her salary could be stretched only so far. Lecture tours, therefore, had become a necessary part of her life. While she enjoyed them, they were extremely strenuous. A statement of engagements for November 2 to February 1, 1938 — with a two-week Christmas break — shows that she spoke in twenty-three cities from Maine and Massachusetts on the east coast to California on the west. In between she crossed back and forth between Minnesota, Michigan, Iowa, Nebraska, South Dakota, Wisconsin, Kansas, Oklahoma, Texas, Ohio, Pennsylvania, Missouri, Indiana and Utah. Lectures were not always scheduled conveniently, and almost all her travelling was done by train. She was paid from one to two hundred dollars a lecture. From November 2 to 18 she made $1,700, plus $10 a day expenses. She told Bill Bierworth that Americans were crazy to pay so much for a lecture but that she would not die poor for she was paying up an annuity.

Her letters to Peat are a mixture of sympathy for his problems and exasperation at his tardiness in paying bills. On January 27, 1937, she wrote:

> Slow, as usual, but here I am at last.
> How would you like "The Good Neighbours" for a title, or "Us?"
> I am finding it difficult to think of a fascinating title for an address on Canadian-American relations. Three weeks in the fall and two in January would suit me very much better than five weeks at a stretch.

In March she was annoyed that her expenses had not been paid:

> I know you are busy and greatly troubled, and I don't want to add to your difficulties. You have been so especially good to me. But, please, what about the expense money?
> I used the earnings which you enabled me to make to pay off two life insurance policies. Like every other fool, I am trying for security in my old age. So that, so far as cash is concerned, I am no better off than if I had not been working in the U.S.A. this fall and winter.

Nothing much changed, however, and on February 25, 1938, she wrote to Peat:

> Your letter of February 19th was a disappointment. As a matter of fact, I had to go to the Bank and borrow money to pay the balance of the life insurance. I feel that it is unfair.
> I suffered enough in the making of the trip, and particularly in finishing it after a bout of 'Flu and with the House in session, without having to suffer financial embarrassment at the end. Carrying my financial worries is burden enough for me without sharing yours, though I did try to save you by taking the Challenger from San Francisco instead of the Overland, as routed.
> I do sympathize with you on having to face three cancelled tours on your returning home, and I know that your business is one of continual adjustments and irritations. But this is at least the third time that I have had to either take less money than our agreement gave me or wait for the money, or both.
> Even that would not bother me if I were positive that you were not just putting something over. I admire your initiative and energy, and very pleasing personality, but I am just never sure that you are not taking advantage of my integrity.

The next month she is clearly tired of the lecture circuit:

> Thank you very much for your letter of February 28th and the cheque for $500.00. It has meant a great deal to me, and if in my old age I can sit in comfort, you will have the satisfaction of knowing that your cheques of this last two years have paid up the pension policies which made it possible.
> I am glad you are angry at me for reflecting on your integrity. It reassures me.

I don't know what about this fall. I certainly cannot break into October here and there. These occasional speeches are just that. And four weeks, all told, is the outside limit. No more January speaking for me. I am still tired and am not really doing the work in the House that I should do. It is not fair to my constituency and I will not do it again.

Democracy needs the best we can give it, if we are going to save the thing. If we have another "war to save democracy" it will be a goner. The last one half did the job.[17]

Her speaking tours were immensely popular. The *Dallas Journal* called her a "sensation." The *Border Cities Star* said she was obviously the idol of young women and the admiration of old when she talked to the largest audience ever seen in the ballroom of Windsor's Prince Edward Hotel. People wrote flattering letters and she responded in spite of her busy life.

The following year doctors warned her that she had a "tired heart" and advised her to take a six-month rest, which she did not do. She cut out some activities, though, and did not renew her contract with Peat.

On the lawn of the Macphail home in Ceylon, 1935: left to right, Agnes' mother Henrietta Macphail; James Palmer; James' sister Helen; his aunt, Mrs. Harry Ramsdale; Sadie Ferris, the Macphails' house-keeper; and Agnes

Chapter XI
Approaching War
1937-1938

"By motoring seventy miles over skiddy roads," Agnes told her constituents in February 1937,

> I managed to catch the Sunday night train back to Ottawa. I think the Owen Sound-Toronto line must be about the last one in the province not having a Sunday night train. Wouldn't it be a good idea to do as is done from Huntsville down, eliminate the Monday morning train and run one Sunday night instead? . . . The train is so much safer and more comfortable in winter weather. I felt I was travelling de luxe when I got on the parlour car at Oro Station. The train doesn't whirl around on the ice, at any rate. The subject is very much on my mind, since I have to do the driving stunt again this Sunday. [Her mother was ill.]
>
> This week was pretty much devoted to a discussion of Canada's foreign policy, need of amendments to the B.N.A. Act and estimates. Mr. Woodsworth's resolution asked that Canada remain neutral in case of war, regardless of who the belligerents might be; that no profit be made out of supplying war munitions and materials and that the Canadian government should make every effort to discover and remove the causes of international friction. . . .
>
> Mr. King was in agreement with Mr. Woodsworth so far as the desire for peace was concerned, but he said he felt Canada should, in a world armed to the teeth, spend money on defence. But he assured the House that the estimates had not been framed with any thought of participation in European wars. The manufacture of munitions ought to be carefully watched in order to prevent exorbitant profits, but should not, Mr. King thought, be a publicly owned enterprise.
>
> He would not bind himself to a neutral position but would leave the decision to be made at the time by Parliament.
>
> As I pointed out later, unless we make very careful preparations for neutrality, no decision will be necessary — events will decide. "If we wait until the last moment to make our decision we shall not decide for neutrality because there will be the pull of the military caste, of sentimental imperial ties, and many other things influencing us. If, then, we are going to consider it, we should consider it now."
>
> I could not bring myself to agree with Mr. King's professed faith in the British government as a "peacifier.". . . While I have great faith in the masses of the British people, I have little or none in the ruling caste, and said that I could not feel they would consider what was good for Canada any more than they would consider what was good for the masses of the people of Great Britain. They were

activated by their own peculiar interests. Mr. King's speech made in Geneva in September was, I thought, a particularly courageous and clear-headed utterance. The one made in the House the other day was much more political in character.[1]

War and peace were the theme of her next letter too:

The very large increase in defence estimates threatens to be the most contentious matter which will come up this session. The Hon. Ian Mackenzie, Minister of National Defence, will shortly introduce estimates totalling over 33 million dollars, an increase of 16 millions.

The matter has not yet come before the House, but the Government, apparently anticipating opposition, has used every opportunity of creating a favorable atmosphere for them when they finally arrive. Several such have occurred this week. There was the continued debate on Mr. Woodsworth's neutrality resolution, Mr. Heap's suggesting that we ask Mr. Roosevelt to call a world conference and Mr. Douglas' motion suggesting that, in the event of another war involving Canada's active participation, every agency, financial, industrial, transportation or natural resources shall automatically be conscripted for the duration of such a war. Leading government members used each of these as an excuse for making strong, almost belligerent speeches in favor of the huge military expenditure.

Other prominent issues of the week were the Home Improvement Bill and another all-day discussion on the necessity of amending the B.N.A. Act. . . . I cannot believe that we are supposed always to be bound by the brains of the Fathers of Confederation. They had very excellent brains, and they used them in their day and generation; and I have no doubt they thought that we would do the same. I feel that if they came back today they would be thoroughly ashamed of us. I cannot have any respect for anyone who is still relying solely on the grandfather's brains. . . .

When the British North American Act was written, no provision was made for its amendment, so that in many things we are still bound by the thinking of wise and good men who lived many years ago, before the industrial age, and who could not possibly foresee the needs of this day.

Mr. Bennett assumed that the federal government had the power to enact legislation regulating hours of industry, establishing a weekly day of rest and determining minimum wages. But in a recent judgment in the Privy Council [of Great Britain], it was determined otherwise. Uniform legislation for all the provinces on these and many other matters is needed if there is not to be a constant shifting of labor to the provinces with the greatest security and of manufacturers to the provinces with the lowest costs. . . .

In my opinion, division of authority with lack of power on the part of the federal government, is doing more than anything else to make democracy ineffective in Canada. Unless the changed conditions of today are to be taken into account by the Privy Council to a degree that affects their decision, the B.N.A. Act must be amended. If the

*provinces have to carry the burden of the ever-increasing social legisla-
tion, then their right of taxation must be greatly increased. But even that
would not result in uniformity of social services over the whole
country. . . .*

*In debates touching on preparation for war all the old fears are
being revived — that Canada is not safe from Germany, from Japan
and I suppose from Russia. And phrases I thought never to hear again
are used repeatedly: "Preparedness brings peace," "Make the world
safe for democracy," and even that old boner "We must defend our
women and children."*

*The Right Hon. Ernest Lapointe made an impassioned speech, partly
in defence of the military estimates which were not before the House,
and partly in bitter criticism of Mr. Woodsworth's speech and attitude.
While on the one hand, Mr. Lapointe claimed that the increase in
defence estimates is intended for the defence of Canada only, at another
place he implied, if he did not say, that complete neutrality on Canada's
part would be equivalent to breaking from the Empire and the League.
They seemed to me two irreconcilable statements.*

*The Secretary of State, Mr. Rinfret, went further and confessed that
he was too good a Britisher to say that if any part of the Empire were
attacked Canada should not go to its aid.*

*A Social Crediter, Mr. Johnstone of Bow River, not to be outdone in
patriotism, expressed the view that Canada should have the biggest
army, the biggest navy and the biggest air force and yet keep them all
in Canada when the war breaks out. Most countries are content if they
excel in one of these fields, but we are to out-Britain Britain on the sea,
out-Russia Russia in the air and out-Germany Germany on the land.
After all that, surely we are safe in our beds.*

*Mr. Woodsworth, in closing the debate, urged us not to be deceived;
"Armaments mean war. . . ." Frankly, I am afraid of the influence the
coronation ceremonies may have on those Canadians who go to London
to represent the government.* [2]

In her next letter she told how upset she was that the flu would keep her from
addressing a peace meeting in Toronto and from attending several social engagements:

*Usually these articles are dictated in my office on Saturday morning
direct to the typewriter, or rather to a very efficient sec'y who manipu-
lates the typewriter. But this time the layout is entirely different. I am
lying comfortable in bed, just having finished a bowl of gruel, and am
now all set to talk onto the portable typewriter an article which promises
to be short and not very interesting. (I want to tell you the name of my
secretary and how she happens to be mine this session, but she won't
have it.)*

*The flu never passes me by. I have a fairly good dose of it and it
struck me at a most inconvenient time, causing me to miss the only
break so far in the monotony of the session. . . .*

*It's a bit of bad luck that the flu has caused me to cancel two of the
most interesting dinner engagements I have had this season. The Hon. T.*

A. Crerar and Mrs. Crerar are entertaining at dinner tonight at the Country Club for the Hon. Percy Pease, the Deputy Premier and Minister of Lands of Queensland, Australia and were good enough to invite me, and on Thursday (the day the chills and fever started), Mr. Fraser Elliott, Chief of the Income Tax Branch of the Department of National Revenue, and Mrs. Elliott, entertained in their beautiful new home, and I was one of the absent guests. (And a new dinner dress is still in its wrappings.)

But more serious is the cancellation of the emergency peace meeting, or at any rate my part in it, at the Uptown Theatre, Toronto, on Sunday afternoon. I do dislike not being able to keep my speaking engagements. I feel, possibly, an undue sense of responsibility about them. But unless the temperature becomes normal very rapidly, I will be in this same place tomorrow, rather than discussing "Do we want increased armaments in Canada" at the Uptown.[3]

As far as Agnes was concerned, "democratic socialism" was by far the best form of government. Trips to such countries as Denmark and Sweden served to strengthen this opinion. In a debate on housing policies in 1937, she said:

I want to take a few minutes to tell the House something about housing as I saw it in Sweden. . . . I was not able to be in Sweden as long as the honorable member for Greenwood (Mr. Massey) —

Mr. Martin: Were you there together?

Miss Macphail: No, nor at the same time, I am sorry to say. But I was very much struck by the housing enterprises, and spent a good deal of time seeing them. It is hardly believable that one third of the city of Stockholm has been rebuilt since 1921 as part of the tremendous building program by which Sweden sought to overcome the depression. That was a building program which in my opinion was carried on at the right time . . . some by federal assistance, some by municipalities entirely, and some by co-operatives. . . . housing in Stockholm is not particularly cheap; it is a difficult city for building. To begin with, it is built on fourteen islands; it is rocky; the cost of the numerous bridges and of the blasting necessary in making excavation makes it expensive and housing was too dear. That I think is one reason why they have developed such splendid cooperative schemes, because it is not so long ago that housing cost almost fifty per cent of the average income, which was much too high a proportion. This led to a great deal of investigation. . . . One thing I found very interesting was that they have houses for elderly people of slender means, started by what they call the flower fund. Instead of sending flowers to show respect at a time of bereavement, people send to the flower fund and with that fund apartment houses have been built for elderly couples. These apartments have a central dining room, and trained nurses in attendance. . . .

Then I went through some apartment houses built to accommodate five hundred families, who had three or more children. The federal government was anxious that children should not be raised in slums, with resulting ill health and juvenile delinquency. Working with a cooperative concern they built apartments for families of different sizes. Where the parents cannot support the children as the state thinks they should be supported, for a family of three . . . the federal government pays thirty per cent of the rent. If the family consists of four children the government supply forty per cent of the rent, and for families of five they supply fifty per cent. . . .

In Sweden over twenty-five per cent of all married women in Stockholm work outside the home. They have built houses designed for such families. In connection with the apartment house there is a nursery. . . . There are facilities to care for the children, sleeping rooms, play rooms and kitchen for the preparing of three meals daily for the children, and a trained nurse in attendance. The particular one that I visited had a central dining room, and a gymnasium which the families in the house could use not only as a gymnasium but also as a concert and lecture hall. . . .

We spent the better part of two days looking into the magic houses. Certainly they go up like magic; some of them, as far as the framework is concerned, are put up in almost a day. . . .

The corporation of Stockholm employed architects who designed many types of these cheaper houses. Then they prepared standardized material, and the workman who wanted such a house could start building it with practically no cash deposit. . . .

There were many things to show how proud they were of their houses. . . . Certainly they will never become slums; the pride of ownership will prevent that. I did not see any indication that there was not as much pride of ownership in the apartments, but there is something about walking out of your own door into your own garden that you cannot get in an apartment. But in their wisdom the Swedes have tried to fill this gap in the life of people who dwell in apartments. In both Denmark and Sweden, as a matter of fact, anyone living in an apartment can, if he wishes, have a garden plot on the outskirts of the city, with a garden house on the plot. They are really things of great beauty because roses grow very easily in both these countries. The garden house is often as pretty a little place as any summer house could be. Of course it is very small; it is intended only for holidays and Sundays, when the apartment dweller comes to enjoy his garden.

I did feel, after visiting Denmark and Sweden in particular, that in matters of housing and health, as in many other things, they were setting a pace for all other countries, and I think we have a great deal to learn from their experience.[4]

In a February letter to her riding she describes the Finance Minister:

Once, Charlie Dunning [Finance Minister] was the farmers' spokesman — the voice of the prairies — Western Canada personified. But Charles Avery Dunning, who, in correct morning attire, addressed the House for two hours and forty minutes in presenting the budget, was not the same man.

Thus, the change has been gradual, but constant. Today he is a man of the world; very able, as he was in those old days, but with the poise and assurance and a commanding presence in addition. Where once he argued, now he simply states. All this is discernible to the members and the crowds in the galleries as they listen to his powerful speech.

But to those who see, the change can be detected by the angle at which he wears his derby. No, not at a tilt; that would be defiance — tilting at windmills and all that. I mean an angle, the correct angle, with the carefully brushed hair out at either side; with just that smooth, well-groomed look that one sees where the princes of finance and industry gather; or, by the impressive white, voluminous scarf and the conservative, eminently correct, tailored overcoat. Not that he wore these in chambers, you know, but one sees leaders walking up the boulevard.

But I like Dunning. It's just that I'm telling you there have been two of them, and I liked the first one better. . . .

The week has held several enjoyable events. We heard Lena Madesin Phillips of New York City who is International President of Business and Professional Women of 24 countries. She addressed the local club here. She is a remarkably clever speaker, a woman of outstanding personality. It was a great joy to have a visit with her.

Then, too, the Cabinet Ministers' wives entertained on Wednesday, the one free evening of the week, in the Parliament Buildings, with dancing in the Railway Committee Room and refreshments served in the Speaker's quarters. Since this was the first such gathering in two years, it was particularly appreciated. I had a thoroughly good time and the others looked as if they were having just the same kind of a time.

On this day, I broadcast for the first time over an international linkup — Great Britain, Canada and the United States. Lady Astor speaks from England and Congressman Caroline O'Day from Washington, the subjects touched upon having been suggested by the sponsors. I hope I may not be so nervous that I gasp and splutter. Any broadcast is bad enough, but an international one will be frightful.[5]

In March 1937 she discusses changes in the Prime Minister:

Mr. King has gone to Washington to talk over common problems with the President. And to rest, in preparation for the herculean task of representing Canada at the coronation and the Imperial Conference. Since technical experts did not accompany him, the conversations with Mr. Roosevelt are likely to be general. . . .

The Prime Minister is tired. Since the exhaustion of a general campaign only sixteen months ago, he has, in addition to leading a government with a too numerous following (think of all the jobs all the members want for all the supporters) he has represented Canada at Geneva, engaged in conferences in Great Britain (think of the heavy luncheons, dinners and endless flow of polite conversation) and he has negotiated the Canadian-American trade treaty.

Does standing still make you tired? It does me. Yesterday I stood thru' three speeches in Montreal. Toward the end I began looking for the least hazardous direction in which to fall. But the professor stopped at exactly the right moment; putting my 160 pounds behind my elbows, I was able to reach fresh air in time.

But Mr. King, the Prime Minister, was required to stand, dressed in tight, gorgeous but undoubtedly uncomfortable Windsor uniform the day of the opening, through the interminable reading of the speech from the throne in our two languages. And on the following evening, when youth and beauty came to bow to Their Excellencies (I, possessing neither, was comfortably at home in bed), he actually stood for four hours, almost motionless, except for the slight swaying which showed his extreme fatigue, toward the end of the trying ordeal. I venture to say it was many days before Mr. King felt himself again. . . .

Government is becoming an increasing burden, and the leader of it should be spared wherever possible, particularly in non-essentials. I wish for Mr. King full restoration of his vitality. [6]

Another letter touches on her own personality:

Habit is an impelling force. We should carefully watch our thoughts, our acts, our habits. Habit becomes our master. If it's a good one, we are carried forward by the momentum of it to accomplish what without habit would have been an impossible task. Let me illustrate.

For years now I have been writing an article a week for the home papers. It was a tremendous effort, requiring preparation and a good deal of time. But week after week I ground them out — poor stuff, often. The habit grew. The work became easier, bringing each time a satisfaction to me. It completed the week, somehow. It became part of the fascinating, irritating and yet satisfying parliamentary life.

Unexpectedly, I was called home on Friday, on account of a worsening of my mother's condition. She has been seriously ill for months. I had done nothing at all on the weekly stint. In the haste of getting off, I asked my secretary to inform the editors that no copy would go forward this week. But I reckoned without the strength of a long-established habit. When I had spent some hours with my mother and found her free from pain, though extremely weak, had a consultation with the doctor, had shopped for the household, had established a second nurse, my mind reverted to the unfinished task of the week.

Habit was strong enough to carry me from the supper table in my home in Ceylon into an automobile, into the over-night train at Toronto, into a taxi which brought me to the door of the Parliament Buildings, on to my feet, to my desk this Monday morning, from where I now talk to you. [7]

Her next letters discuss a variety of topics: loan companies, luncheon invitations, long-distance flight:

March 25, 1937

The difficult years which we hope are behind us have been a harvest for small loan companies which arrange credit for people suffering from great financial stress. At least two of them have been before the House this session asking for changes in their charter. Both the House of Commons and the Senate have shown strong opposition to the rates charged. For instance, one company named a

2% rate per month which sounds easy but actually runs about 27% a year. Families that fall into the toils of such concerns must have the utmost difficulty in extricating themselves. . . .

I said I couldn't see how people who were unable to pay their debts without borrowing could pay them by borrowing from one of these companies and at the same time pay the additional moneys resulting from 27% interest. One of these companies had carried on a persistent lobby in favor of the bill, and that, I said, always made me suspicious. If the act was as good as they claimed it could rest on its own virtue. . . .

You will know how sometimes you will get several interesting invitations together; they sort of bunch up. This week was such a time to me. For the first time I went to dinner at Earnscliffe, the Ottawa home of the British High Commissioner, Sir Francis and Lady Floud. It was a particularly enjoyable event, the number being small enough to allow for general intermingling of the guests and unhurried enough to permit of conversation.

In the middle of the week, two professors from St. Lawrence University of Canton, New York, motored over, bringing with them ten students who are majoring in government. They came to see the Parliament of Canada functioning and to absorb as much as they could of the atmosphere. I was glad to be able to arrange a luncheon for them in the parliamentary restaurant and to see that they met several members. It's not a bad idea, which Canadian schools might well emulate. I said so to a professor from McGill who was calling on me and he cynically replied: "Not if you wish them to continue studying government."

The wife of the Speaker, Madame Casgrain, who, like Her Excellency Lady Floud, is a personality in her own right, gave a most enjoyable luncheon to a number of women — I should think thirty or more. . . . the table was beautiful with its masses of spring flowers in silver bowls and specially created service. Since the room faces out on the beautiful Gatineau country, the eye as well as the stomach feasted, and more important still, we were stimulated and encouraged by the flow of good talk, which showed that these women are thinking critically and constructively about current national and international matters.

Their Excellencies, Lord[8] and Lady Tweedsmuir, had arranged for a large tea early in the week, but on account of an epidemic of "flu" which laid low seven members of the Vice Regal group, it was postponed till Friday. I felt that Their Excellencies should have been thinking of themselves and having a slow convalescence rather than exhausting themselves with guests, and so many guests. They are delightful people, so intellectual and yet so human and friendly that I quite forgot myself and urged that they take rest and care after this dangerous flu; and all this as I made my curtsey in the line, which with me is never more than a badly executed bob.[9]

April 1, 1937

Morning sittings begin Wednesday, a clear indication we are hurrying to a close. Some optimistic souls think the House will rise about April 3rd, but that is impossible, unless the legislation still to be dealt with is thrown overboard. It might be possible to finish by the 10th, working mornings and Saturdays. Rumor in the lobbies has it that the Big Chief laid down the law to the Whips — either we finish by the 10th or we come back and swelter through July.

When Gerry McGeer was Mayor of Vancouver as well as member of the House of Commons, he flew back and forth between the Capital and our growing Western metropolis, but to do it he had to cross the international border and use American airships. Now he and Denton Massey, our other flying member, will soon be able to cross this great country of ours in Canadian airships.

Already one can fly from Ottawa to Montreal. But to ensure more extensive service, the Hon. C. D. Howe, Minister of Transport, has moved for the incorporation of a company to be known as the Trans-Canada Air Lines, which concern will have authority to establish and operate air lines and services across Canada. . . .

According to Mr. Howe, the corporation contemplated by this bill is to be organized as a private venture. It is not the intention of the government to own directly any stock in the corporation. The agency for organizing it is the Canadian National Railways. The C.N.R. will underwrite, in the first instance, the stock of this company and distribute it among firms at present engaged in aviation in Canada, which wish to participate. This company will fly only the main arteries of traffic across the country and such others as are designated by the government as being of national importance. It is not the intention to interfere with existing operations. . . .

The cost of operation of a coast-to-coast service is estimated at about a million a year. . . .

The Easter recess of one day was the shortest on record. But the brevity of the holidays was more than compensated for, for me, by pronounced improvement in my mother's condition, and by a very festive birthday. The member for North Grey, Mr. Telford, wished me many happy returns with carnations, the largest, spiciest and pinkest I've ever had (long may he reign!). Madame Casgrain, wife of the Speaker, sent quantities of mixed spring flowers. The gardener, whose mother's name was Macphail — what a lucky break — brought potted tulips and schizanthus. My secretary (who has a forgiving nature) expressed her good wishes in pansies. Due to the co-operation of the railway employees, some of all of these reached my mother fresh and beautiful.

Jean Francis Pouliot, often called the bad boy of the House, but my courteous and respected friend, gave me some very fine French perfume. Other friends catered to my weaknesses by giving me a pair of bracelets, cups and saucers, gloves, initialed handkerchiefs, a silver frame for Mrs. Black's picture, a carved trinket box (by the carver), a carved moose, books, cards and letters.

Who wouldn't have birthdays? [10]

On September 24, Agnes' mother, Henrietta Campbell Macphail, died in Ceylon at the age of seventy-three. True to the expectations of the day, Agnes, the unmarried daughter, looked after her in her last illness. Parliament had not sat since April and she cancelled a lecture tour.

In her youth Agnes had been impatient with her mother and more impressed by her father and grandmothers, but as she grew older she appreciated her mother's qualities. Still, a mother's efforts are often taken for granted, and after her mother's death Agnes mentioned suffering from "vain regrets."

In 1938 the Honeymoon Bridge across the Niagara River collapsed; the first Superman comic strip appeared; and Malton airport was opened in Toronto. Dr. Norman Bethune, the Owen Sound Collegiate classmate of Agnes, joined the Chinese Communist Army and formed the world's first mobile blood transfusion unit. On a questionnaire answered by students of Toronto secondary schools, Agnes Macphail, M.P., was voted the greatest Canadian woman. The third session of the Eighteenth Parliament ran from January 27 to July 1.

In February Agnes asked for pensions for soldiers' widows:

> *This morning I received a letter from the Durham District Veterans' Club setting out in detail the case of the widow of a returned soldier who died in the late summer. He had been getting a pension for himself and family of $85.75 and at his death this terminated. That widow and her two children — a boy and a girl aged nine and eight — are left without any income. The ex-soldiers in the town and district of Durham wrote me on behalf of this woman, and advanced the arguments which have already been presented to the committee.*
>
> *There is one other thing which as a woman I feel like saying for these women who cannot be here to speak for themselves; that is that they have had in many cases a particularly difficult life, caring for men who were ill. In this case the man had a leg amputated; he was in hospital twenty-five months afterwards and was never able to work. These women have a trying life taking care of perhaps ill and in many cases irritable patients. They have not the same chance of providing for their children, because so often the income is small. It is hard on a mother to see her children not getting all the advantages that she feels that under other circumstances they might have had. I have talked to so many women — or putting it the other way, so many have talked to me — about this particular problem of the strain on the nervous system of always living with a person whose nerves were shattered by an inhuman experience, the experience of war. The wives of these soldiers have themselves served their country in a way that is not easy, not in the field it is true but by being the person who provides the tenderness and understanding and home life for men who did serve in the theatre of war and have come back wrecks from that experience. And many who look well are still nervous wrecks. When the husband goes, these women face the new problem of not having anything with which to provide for their families. At least I think the department should have discretionary power, and where a mother is left with children and no way to provide for them she ought not to be asked to go on relief. We are*

not fair in asking that. Eventually I believe something will have to be done; so if eventually, why not begin now? [11]

During a debate on old-age pensions she asked again for help for the disabled:

> *I wish to speak briefly upon the needs of another class of Canadian, namely those who are totally disabled, and I am thinking particularly of people who are so crippled that they are unable to sit but must lie prone; of others who can sit but cannot walk; and yet others who can walk only a few steps. It may be that I have come in contact with more cases of this kind than most hon. members; in any event I have definitely come to the conclusion that they are people who need help, even more perhaps than the blind, because they suffer so much and have no hope of ever being able to provide for themselves. . . .*
>
> *In my constituency is a man who, when a boy, and still at public school, was afflicted with some rare disease which left him totally unable to walk, or as years went by, even to stand up. He is now in his forties, and most of the time since his youth he has been compelled to lie prone; he can scarcely feed himself. He is very intelligent.*
>
> *He lived with his aged mother who cared for him. At the age of eighty she died, before his eyes, of a heart attack; he, though seeing her, was unable to do anything except call for help, and help had hardly arrived before his mother was gone. Her death left him with no one to care for him. . . . he had lived in the village all his life — but the only thing that could be done was to take him to the hospital, which happened to be at Hamilton. I wanted to have him live in his own village, because I knew it was breaking his heart to have to go away; but I found that the amount which the municipality were willing to contribute for his support would not be supplemented if he remained in the village, but only if he was taken to hospital in Hamilton; I am not familiar with the institution but I believe it is a place for incurables. In the summer when in his home village he was put in a sort of bed which can be wheeled outside, left there during the day and wheeled inside in the evenings, so he spent his summers in the garden where his friends and neighbours called and talked with him. His case brought home to me what a cruel thing we had done to him although nobody intended to be cruel. From his public school days until the present time he has not been able to live anything that approaches a normal life; but in his own little cottage in his home village he really was happy; he had his radio; friends came in to read to him, talk to him and treat him in a human way. Then suddenly he is taken away, and as far as I can see — and I have tried to do everything I can — there seems no way of getting him home again. Last year some of his friends were able to take him home for a day or two, but it is not possible for him to remain there.*
>
> *I will cite another case in my constituency. This woman developed in her forties what seemed to be ordinary rheumatism and it got worse and worse. She is now over seventy and can neither sit nor stand, though she could live for many years. It was a progressive*

disease and each year she got worse. You can imagine how much it cost to care for a patient from some time in the forties to say the age of 72. This woman could now get an old age pension, but she lives on a farm. All this time she has suffered so much that one wonders how she can continue to live. Her stepson has taken care of her in a loving and admirable way. He has farmed the land and when he could afford it has kept help; when he cannot afford it he cares for her himself. She told me that she could apply for a pension; but she would have to sign away the farm on which they live, and she said that she could not have it taken away from her stepson, who has done so much for her. She therefore goes on suffering and hoping that the end will not be too long delayed. That has been her condition for many years. These happen to be personal friends of mine, but I am sure that hon. members can all call to mind similar cases.

On Saturday I got a letter from a young man in Quebec who says he is twenty-eight and for sixteen years has been unable to walk. His story is much the same; there is no one to take care of him and he does not know how in the world he is to be supported. There is no pension for him; he does not know where to go, and he wishes to know whether something can be done for him. . . .

I do not want to prolong the discussion. The need to act is clear to everyone. I was glad we did something for the blind; though it took us a long time we eventually got around to it. People who are totally incapacitated and are thereby denied the happiness of a normal life which the rest of us enjoy and who, moreover, often suffer excruciating pain, ought not as well to be worried by economic difficulties, and I submit that at the earliest possible date we ought to extend pensions to totally disabled persons.

People will ask where the money is to come from. Well, just recently I have been reading in the Star Weekly of Toronto the story of some of these birds of passage, rather wealthy birds who flit to the Bahamas. One of them is Mr. Harry Oakes, and he was justifying his flight on the ground that he might avoid taxes. I read that in the same island there was that eminent banker whom we all had the privilege of meeting in the banking committee many years ago, Sir Frederick Williams-Taylor. I read that Sir Herbert Holt also had gone to the Bahamas. If they care to go there it is all right with me; but at least I would see, if I were in the seats of the mighty, that they did not take with them all the great gifts which this country has so richly bestowed upon them, and that from such people income tax should be taken to such an increased extent as to afford large sums of money to be used in alleviating the suffering and mental distress of these our unfortunate fellow citizens. One should not become too perturbed at these newspaper articles; it is likely to cause high blood pressure; but if I did become agitated by such reading matter I would have been particularly violent when I read about these three men. This man, Harry Oakes, took the trouble to give an interview in which he defended himself. I thought he might have spared us that. I suggest that allowing these people of great means to avoid taxation

by going to the Bahamas or elsewhere is an affront to all hard
working and destitute Canadians, and I hope that something will be
done about them before very long. [12]

Many Canadians shared Agnes' negative opinion of "tax payers who escaped
their obligations" by going south. One, Clara McNeil Johnston of Rorketon,
Manitoba, wrote:

It is with considerable interest that we women of the West have
watched your career, and I have thought so many times, how quick
human nature is to condemn, but how slow to commend! While to
progressive minds throughout Canada, your name has always stood
for intelligence, high ideals and justice for the masses, it is only since
your recent denouncement of those wealthy tax-payers, who escape
their obligations by seeking a warmer clime, that I felt I must write
and congratulate you.

So few have the courage of their convictions. Those who do,
receive only contempt from the rich and no thanks from the poor.
How we cling to our chains! However, I suppose only the patient
work of educating the Nation to its needs, will ever bring about a
change of system. I am sure it must be a discouraging procedure,
especially in the face of present conditions with governments howling
for more armaments, and the whole world in danger of martial
conflagration. I am only sorry that the other female member of the
house does not entertain the same economic convictions as you do,
for what splendid results might be achieved with her co-operation.

Please allow me to tell you that we admire you for your fearless
attitude, your defence of the common people — and the fact that you
are a woman and have the fortitude to speak for us. Behind you, I
know, you have a vast body of Canadian women, who while they
make no demonstration of the fact, support you, silently, but with
sympathy, and a great hope for the future. [13]

R. B. Bennett announced his retirement in March of 1938, and "the House,"
said Agnes, "received the news with regret."

The House of Commons will suffer a severe loss when the Right
Hon. R. B. Bennett retires. [14] *His knowledge on all subjects coming*
before this body is phenomenal. In opposition he is helpful, many
times assisting cabinet ministers and often, too, frankly agreeing with
government policies, making no pretence of opposing for the sake of
opposition.

Mr. Bennett's dictatorial manner, when leader of the government,
and his failure to develop to the utmost, the capabilities of the mem-
bers of his party is, I think, rooted in his great abilities. He can do
each task so much more efficiently and with so much less irritation if
he does it himself; so he just does. He often reminds me of a very
efficient mother, who, because she can do things so much better than
her family, does all the work, to their detriment.

At his going, we will lose, too, the most colourful personality in
the House. He displays before our eyes the whole gamut of human

emotions according to his mood. In a happy mood, he teases and cajoles the House; again, he earnestly and forcefully builds a logical argument and where an impartial decision is needed, he can exhibit judicial qualities. But, when aroused, he can storm and rage as can none other.[15]

When he left Canada the following year to retire in England, Agnes wrote:

The Right Honorable R. B. Bennett has left us; the last honoring dinner has been eaten, the last speech made, the last flower-girl publicly kissed, the last hand clasped and the ship has borne him from our shores. We suffer a great loss; we in Parliament; we in Canada. Every day in this place we miss his unique ability, his inexhaustible store of knowledge, his smooth and easy flow of language, his vivid personality. It seems incredible, but Richard Bedford Bennett will rise in the House of Commons no more. . . .[16]

By March of 1938 the threat of war loomed large and Agnes wrote:

In Parliament — the Senate and the House of Commons — many matters have been talked of, numerous pieces of legislation advanced a stage, several committees have sat and in all offices the increasingly heavy routine business has been carried on. But wherever members meet — in lobbies, the corridors, the cafeteria — it was not of these they talked, but of the growing gravity of the European situation. The strain is felt by everyone. We live in an atmosphere of foreboding and, in the face of it, with millions dying in Asia and Europe and with the threat of even vaster destruction, efforts seem futile and our daily tasks insignificant.[17]

Insignificant or not, daily living was not all gloom. Agnes was a devoted aunt and enjoyed her three young nieces. The girls returned her affection. In a speech at the opening of the Agnes Macphail Public School in Scarborough, Lena Bailey McCracken reminisced:

The history books will refer to her as Agnes Macphail — first woman member of Parliament, but we remember her as Aunt Aggie who, when we lived on the farm, gave us rubber boots. We loved those boots so much that we took them to bed with us every night for two weeks.

We remember the birthday party when she rented a pony for us as a special treat. She was an excellent horsewoman herself and loved horses, but we were frightened and we all sat down and cried. Aunt Aggie was disgusted with us, particularly when the pony ran away. . . .

We remember Sui — her housekeeper during World War 2. Many of you are too young to remember that Canada's treatment of the Japanese-Canadians during World War 2 was nothing to be proud of. Sui was Japanese, but Aunt Aggie did not show the popular war hysteria. She and Sui shared a mutual trust and support for years. . . .

We remember Aunt Aggie as a person who gave of herself. She talked about her beliefs and she spent her life trying to achieve those beliefs. We remember her with a bit of awe, with respect, and with a great deal of love and pride.

On February 27, niece Jean Reany thanked Agnes for gifts she had sent her.

Thanks ever so much for the lovely bracelet and book. I'm sorry Jean [cousin Jean Bailey] lost her bracelet. She'll have to be careful of other things in future. We had our school concert on Thurs. and Fri. nights. I had to play the piano for the rhythm band I go[t] through it all right. I was in two choruses. The Saturday before last we went to a show in Port Elgin but just took on the show and I never noticed the name of it but it was real good with Jack Okee in it. Yesterday was so nice that Mother and I decided to go to Port Elgin. Next Saturday if nothing happens we're going to Dundalk [where Agnes' sister Lilly, Mrs. Hugh Bailey and her twin nieces, Jean and Lena lived]. I wrote to Lilla Belle today and I didn't know her address so I'm giving it to you. Will you please give it to her (would you like too) I hope we'll see you soon. [18]

In March and April all three nieces visited. On March 31 Agnes wrote:

I had the pleasure of having my sister, Mrs. W. M. Reany and niece Jean Reany of Southampton, visit me for a few days. From Jean's twelve-year old point of view, Parliament was pretty dull, but she found the birthday party [Agnes' forth-eighth] and gifts interesting, especially the birthday eve party, its cake with my name in frosting, 17 candles for my years in Parliament (how diplomatic!) and the sheiks who sang in costume "Happy Birthday to you." Jean enjoyed the great variety of "eats" and then slept like a top. Oh, to be 12 years old! The flowers are still beautiful. But nothing is more appreciated than the kind and affectionate letters from my friends in Grey Bruce. [19]

Early April was the twins' turn to visit and Agnes reported:

The week wasn't all work. Mr. and Mrs. Hugh Bailey (my sister Lilly) and their twin daughters, Jean and Lena of Dundalk, visited me. In a couple of days we crowded in sightseeing, entertainment, meeting parliamentary people, listening to debates, shopping and one show (Deanna Durban). The twins liked swimming in a luxurious pool at the Chateau Laurier a lot better than they did the debates. But their school teacher aunt saw that they acquired some knowledge of the set-up of government. [20]

Possibly because of her three nieces, Agnes was especially fond of little girls. In 1939 while talking on the CBC she related an experience with a parliamentarian and his young daughter. She used it to illustrate a point in her speech, the topic of which was, "How far can women help solve national problems?"

Just the other day I went into the reading room of the House of Commons and there encountered a delightful M.P., a lawyer, and his little nine-year-old daughter. . . . I said: "Where does she come in the family — the youngest?" He said: "No, the older — I have only

two children, a boy and a girl and the boy is the best." I was star-
tled and this in May, 1939. But controlling my countenance as well
as I could — a job I do badly — I said: "I am very fond of little
girls — they are my favourites." I wanted to save that child from a
scar she will carry for life. But the father wouldn't have it. He said
to his daughter: "You think the boy is best don't you?" And she
sullenly answered: "Yes." That story illustrates perfectly why women
don't have more confidence. . . . It is unforgivable. [21]

Chapter XII
Royal Visitors
1939

In 1939 King George VI and Queen Elizabeth visited Canada. The King unveiled the National War Memorial in Ottawa. On September 10 Canada declared war on Germany. The First Canadian Division landed in England before Christmas. The fourth session of the Eighteenth Parliament sat from January 12 to June 3, and the fifth session from September 7 to 13 for the purpose of declaring war.

On January 19, 1939, Agnes wrote:

> Parliament has been opened, the formalities observed, the brief sittings of an hour and a half one day and an hour the next concluded; but had I missed all the opening ceremonies, I would know that we are underway by the skirl of Tom Reid's pipes. Every evening after supper (dinner) the mood of the Scottish member for New Westminster pervades the corridors and courts in laments, fighting songs, or ballads of sentiment. It's a homecoming sound.

> The crowds for the opening seemed greater than usual. Even the space in the inner Senate lobby, formerly used by members who, tired of straining to hear the King's speech fell back there to visit with each other, was filled with women in evening dress, leaving only a narrow corridor through which the members could pass, to occupy the restricted space behind the bar of the Senate (brass bar). Just a little more crowding would eliminate the members.

> This year I had the same feeling of revulsion that I experienced at the opening in my first years here — richly gowned women, strapless, backless gowns, uniformed and bemedalled men, with the hierarchy in purple, chief justices in scarlet and ermine and, in short, the whole elaborate ceremony. It would be a lovely pageant if it were an expression of Canadian life. But it is too sharp a contrast to the struggling agriculturist, the industrial worker, the unemployed, the single transient. It makes one realize the truth of the statement that "one half of the world doesn't know how the other half lives."

> Couldn't something be done to have really representative Canadians attend the opening? By representative I mean farmers, industrial workers, teachers, unemployed, miners, senior students, clerical workers. The difficulty is that the same people come year after year; Ottawa people, civil servants, the official set. I would like to see one gallery set aside for Canadians who come from long distances and co-operation on the part of railways to enable people of small or non-existent means to attend. A young Alberta teacher, who was my guest last year, was thrilled by the spectacle. . . .

> Usually the speech is a forecast of legislation. This year it was that, augmented by long explanations of how well we have solved our agricultural and unemployment problems! rejoicings over the much

anticipated visit of Their Majesties, and the official visit paid by the President of the United States.

The speech expressed satisfaction that Canada is still friendly with all nations, but showed anxiety over aggressive policies which are disturbing every part of the world. And on this observation, it hangs increased appropriations for defence and the formation of a purchasing board for the defence services, "To ensure that, where private manufacture is necessary, the profits in connection with such are fair and reasonable." . . .

It seemed to me that at the first sitting there was a note, a clear note of sincerity and good will. Certainly the tributes to the two members who have died since the last session, Sam Jacobs of Montreal and David Beaubier of Brandon, were heartfelt and genuine. Both men were fine types and worthy of praise. Sam Jacobs was distinguished by his wisdom, broad sympathies and keen but kindly wit. His was a vivid spirit that will be long with us. I cherish the memory of my friendship with him.[1]

In her reply to the Speech from the Throne, peace-loving Agnes finally admitted that aggression had to be stopped. She said there was a growing conviction that we could not forever give other countries away.

All over the world, we are seeing liberty, freedom and personal security being swept away for thousands, yes even millions of people. We see democracy backing away before the onslaught of fascism. What surprises me more than anything else is the fact that the conscience of the world has been seared to such an extent that we can endure the tragedy of China, the betrayal of Czechoslovakia and the unparalleled agony of Spain without doing anything about it. We even see Great Britain and France, countries which we thought were great democracies, aiding the fascists to overthrow the Spanish government by means of the non-intervention pact. Quite apart from what was in our innermost hearts, we listened to the Prime Minister of Great Britain being lauded the world over in the name of peace, or this new word "appeasement," for having delivered democracy into the hands of the fascists in response to a gigantic bluff on the part of the greatest dictator of them all. In many countries we see thousands of people who are striving to get away from fascism, who want to be allowed to enter the free democracies. An Austrian woman who was my guest yesterday told me that the actions of the leaders in the fascist countries did not break the spirits of the people as much as did the indifference of the democratic peoples like ourselves.[2]

The plight of refugees was of increasing concern and Agnes kept her constituents informed:

The Austrian, Madame Anna, was a joy; an amazon of a woman, with an unquenchable spirit. Her husband was very rich. He stayed to save some treasures and lost his life; was killed by the Nazis. She escaped with her two daughters through Switzerland, just in time, and

*with them and others, is going to settle on Vancouver Island, to farm
and carry on handicrafts. In her little colony there will be both Jew
and Gentile; German, Austrian and Czechoslovakian. She loves
Canada. I am sure we all hope she may continue to. I felt an unusual kinship with her.[3]*

Again she wrote:

*Many have the feeling that these friends of democracy in Czecho-
slovakia, Austria and Sudentenland should find a refuge from persecution in the democracies of the world, and that we have a duty
toward them. Mr. Crerar, Minister of Immigration, made a statement
the other day that an unspecified number of Sudeten Germans, anti-
Nazi, would be admitted to Canada, regulated and carefully examined
before leaving the other side. Each family, averaging four, would
have $1500 on arrival, provided by British and French funds and
would be settled on suitable lands by the colonization department of
the Canadian railways. He said that 95% of them are Catholics; this,
possibly, to reassure Quebec.*

*Mr. Crerar's statement had to do with farmers only. I asked him
what provision was being made for the admission of scientists, musi-
cians and professors of note who did not come under the statement
he had just made. He said that in some cases, where the merit was
outstanding and it was felt that a contribution would be made to
Canada, the government gave permission to enter by Order-in-
Council. . . .[4]*

*The plight of refugees formed the greater part of the subject
matter in the address made by Mr. A. A. Heaps, one of the three
Jewish members in the House of Commons. He made a controlled
but moving appeal to the Canadian government to offer asylum to the
persecuted; not only for his own people. He said: "Never in the
history of mankind have human beings been treated so barbarously
as at the present time by fascist powers. . . . Families which have
been rooted for centuries in the land in which they lived had been
deprived and robbed of everything they possessed and ordered to
leave the country — their only crime being that their racial origin or
religious beliefs were distasteful to the powers, or their democratic
principles were unwelcome in totalitarian states. The pitiful plight of
these people has aroused international concern. . . . Canada has yet
to take her place with other democratic countries in showing her
sympathy in a practical manner.[5]*

In April, Agnes noted:

*All members and senators are having solicitations made to them
on behalf of refugees, particularly from those countries which the
dictators have recently swallowed. Some refugees are Jewish, others
are Christian anti-Nazi and anti-Fascist, both Catholic and Protes-
tant. The government has not had a liberal policy with regard to
these stricken people, although, through Mr. F. C. Blair, the Director
of Immigration, on whose recommendation apparently, the Minister,*

the Honorable Mr. Crerar, always acts, quite a number of highly educated or skilled people have been quietly admitted. But so few compared to the awful need. I had a note from Nellie McClung yesterday in which she says: "Agnes, this refugee problem is getting me down. . . . See the United Church Observer, March 15, the editorial. We must do something or be forever disgraced. . . ."

The Chairman of the Canadian National Committee on Refugees, G. Raymond Booth of Toronto, stated the other day that a million people are seeking sanctuary as a result of the activities of Hitler and Mussolini and he deplored the fact that Canada was doing nothing.[6]

Contracts were being awarded for the manufacture of armaments, and the government was being accused of "patronage, profit and possibly corruption" in connection with them. The Bren gun contract was hotly attacked in the House.

We have had a week of it! A week of guns — machine guns — Bren machine guns — "big guns!" They rat-a-tat-tatted, volley after volley all through the week, until one's head reeled. It was a fearful war, with attack and counter-attack. We are temporarily resting behind the lines but will move in again on Monday. . . .

The real issue in the controversy seems to be that the government has gone back on its former position of the manufacture of armaments under public ownership without profit, and has been inveigled into private manufacture, with patronage and profit, by the persuasive Major Hahn.

We have just had the most exciting debate of this Parliament. Such name calling, lava tempers, jeering and pounding of desks!

The attack on the government was well handled by Manion, MacNeil, Stevens, Douglas, Cahan, Coldwell, Massey, Homuth and others. They claimed that patronage had been the determining factor in awarding the Bren gun contract. They claimed that young Hugh Plaxton, M.P., had told the Prime Minister that a group of his friends were fully equipped to manufacture the Bren gun when they were not, and when two of them were his own brothers.

They claimed, further, that Plaxton toted around Major Hahn, the promoter of the idea, introducing him to the Dep. Min. of National Defence, LaFleche, and later to the Minister of National Defence, Mackenzie, procuring a letter of introduction for him from the Minister to the Canadian High Commissioner in London, Vincent Massey.

They claimed that pressure was brought to bear on the Prime Minister, in his capacity as Minister of External Affairs by the Department of National Defence, to induce him to sponsor Major Hahn in London by means of cabled instructions to Vincent Massey. (There is a possibility that the Prime Minister, personally, had little to do with the cable.)

They claimed that Major Hahn's plant (the John Inglis Company) was a broken-down boiler factory, closed two years, and that Hahn's experience as a washing machine and radio manufacturer did not qualify him to go into the field of precision steel, nor did his experience in liquidation commend him as a financial genius.

*They (the attackers) claimed that the British Government hung
back, not relishing dealing with an individual; wanting, rather, the
manufacture of the guns to be carried out in government-owned
plants in Canada, but, due to constant pressure from the Canadian
government, finally gave way and agreed to do business with Major
Hahn. They claimed that no other manufacturer was given a chance.*

*They claimed, too, that the contract, as signed, was a good one
for Hahn but not good for the Canadian government and that one
section of it provided for the payment of $20,000 expense money to
Major Hahn and his associates for preliminary work in obtaining this
very lucrative business for themselves — a four million dollar order.*

*The Hon. Ian Mackenzie was called careless, negligent, incom-
petent, improvident, incapable of his high office, and his resignation
was suggested.*

*No one could watch the Rt. Hon. Mackenzie King through this
very contentious debate and yet believe that he approved in his heart
of what had been done by the Minister of National Defence in regard
to this contract. He looked sad. He listened to every speech and he
certainly wasn't happy when Ian Mackenzie was speaking. (It was
nauseating.) It was only when the battering guns of the government
defence — Gardiner, Howe, Slaght, Bradette, Pouliot and particularly, Gerry McGeer — were turned on its critics that he relaxed and
smiled. His relief and almost enjoyment was especially noticeable
when Gerry McGeer was making his telling defence. Gerry has both
wit and weight and on this occasion he employed both in the service
of his party. Messrs King, Lapointe and Dunning, the big three,
smiled, waved and visited their thanks to Gerry; a great victory for
the monetary reformer.*

*After Colonel Drew's charge, in an article in Maclean's Maga-
zine, that there was patronage and profit and possibly corruption in
connection with the Bren gun contract, an inquiry was set up under
Mr. Justice Davis, one of the Supreme Court Judges. The investigation went on for weeks and finally Justice Davis made his report
based on the evidence. He made two principal findings: first, that
there was no evidence of corruption and, second, that a defence
purchasing board be established which would report to the Finance
Minister, or the Prime Minister.*

*The second recommendation does seem a clear inference that Mr.
Justice Davis was not satisfied with the manner in which the Defence
Department had handled the Bren gun contract.*

*He also stated: "It will be for those charged with the respon-
sibility of dealing with the facts (that is, the government and parliament) to examine and study them and take such action, if any, as
they may see fit." [7]*

Around this time the *Dundalk Herald* reprinted an article by Jessie Allen
Brown describing her first meeting with Agnes. The writer said she felt she
already knew her because she had heard her on the radio, had read her weekly
letters and her speeches in Hansard. She was surprised to find her such a good

looking woman and said her photos did not do her justice. Her eyes were most attractive — "large, dark brown and very much alive. They accent her greying hair most becomingly. She has developed into the very smart well-groomed type."

Brown said that both she and Agnes were students of Ralph Waldo Emerson. Emerson's essay on "Compensation" had been a definite influence in Brown's life, while his essay on "Self-Reliance" had been important to Agnes. "Somehow one would expect Miss Macphail to believe in self-reliance."

Agnes told her that "if she had the money she would like to provide a half-way house [for ex-prisoners] where those who could not find work could come and live and work until they found steady work outside." [8]

Agnes' long battle for prisoners' rights was bearing fruit. In her letter of March 16, 1939, she wrote:

> The Penitentiary Bill, providing for a commission of three to take charge of all penal institutions in Canada, passed the Commons, and is now in process of being passed by the Senate. You will recall that last year the Senate defeated a similar bill. Mr. Lapointe met with some difficulty when the lengthy measure was before the House, but it did not prove serious, and the Conservatives gave a good deal of support, which is important in view of Mr. Meighen's antagonism last year.
>
> The plan is that the new commission, which the Minister has promised, will be men of high calibre, will reform the penitentiary system along the lines laid down by the Royal Commission. They made eighty-eight definite recommendations which, when carried out, will give us a penal system which reforms as well as disciplines the anti-social members of society confined in prison. Almost all prisoners are released at some time, and it is necessary for the protection of society that they be turned from their destructive ways.
>
> The House was extremely gracious to me, all members joining in the applause when J. R. MacNicol, Conservative, Toronto, and Denton Massey paid tribute to my pioneering for prison reform. In acknowledging the tribute I said: "It is a triumph for democracy that the Hon. member for Davenport (Mr. MacNicol) and I should find ourselves in agreement. I can remember that many years ago, when we were both new in the House, the respect, regard and something close to affection which we now feel for each other, were conspicuously lacking [in 1933 he had accused her of sedition]; but through the years it may be we have changed and now we . . . are saying identical things on this great social problem. I do appreciate his kindness. . . . The kindness of the hon. member for Greenwood (Mr. Massey), is not so remarkable, since our friendship has been well known from the beginning. . . . [9]

Two weeks later the international situation was again the subject of her letter home:

> The international situation is the chief topic of conversation on Parliament Hill. It is in the background of everyone's thinking all the time. Yet it is seldom the subject of debate in the House of Commons. An exception to the rule of silence was made early in the week, when all the leaders made brief statements.

Agnes during her last years in Parliament

Mr. King, at the very beginning of his statement, said that he had been taken to task "for some guarded reference" made earlier on the European situation. This amused me very much for if Mackenzie King ever made anything but guarded references, I have unfortunately missed them.

The form and place of the latest disturbance in Europe was a surprise to him, the Prime Minister said. He called the capture of Czechoslovakia by Germany, wanton and forcible and said there were few countries which do not regret the fate of that gallant and vigorous nation, and still more the evidence that a great country does not honour its pledges.

In referring to Mr. Chamberlain's [10] speech at Birmingham, he repeated the questions posed there: "Was this the end of an old adventure or the beginning of a new; the last attack on a small state or the beginning of an attempt to dominate the world by force?" Neither Prime Minister ventured an answer. But, in response to Mr. Chamberlain's suggestion of a consultation with the members of the British Commonwealth, France and other powers, Mr. King said: "So far as Canada is concerned, the government is ready at any time to take part in such consideration, to join in consultation with the United Kingdom and such other countries as would be appropriate.

It is important to sift rumour from fact, to know whether trouble comes as a result of agitation and propaganda, or economic pressure, or of military force, the Prime Minister thought, and equally important to know exactly what policies are being suggested to meet the situation. . . .

"If there were a prospect of an aggressor launching an attack on Britain, with bombers raining death on London, I have no doubt what the decision of the Canadian people and Parliament would be. We would regard it as an act of aggression, menacing freedom in all parts of the British Commonwealth. If it were a case on the other hand of a dispute over trade or prestige in some far corner of the world, that would raise quite different considerations."

In concluding, Mr. King said that in spite of the shock to the world's confidence, there was no reason to despair of peace or to cease working for it, and he warned the totalitarian states that they could not win over the "limitless moral and material resources" that would be arrayed against them."

My personal concern over the international situation is great, but I cannot say that I am surprised by the recent action of Hitler. Before Munich, he had shown that his pledged word meant nothing to him and I could not then, nor since, understand people who trusted in his assurances. It seemed to me that the three aeroplane trips by Mr. Chamberlain to Germany to visit Hitler could have no other effect than to still further inflate his colossal ego. It was a psychological blunder and in addition, an economic one. We handed him the great fortifications of Czechoslovakia and the Skoda works on a silver platter. We speedily armed our enemies. I remember the Duchess of Athol saying on the day Chamberlain took his first flight: "Hitler will not stop until he reaches the Black Sea. . . ."

If all goes well, I will have been to Vancouver and back before this article, which has been written piecemeal in a very hectic day, is printed. I leave at ten o'clock tonight on the Good Will Flight of the Trans-Canada Airways. We expect to arrive in Vancouver at noon tomorrow and leave again on Sunday early evening. It seems impossible, but next week I will tell you about it. It is an exciting way to celebrate one's birthday.[11]

In April she flew to Vancouver:

This week we suffer from an embarrassment of riches. The trans-Canada flight, the Eastern Canada agricultural conference at Montreal, an outstanding debate on foreign policy, the completion of the trade agreements and the forecasting of new legislation. It is impossible to deal with it all. But we start with the flight.

Quite apart from the novelty of flying to Vancouver and back in an incredibly short space of time, the importance of it to Canada justifies putting it first. Once more space has been eliminated and the evolution of transportation has taken a stride forward. Some people still living will remember the whole transition: from foot travel to ox carts, stage coach, railway trains, automobile to airplane.

Mail service, trans Canada, has been in effect for some time, but the carrying of passengers started only on April 1st. In the week or two previous to that date, a number of goodwill flights were arranged by the Hon. C. D. Howe, Minister of Transport, to whom great credit is due in the initiation and administration of the service. People from the West Coast were brought to Ottawa and representatives of the Eastern provinces, the Parliament of Canada and the Press Gallery (no senators went) were flown to the Pacific, with civic receptions, broadcasts, interviews and photographs at both ends.

Only having been in the air (in an airplane) once before, I was anticipating with a great deal of pleasure and excitement the take-off at ten p.m., March 24th. But so many unforeseen incidents intervened — a busy day, a late birthday dinner, a delayed starting for the airdrome, a wrong turning (the roads have not yet been marked), doubtful driving between snowbanks at least ten feet high, an almost impossible turning of the car, a flat tire, a long run on foot to the main road again, the hailing of a car and final arrival — that I sank into the comfortable seat of the plane with my only sensation that of relief.

The take-off, when it came, brought joy to be above the snow, past all the bother of starting. Each time the plane takes to the air, one gets a sense of power, a lift to the spirit, comparable to driving a powerful car but much more so. While the ship taxies down the long run-way before it turns into the wind to be off there is a decidedly uncomfortable sensation of leaning too far backward, but as we leave the ground the tail comes up and we feel on even keel again.

Ottawa lay beneath us like a jewel. Gerry McGeer, Les Mutch and I, the three M.P.'s on board, looked for the Parliament Buildings, and there they were, a little cluster of lights in the black oasis of their lawns. Tommy Wayling and Evelyn Tufts, representing the Press Gallery, with us exclaimed over the beauty of the lighted Champlain Bridge and the Driveways. But, in a moment, the swift silver ship had swept us beyond the Capital City and, straight as the crow flies, we were on our way to Vancouver, a distance of 2,301 air miles.

Looking around the plane, I found that it was built very much like a bus, only narrower, one passenger to each seat, with a narrow aisle down the centre, with small racks above not sufficiently large to hold luggage or coats, but each passenger had a pocket on the wall, just like a door pocket in a car. The stewardess came around offering to wrap us up in lovely soft blankets. Our coats had all been put away on hangers in the stern or tail. She was a very attractive girl, with a French accent so slight that Mr. Mutch said to me, "It may be accent or it may be charm," and then to her: "How sick does one have to be to get attention?" Quite soberly she asked: "Are you sick?" She then gave us gum to chew. We were instructed to chew it when arising or coming down, to help the eardrums to adjust to the changing air pressure.

Then, before I am accustomed to it, we are at North Bay, where, unfortunately, we lose Commander Edwards, who is on his way to Toronto and pick up Mayor Day of Toronto, Ontario's representative, who proved to be a popular and interesting addition to the party. Everybody liked him.

A little sleep. The very comfortably padded chairs tilt to a reclining position. About 1.20 a.m. the stewardess gave us a light lunch: a tangerine, cheese sandwich and coffee. The coffee woke us all up. I recommended ovaltine for a middle-of-the-night drink. It was snowing and sleeting a bit and the wings and tail were coated, making it necessary to come down on the emergency landing field at Wagaming, for de-icing and refueling. And, after that, only two stops to Vancouver.

At Winnipeg, Mr. Les Mutch, M.P., was happy to see his wife and eleven-year-old daughter at the airport, at 4.20 a.m. our time. I had the pleasure of meeting them and being photographed with the Mutch family. There, in Leslie's stead, we picked up the Hon. John Bracken, Premier of Manitoba, who was perturbed that clouds between us and the earth prevented us seeing the checkerboard of the prairies. We never caught a glimpse of either Manitoba or Saskatchewan and the fog kept us from landing at Regina, which is the usual practice, but just before reaching Lethbridge we had a peek at Alberta and did not "sit down" again until we arrived at Vancouver's famed airport.

The air was very bumpy going over the mountains and to get out of it, the man at the controls climbed to 16,000 feet to cross the Selkirks, then dropped to 14,000 over the Coast Range. At such an elevation one does not move around. The head is giddy; the same effect as champagne the stewardess said; and one breathed consciously, not gaspingly nor uncomfortably, just breathing, and looking at the mountains is enough.

As we got near Vancouver, the lower air cleared and we saw below the magnificent panorama of the Fraser Valley. And then Vancouver, its green grass and spring flowers, and eager, friendly crowd to welcome us. It seemed impossible to believe that only fourteen hours before, we had left the winter and snow of Ottawa.

Well, first, soap and water, and lots of it. On landing, nothing interested us so much. Why should we have felt so travel-stained sailing through the clear upper air? We did, anyway, and our scrubbing delayed the civic luncheon.

By the time everyone present made a speech, on the wonders of the flight — the miracle flight as it was called — and the beauty of Vancouver, the excellence of their M.P.'s, especially Gerry, it was four o'clock and it felt as if by some misadventure we were back in the Commons again, hearing speeches and more speeches.

But no. We were going driving, through Stanley Park and following the luscious spring beauty along the sea; buying flowers at flower-stalls (daffodils, 3 dozen for 25¢), or having them given, seeing Chinatown, the marvelous C.N.-C.P. hotel and Gerry's magnificent City Hall. And then, to bed.

After a delightful Sunday, on which everyone was on his own, we left at ten minutes of seven in the evening and arrived at the airport at Ottawa the next day at twelve noon. The trip back was smoother and two hours shorter on account of the prevailing west winds assisting.

We spent the week-end in Vancouver without missing one sitting of the House of Commons. It doesn't sound possible, but we did it.

Three clear impressions. The complete trust the passengers had in the mere youths who piloted the planes. Youth is certainly at the controls in the air and if we can so completely trust the highly trained and very young in this element, why cannot we use their initiative, idealism and courage in the reconstruction of our social order. Youth wants to serve.

A truer idea of success is coming. High pay and shoddy work will no longer be good enough. The ground crews and the air crews will be judged on their perfect performance, their absolute integrity, and nothing less will be success.

Canadian unity will be served by this rapid transportation. The great distances which made one part of Canada seem foreign to another are wiped out. The amazement and delight which the French-Canadian Montreal alderman on our ship expressed repeatedly over the grandeur of British Columbia and Vancouver indicates the effect of Canadians seeing Canada. [12]

"Spring has come," said Agnes a month later,

that's by far the most important thing. If we weren't so civilized, we would quit working to enjoy the sun, just as we do when a loved and long-absent friend returns. But, no! We go about our various tasks, hurried and harassed with the stress of life. It's all wrong somehow.

We, the M.P.'s (who waste the taxpayers' money talking, à la McCullagh!), had a busy week, shut carefully away from the sun in a most luxurious prison.

The budget came down. . . . The budget speech is a highlight, possibly the highlight, of a session. But this year, when few tariff changes were anticipated, because of the three-way trade agreement between Canada, Great Britain and the United States, less so. And, with the great social burdens to be carried, much reduction in taxation was unlikely.

The interest of the members centred, then, on the Hon. Chas. Dunning who, as everyone knows, suffered a breakdown in health last summer. The preparing of the budget and the delivering of it require tremendous energy, and there was some anxiety lest it prove too great a strain. There need not have been. It was excellently done. Mr. Dunning is a distinguished man, who stands high in the regard of his colleagues. He is extremely able, hard working and his integrity is beyond question. But he is conservative in his outlook and he brought down a conservative budget.

The one surprise was encouragement held out to industry to make capital expenditures by way of enlarging plants, installing new machinery and equipment, and generally branching out. The encouragement takes the form of reduction in income tax equal in amount to ten per cent of the cost of the expansion. (If that doesn't beat you, when we now have plant and equipment sufficient to glut the market! Consumers with money is what we need.). . .

Mr. Dunning enunciated a great truth, which is not yet generally realized. It is: "If the people as a whole and business in particular will not spend, the government must. It is not a matter of choice but a sheer social necessity. The alternative is a greater burden of relief and greater dangers from deflationary sources. . . . We dare not, we cannot contract our expenditures until our industries and our people generally are spending more freely."

The day that the Hon. Ian Mackenzie made his speech on national defence I was preparing my script for the C.B.C. broadcast over a national hook-up on "Education in Rural Life" and it is perfectly amazing the amount of time one can spend on a twelve minute radio address. I did the script twice. After the first one I had an audition at the CBC studios which was heard by H. H. Hannam, G. C. Coote and Robert Anderson, the expert in charge. They laughed so much at my stilted language and I was so provoked and amused at myself that I reconstructed the whole business and so missed the Hon. Ian's address.

The defence vote is raised from 35 million last year to 63 million this year, and particular stress was laid on the air arm of defence. It was stated that there are 210 planes now with 109 to be delivered soon. Many of these are used only for training. Pilots for the Royal Air Force of Great Britain will receive training in Canada, particularly at Camp Borden and Trenton. In addition there will be a greatly expanded training scheme for Canadian forces. [13]

In the House on May 8 she urged Parliament to give Canada's surplus wheat to the hungry of the world:

> *It seems a sad thing to me that we should go on saying that we have a great surplus of wheat . . . and yet in a civilized country like Canada and in a fairly civilized world there are great numbers of people who are not getting enough to eat. . . .*
>
> *It may seem a wild idea, but why could not the government buy up a large quantity of wheat and go into the public ownership of at least one mill? They could then turn out a vast amount of flour and wheat products and these could be distributed to everyone in need, whether or not they were on relief. . . .*
>
> *Perhaps the Minister of Trade and Commerce will agree with me when I say that Canada has not begun to do her duty in taking care of the starving people throughout the world who are in their present condition because of their loyalty to democratic ideals. . . . Apparently all Canada has donated is dried cod fish — I knew the government was fairly dry — to the value of $10,000. We read of what has been done by countries the size of Sweden, Norway, Denmark and New Zealand, and yet we have done so little when wheat is bursting our granaries and elevators to such an extent that we do not know how to dispose of it.*
>
> *Surely Canada could give generously of her wheat. I do not think anyone will deny that this commodity is needed by refugees, not only children but adults, from Spain and many other countries. The burden being borne today by France is terrific. She is bearing a burden which should not rest entirely on her shoulders. Other countries, including Great Britain, are doing a great deal towards the care of refugees. Canada has great open spaces; we have more wheat than we know what to do with and I do not think we are doing what we ought to do. I feel that the government of Canada could and should send large quantities of wheat to help refugees wherever they may be found. There are tremendous numbers of men, women and children who are in refugee camps here and there all over the continent of Europe. It may be said that this would not make much difference, but it would make some difference. At any rate it would show that we have the spirit of helpfulness.*[14]

On May 13 during a debate on supply and national defence, Agnes warned Canadians to be wary of Nazi propaganda and said the Department of National Defence should "address itself with a good deal of vigour to the problem." She continued:

> *It was heartbreaking that we should have come again to a time when we must talk about spending large sums of money for defence. Just ten years ago now, in 1929, we thought there was a real chance that never again would we have to go through a bath of blood; that the world would never again act in such uncivilized and barbaric fashion. There was real hope we had done that for the last time. No one can discuss the question of Canada's defence and the situation in the world as it is today without wondering when we shall ever learn;*

without wondering whether, if we have another war — and it looks as though tha: is what we are preparing for — we shall be any wiser at the conclusion of it than we were when we wrote the treaty of Versailles. I have reached the point, as I think a great many others have, where I wonder how much we shall have to suffer before we learn that trying to eternally punish will not get us anywhere. If we had started being wise at the end of the last war, possibly we could have avoided spending the money that is about to be voted.

I should like to say how much I appreciated the speech of the hon. member for Vancouver North, who stressed a point which for a long time I have felt needed stressing, namely, that if we are going to address ourselves to the defence of Canada, it must be in co-operation with the United States. It is really ridiculous not frankly to admit it. We have common coastlines; and if we are going to defend the east coast and the west coast it is only reasonable to expect that it should be in cooperation with the other great nation sharing that coastline. Quite frankly, if we do have a real problem in Canada — for which I do not look — I think we shall have to rely on the United States and ourselves. . . . I do not believe Great Britain considers coming to our defence. A great many people would not agree with that, but I believe if the unhappy day of invasion ever comes, Great Britain will not come to our defence. As a matter of fact we could hardly expect her to defend the dominions, which are spread throughout the world.

If we are going to continue spending very large sums of money, such as $63,000,000 — and that is a great deal of money — I think we have to convince the people of Canada that this money is being spent wisely, carefully and perfectly honestly. . . .

I wish to stress for a moment the fact that it is but a form of hypocrisy to say that we want to defend Canada and at the same time allow powerful interests in this country to go on arming the nations against which we are preparing to defend ourselves. It is not honest; it is not sensible. Either we must stop sending munitions and materials to make munitions to the countries we fear, or look continually foolish to ourselves. . . .

The government has a very grave responsibility, and should be completely frank with parliament, or with a committee of parliament. It should be frank with the people of Canada and state whether it will follow British policy wherever it goes, spend the money of Canada and offer the lives of Canadians to defend British policy, or whether it intends to use the money to defend Canada's shores. Those are very different policies, and, as the hon. member of Vancouver North has said, it is high time we knew which one we are pursuing. [15]

It is hard to imagine today the impact of the visit of the King and Queen on Canadians in 1939. In those unsophisticated times kings and queens belonged in the realm of fairy tales and history books and to see a real king and queen, Canadians closed schools and businesses, got up at dawn, travelled hundreds of miles, waited hours by railway tracks and on curbsides to make this fleeting connection with history. That the visit was planned to strengthen Canadian and British ties in face of almost certain war mattered not at all when the magic moment came. Sophisticated or unworldly, sentimental or made of "Scotch granite" as Agnes Macphail claimed to be, Canadians quickly succumbed to the royal charm.

Agnes, of course, shared her "royal" experience with her constituents. Her letter of April stated:

> For a long time now we have been hearing and reading of the visit of Their Majesties, King George VI and Queen Elizabeth to Canada and the United States in May. In the last week the details of their four-day visit to Ottawa have been published in detail, when and where they would dine, the routes over which they would travel, when the National Monument would be unveiled, when the cornerstone of the new Supreme Court building would be laid by the Queen and on and on. But it was not until I received the official invitation to dinner where all members and senators and their wives (no mention of husbands) will have the great honor of meeting Their Majesties, that I really realized that Canada's King and Queen would be with us in three weeks.
>
> The terrible uncertainty of the European situation gave many of us a feeling that the visit might never come off, and with all this talk of German submarines off the coast of Labrador and the rumor of one appearing even in Halifax Harbour and the Dictator's fleet playing in the waters off the coast of Spain, that the visit probably shouldn't come off.
>
> However Hitler's birthday has gotten over our heads without the powers handing him Europe on a silver plate and Roosevelt has spoken wisely and decisively, so possibly we are in for a spell of quiet.
>
> But in my hand I hold an imposing card of invitation [to meet the King and Queen]. . . .
>
> Now the awful problem confronts us (by us I mean women) what sort of dress should we wear? Are there certain regulations regarding the dress to be worn? and if so who is to tell us of them? And how do I get my decorations from the safety vault in Flesherton? Only the owner can use the keys to the safety box and the Bank is so particular that you have to go with the Manager to see the box locked away and sign a statement as to the exact time it was done, even though there is nothing more valuable in the safety deposit box than insurance policies. Anyhow these Decorations must be gotten somehow. I have never worn them before and never expect to wear them again. This horrid infection in my ears and throat has left me so limp that I must conserve my energy for the every day tasks and these extraordinary social events in May. [16]

On May 18 she wrote:

> No one could charge that Parliament has not been busy. Committees sit morning and afternoon, the Commons morning, afternoon and evening, and even the Senate does two sittings a day. And the subjects before Parliament have been important; the Mortgage Bank,

wheat and more wheat, acreage bonus, national defence, as well as many odds and ends.

But through it all there is a feeling of distraction; a sense of expectation. The King and Queen are coming! Ottawa is working day and night to make the Capital beautiful. Miraculously, full grown trees appear where none were. Street car lines are torn up, new pavements put down, unsightly buildings demolished or screened with evergreens, acres of new sod laid, public buildings richly decorated and the routes over which Their Majesties will travel made gay with bunting, flags and banners.

It is almost an impossibility to decorate buildings as immense and beautiful in themselves as the Parliament Buildings, but a valiant attempt has been made by hanging a reproduction of the Imperial Crown, seventeen feet high, above the main entrance, and smaller copies of the King's Crown over the Commons entrance, and of the Queen's Crown over the Senate, the jewels being colored lights, and all three flanked by the flags of the Empire.

With our six invitations to formal functions, with prescribed attire, it is personal decorations that worry some M.P.'s. The other day a knot of Liberals who sit in the "rump" — the overflow to the left of the Speaker — were chatting and laughing as I passed behind the curtain near them. When I enquired what the joke was, one of them said: "We have just been downtown to the milliners buying Walter a silk hat to wear to the garden party." I said I would watch for him to see how he looked in it and they chorused: "That's why we are going."

A young Conservative M.P. rather shamefacedly said to me: "I got my first Prince Albert. I hope my county never hears of it." And a C.C.F.'er said he couldn't go to the dinner, although he had fought with the King's forces for four years, because he had not "tails" and didn't feel justified in buying them, with so much unemployment and misery to be alleviated. I suggested that he rent a suit, but he said he would never come to that. Another member of the C.C.F., who had been induced to order evening clothes for the dinner, says they make a fool of a man — the evening clothes.

Mrs. Black, who always dresses beautifully, is greatly concerned over the dress I am to wear to the most important function, the government dinner for the King and Queen. She had suggested that I go to Montreal on Saturday morning and when I came to my seat in the Commons that morning, she called across Mr. Woodsworth, who sits between us: "Why didn't you go to get your dress?" "I couldn't," I said. "National defence estimates on. Lunch at the Country Club with Rt. Hon. Geo. P. Graham and this everlasting newspaper article to do." Whereat Mrs. Black shook her head sadly and said: "You do take yourself seriously." Mr. Woodsworth pooh-poohed the idea of taking time off for such frivolity. But the question that haunts me is, what do I wear to dinner?[17]

Agnes told friends she was not going to spend money to get a new dress, but she did. "And," said a friend, "I recall it as being navy blue and very beautiful."

At last the great day arrived and Agnes wrote:

For three magic days the King and Queen of Canada lived in our midst. Their coming lifted the people out of their everyday humdrum lives to a pinnacle of rapture which had to be seen and sensed to be believed. Before Their Majesties came, one would not have thought that prosaic Canadians, and particularly cold and critical Ottawans, could lose their self-consciousness in a unity of acclaim but so it was. It looks as though the King's wish, that his visit may give Canadians a deeper sense of unity as a nation, will be realized.

Knowing that I was to have a close-up view of the King and Queen later I made no attempt to get near them during their eight mile drive from Island Park Station to Government House, but with a friend drove on the other side of the Canal along the beautiful Driveway, where again and again we got a clear view of the caval-cade. First came the red-coated, brass-helmeted dragoons on their spirited and beautiful horses, then the open coach, drawn by four horses, in which Their Majesties rode, followed by more dragoons and eight automobiles carrying high official dignitaries.

As they passed between densely packed lines of people, a cheer rippled along following rather than preceding the Royal carriage. It was as though the people were too intent on gazing on the radiant Queen and dignified King to cheer until they had passed.

That was Friday morning, May 19th.

At three o'clock of the same day the King came to meet his Canadian Parliament for the purpose of giving Royal Assent to seven Bills. After the dignitaries of state and church, the judiciary, senators and wives of parliamentarians, in formal attire, were seated "on the floor" of the Senate Chamber and the galleries filled, the King entered, dressed as a Field Marshal of his Empire, holding high the hand of his lovely Queen, as he escorted her to the throne dais. Then the King commanded the Gentleman Usher of the Black Rod to call the Commoners to his presence. We had been asked to be in our places a half hour early to await the call and at length we heard for the first time the words "His Majesty commands the Commoners. . . ." On the heels of the King's messenger, the Commoners eagerly left their Chamber, headed by Mr. Speaker, and, with more quiet and decorum than we have ever exhibited before, made our way to the Senate Chamber, where, standing behind the bar — the brass rail which separates the rabble, the Commoners, from the seated assem-bly — we heard the King's speech.

It was a good speech, clearly spoken, containing these three significant statements:

> *". . . the unity of the British Empire is no longer ex-pressed by the supremacy of the time-honored Parliament that sits at Westminster. It finds expression today in the free association of nations enjoying common principles of govern-ment, a common attachment to ideals of peace and freedom, and bound together by a common allegiance to the Crown.*

> *"It is my earnest hope that my present visit may give my Canadian people a deeper conception of their unity as a*

*nation. . . . I hope also that my visit to the United States will
help to maintain the very friendly relations between that great
country and the nations of the Commonwealth."*

The arrival of Their Majesties, and their departure, was accompanied by a great deal of military fanfare, booming of guns, representatives of Canadian forces in dress uniform, mounted escort and
so on, but what interested the Members and the privileged guests was
not these but the young man and woman who, with simple dignity,
rule over but do not govern the vast, spreading British Commonwealth of Nations. We packed ourselves in as closely as possible,
from the main door down the Hall of Fame, that we might come
close to the King and Queen as they were shown to their car by the
Prime Minister, Mr. Mackenzie King, and the leader of the Senate,
Monsieur Dandurand. There was quite a little wait; then, at the far
end of the great corridor, we saw them coming. And one said to
another, in a flurry, "Do we curtsy; do we bow?" But, almost at
once the whole assembly broke into the most fervent singing of "God
Save the King" I have ever heard, and as that lovely creature, the
Queen, bowed and smiled her way along, everyone forgot to do
anything but look.

It is hard to describe the beauty of the Queen. It is an inner
loveliness which radiates. She is warm-hearted and interested in
people and somehow she transmits her friendliness with even the
most regal bow. It is true that her complexion is beautiful, and her
eyes and her simply dressed hair. It is true that she has grace and
fine carriage. It is true that her clothes are perfect for her on every
occasion. But there is something more than all that; an elusive,
magnetic quality which breaks down all resistance, which wins all
hearts. It is this something which causes crowds to exclaim, "The
Queen, the Queen!"

Saturday was a packed day. The trooping of the color and the
laying of the corner stone of the Supreme Court building in the
morning, the Royal Garden Party at Rideau Hall in the afternoon
and the government dinner at the Chateau Laurier at night. The day
was surely perfect, blue sky, bright sun and yet cool air. It was the
King's birthday or, at any rate, the day celebrated as such, and the
traditional ceremony of the trooping of the King's colors was brilliantly carried out. I am no militarist. I never see the beauty of a
colorful uniform without seeing also the death and havoc of war. But
on this lovely day with thousands and thousands of people covering
every available inch of space on Parliament Hill, and the red-coated
soldiers doing their stuff with precision and grace to the music of
massed bands, it seemed only a good show put on for the King's
entertainment. This idea was emphasized when I heard that the King,
when not chatting with the commanding officer, hummed the airs as
the band played.

We had been warned that those of the invited guests wishing to
see the laying of the corner stone, which followed almost immediately
upon the trooping of the colour, must get through the main gates as

*quickly as possible and walk down Wellington Street, since there was
no chance of getting through. The first out was Mr. Speaker, the
Hon. Pierre Casgrain, and in fun he pompously marched ahead, with
Madame Casgrain, their daughter, Mr. and Mrs. Paul Martin and
myself following down the middle of the street. The crowd massed on
either side, joked with us, calling out: "Poor marching; pick it up
there"; and, on Madame Casgrain's side, to her utter confusion:
"Isn't she sweet?" But she is.*

*When we got to the site of the Supreme Court Building, I was
delighted to find that my seat was only a few feet from the stone
which was to be "laid"; actually lowered by pulleys; so I knew I
would have a very fine view of the proceedings. It was a simple
ceremony. Mr. Mackenzie King handed Her Majesty a trowel, which
the press called both gold and silver but which looked silver to me,
with which she spread cement over the base onto which the great
foundation stone was to be lowered by a workman operating from
above, after which the Queen tapped the foundation stone with her
trowel and declared it well and truly laid.*

*Then, escorted by the Prime Minister, Her Majesty walked to the
speaking desk, where a microphone was concealed, and made her
brief but beautifully phrased and clearly enunciated speech. [It was
the first time she spoke on radio.] It is said that after the speech was
handed to her, she wrote in with pen the sentence: "Perhaps it is not
inappropriate that this task should be performed by a woman, for
woman's position in civilized society has depended upon the growth
of law." By that brief sentence she made herself one with all woman-
kind.*

*I heard a great many people talking of the deep emotion they felt
on seeing Their Majesties — lump in the throat kind of thing. I
thought that the Scotch granite in my nature must be the cause of my
lack of emotion. But now a little scene was enacted which touched
the wells of my being. The Queen came to talk with the three workmen, there to assist in the laying of the corner stone; the one aloft, of
whom I spoke a moment ago, and two others who stood beside her.
The latter were Scots: ruddy, red-headed, obvious Scots. She shook
hands with them and chatted away for a few minutes, with complete
friendliness and no touch of condescension; then half turned toward
the King who was nearby, and he came to shake hands and enter
into the conversation. All this time, the workman up above, a French-
Canadian, was looking down sadly. The Queen caught the look and
beckoned him to come down, and when he started down the ladder
the crowd chorused: "Hurry up! Hurry up!" They did not want him
to miss his great moment. But there was no danger; the King and
Queen were waiting for him and when he came greeted him warmly
and talked with him in his native language. It was the democracy and
humanity of the scene that touched me.*

*5,000 people attended the garden party and five thousand more
could have, so far as room in the grounds is concerned. It was a
pretty sight; the stretches of lawn, broken by shrubberies, rockeries*

and stately trees, with the ladies' dresses making splashes of colour. The men were somber and correct in morning dress with silk toppers. Food was served in three large marquees, with a birthday cake — the King's birthday cake — in each. I was very interested in the birthday cakes and asked a lot of questions about them. Each weighed 300 pounds, was three stories high, topped by a replica of the Imperial Crown, and was decorated with the Rose, the Thistle, the Shamrock, the Leek and the Maple Leaf in white icing. On the huge bottom layer of each cake was a white model of the "Camperdown," the ship on which King George trained as a naval cadet. To my delight, one of the tiny ships about 14 inches long, a lovely thing, was given to me.

Their Majesties walked about the grounds, first together and then separately, meeting some and being seen by all. Part of my pleasure was spoiled by the unthinking people who tramped over flower beds and broke off hyacinths and tulips about to bloom. Such ill manners and lack of respect for other people's property I cannot understand. Other than the garden damage it was a perfect party.

We reluctantly got ourselves away from it with just time enough to dash home and get ourselves ready for the dinner; in my case hardly time enough; couldn't find enough hairpins, taxi waiting, fingers all thumbs getting acquainted with the new dress, putting on "yards" of new gloves. But I arrived in time, almost too excited to see at that moment the beauty of the great ball room in which the dinner was held.

Everybody was in a flutter, finding their place at the table, even though the elaborate plan was handed to us in book form on entering. Eight hundred is a big dinner. But at last I find I am sitting between Joe Bradette M.P., of Cochrane, and Dave Spence M.P., Toronto, while across are Sir Eugene and Lady Fiset and Mr. and Mrs. Pouliot. It was a friendly group and we fell into happy conversation. The half hour which we waited for the Royal party passed quickly. It was an unbelievable experience to be eating in the same room with the King and Queen, but it certainly did nothing to dampen the gaiety of the dinner.

When Mr. Mackenzie King arose and said that His Majesty wished us to be presented we cheered lustily and sang with vigour "God Save the King." There was a real family feeling at that great dinner. The Royal party left the ballroom to have their coffee in the drawing room and then the presentations took place.

I was thankful that my turn didn't come until at least halfway through. It was an awful moment when I heard Mr. Pereira call my name and I knew that the next moment I must curtsey to the King and shake hands at the same time; not an easy feat. But the great moment was made easier by the Prime Minister moving to the King's side and saying: "This is our first woman member." The King said: "Indeed," and smiled. I don't know what I did, but the next moment I was curtsying to the Queen and hearing her saying: "How many women are there in the Canadian Parliament?" I heard myself

*answering in a natural enough voice and felt that my smile was not
so frozen, possibly thawed by the warmth of hers, and I was backing,
safely enough, the five required steps.*

*Sunday morning I awoke and thought: "I can't go to the unveiling
of the national Memorial. I've got to broadcast and the script isn't
ready and, anyway, twenty years after a war is a silly time to be
putting up a national monument. Better to spend the money caring
for the veterans." So, in that frame of mind I worked two hours at
the broadcast. But the crowds poured past my apartment windows,
the bands played and I began to think that half a dozen blocks from
where I sat working an historic event was about to take place, and I
knew that if I could find it there was a reserved place for me. So I
set out.*

*This event drew by far the largest crowd. It is estimated that
100,000 people witnessed the ceremony from the ground, roofs,
window ledges, fire escapes, from every vantage point where a
foothold could be secured. It was a solemn, moving service, with the
King making the speech. It recalled the awful days of the war, the
brave marching away, the thin ranks returning, the sorrow and grief;
and the years since, with their trials for all of us, but especially for
the veterans. An unspoken prayer for peace could almost be heard.*

*When the King's speech, ending with the sentence: "Without
freedom there can be no enduring peace, and without peace no
enduring freedom" was concluded and the last hymn sung, followed
by "God Save the King," Their Majesties mingled among the veterans for more than half an hour, chatting and shaking hands. It was
an event without precedent. The officials were at a loss to know how
to handle it. At first they attempted to keep an advance guard ahead
of them, and the Governor General and Prime Minister tried to stay
nearby, but the pressure of the throng prevented and the only protection Their Majesties had was the affection in the hearts of those who
surrounded them, and they needed none other. Lord Tweedsmuir and
Mackenzie King were jostled rather badly getting to their cars but the
way opened before George and Elizabeth.*

*When I came from the Chateau Laurier, after broadcasting that
same night, into the same square, it was deserted. The Royal train
had gone.*[18]

Agnes with Ontario Premier Mitchell Hepburn at a United Farmers of Ontario picnic during WW II

Chapter XIII
The War Years and After
1939-1954

Parliament prorogued in June 1939, and Agnes told her constituents that everyone was glad that the fourth session of the Eighteenth Parliament

> *had passed into history. It was a long grind, starting on January 12 and lasting until the 3rd of June; almost five months, with only four days recess at Easter and one day for the Royal visit. To make matters worse we sat three times a day since the 11th of May, from eleven in the morning until eleven at night. We are accused of doing nothing but we worked hard at it. . . . And so we disperse to our homes all over this great country, without knowing whether or not we will have an election. The majority think we will. One press man has even the election date fixed for Monday, October 2nd.*[1]

There was no election, however, called for October. A more important event intervened. Prime Minister King called Parliament back on September 7 for the express purpose of declaring war on Germany, and all efforts were mobilized to put Canada on a war-time basis.

By January, 1940, King, disturbed by criticism of his war effort, decided to appeal to the country. On January 25 he called an election for Tuesday, March 26, "the first winter election since Sir John A Macdonald's time. This leaves little over seven weeks for campaigning and it will be difficult going especially in rural areas," said the *Durham Review*.

Angry, as were many parliamentarians, at the House being called and dissolved within hours without opportunity for question and criticism; angry, too, because a winter election meant difficult campaigning in Grey-Bruce, Agnes made the mistake of volubly criticizing Prime Minister King at a time when Canadians felt he should be supported.

At her nomination meeting she charged that King had "put his political career and his party before the unity of Canada." She claimed serious loss of liberties through the Defence of Canada Regulations, some sections of which she described as "Padlock Law made national."

She told the meeting that "Mackenzie King seized on [Ontario] Premier Hepburn's vote of censure on the government's prosecution of the war like the proverbial straw to afford an excuse to go to the country. . . . We had taken him as a leader of the country and he treated us like a cheap politician."

She stated her loyalty to Canada — "a Canadian I was born and a Canadian I will die. We are at war now and there is nothing to do but go through with it as efficiently and quickly as possible. We want equality of sacrifice. We don't want millionaires out of munitions or other war contracts. We want allowances for soldiers' dependents and we want a constructive policy at home to build a better democracy for those who are going overseas to fight."[2]

Her advertisement said that experience was now vital[3], but it still focussed on social issues when the war was Canada's first priority. Her Liberal opponent, Walter Harris, took full advantage of the fact.

A young Markdale lawyer, Harris was married to the former Grace Morrison, daughter of Agnes' old friend and mentor, J. J. Morrison of the UFO. In the past Grace had played the piano at many of Agnes' meetings. Now she was on the other side.

The Harris advertisement read:

I am soliciting your support in this election for the following reasons:

    A. *I believe the King Government has successfully administered the affairs of Canada and should be returned to office.*

    B. *I believe that the Canadian war effort has been magnificent. This united effort was only possible under the leadership of Mr. Mackenzie King, who recognized that his most important duty was to maintain the unity of Canada.*

    C. *I believe that the Government by the appointment of the Wartime Prices and Trade Board has effectively controlled prices and prevented profiteering, a lesson learned from the last war.*

    D. *I believe that if peace comes during the lifetime of this Parliament, as we hope it will, the Liberal Party offers the best means of re-establishing trade in Canada and promoting trade with other countries.*

    E. *I believe that Grey Bruce requires representation in Ottawa by a follower of the party which will undoubtedly form the Government of Canada.*

If you favor such a policy
If you wish the King Government returned
VOTE HARRIS [4]

"Vote Harris" was what electors did. Grey-Bruce went heavily Liberal as did the rest of the Dominion. Mackenzie King was returned to office with 184 out of 245 seats, the largest plurality ever accorded a Canadian Prime Minister.

Walter Harris received 1,689 more votes than Agnes Macphail and 1,507 more than Karl Knechtel.

"The large majority was a surprise to all," said the *Durham Review.*

Nearly everyone had predicted a close run — all three candidates being picked as leaders. By polling day, however, the condition of the roads had greatly lessened Miss Macphail's prospects as she depended very largely upon the rural vote. A surprisingly large vote was polled in the townships and everywhere the trend was to Harris. Even had the back roads been passable for cars, the UFO candidate could not have been elected, as the Liberal vote cut deeply into hers in most rural polls, while the towns and villages [except Markdale and Dundalk] slumped away from her. With good road conditions and a full rural vote out, Miss Macphail would most probably have finished second.

But how different would have been the result if the Bruce addition had not been made to the riding! In the South Grey part, the race was a tight one but Miss Macphail would have been elected with 3493, Mr. Knechtel just 78 behind with 3415 and Mr. Harris third, 315 behind with 3178. It was the bumper Liberal vote given Mr. Harris in Bruce towns and townships which accounted for his sweeping lead over both his opponents." [5]

Walter Harris, who defeated Agnes in the 1940
election

The *Saturday Night* prediction had come true — re-distribution had "scuttled" Miss Macphail. Two days after the election, the *Durham Review* analyzed Agnes' defeat and said that

> *while giving Mr. Harris full credit for his sweeping victory in this riding, many, both here and throughout the continent, regret the loss of Miss Agnes Macphail, for 14 years Canada's only woman member of the House of commons. During the 18 years she has represented this riding, she has given full-time service, her best services, and advertised South East Grey, latterly Grey-Bruce, nationwide. . . .*
>
> *What brought about her defeat after such a long tenure? There were several things. The winter election and snow-blocked roads were a factor, though not the deciding one. The main cause, as we see it, was that the electors, Dominion-wide, believed that Mackenzie King was doing his best for Canada in prosecuting the war; wanted his party's united effort, and said so by supporting his candidates. Miss Macphail alienated a considerable portion of her former Liberal supporters in this campaign by her bitter attacks upon the Prime Minister at all her meetings, and these, somewhat resentful, left her. Some electors considered her too much of a pacifist for a wartime Parliament; others thought that she had had a sufficiently long term as a representative — and another factor — she was up against the best Liberal organization in years and two energetic opponents. The combination was too much for her to overcome, but Miss Macphail is a good loser — her first such experience in six campaigns — and she is taking her defeat gracefully and uncomplainingly." [6]*

Graceful and uncomplaining she may have been in public, but the hurt was deep. In a CBC tape Wilfred Eggleston said that the defeat had been a bitter blow and there were tears in her eyes when she talked to his wife. [7]

She had not expected defeat, yet, strangely, her message to electors before the election seemed almost like the fabled swan's "last song":

> *My friends:*
>
> *Together for 18 years — 18 years this very month — we have done a unique job in the Parliament of Canada.*
>
> *Together we have carried on a successful experiment in genuine democracy; no party funds or party discipline has come between us. Without remuneration other than your satisfaction of enjoying the privileges of democratic citizenship, you have carried cheerfully and effectively the work of organizing the poll, the meetings (50 in this campaign), advancing our ideas in conversation with others, and the highly important job of getting the vote polled.*
>
> *It has been a brave and glorious adventure which has brought hope to countless people who live far from us. Many M.P.'s have said to me: "The people in your riding are remarkable; they don't have to be bought by jobs, promises and patronage." Grey Bruce gives me faith that the "better Canada" we envision (the Canada of security and the Good Life for all) can be achieved.*
>
> *Whatever I have been able to accomplish has been inspired by my*

pride in and gratitude to you, the electors of Grey Bruce.[8]

It was easier to blame defeat on winter conditions than the defection of friends, and Agnes reminded the *Durham Review* that when King had "told an astonished House of Commons that there would be a Dominion election in March," [she had] interrupted to prophesy that 'the roads would be piled up fence high.'"

Recalling the 1940 campaign, William Bierworth, then Secretary-Treasurer of Grey Bruce's UFO-Labor Association, said: "The back roads were not ploughed at that time. Joe Crutchley, President of the Association, and Agnes set out one afternoon to go to a little place called Vesta on the 12th concession of Brant. They drove their car on the highway to a mile north of Elmwood. I arranged for a man from Elmwood to take Joe in one horse and cutter. I took Agnes in another. I had a two-gallon container full of hot water to keep her feet warm." When they came to a particularly steep hill Agnes was worried that the horse would not make it, Bierworth said. When he not only made it, but "ran up the first half of the hill," Agnes was impressed.

The weather had never stopped Agnes. It had not stopped the horse. That it stopped voters was a fact she found hard to accept.

Many people expressed regret at her defeat. Andrew Hebb, editor and proprietor of *The Newmarket Era*, wrote:

> *My wife and I both heard with a real sense of disappointment of your defeat at the polls. We feel we have lost a representative in Parliament. I sometimes wish my mother (died in 1920) could have lived to know of your distinguished career in Parliament. A medical practitioner, starting out in 1898, she was often inclined to be a little contemptuous of this "world of men" and was very keen to see women taking a greater part in the affairs of government. She would have been delighted with all that you have done.*
>
> *Trusting that it will not be long before you are back in the saddle again. . . .*[9]

Dr. Minerva E. Reid said,

> *This is to let you know that I consider it a calamity for all the women of Canada that you are not returned as the member for Grey-Bruce. One hears this on every hand from both men and women.*
>
> *Do not be discouraged and do not decide any future courses too hastily.*
>
> *I have heard over and over again from members at Ottawa and from newspaper men that your statesmanlike behaviour during your years of public service have set a standard for all members of parliament to emulate.*
>
> *That is something for which the women of Canada should be grateful.*[10]

Alderman Adelaide H. Plumptre wrote:

> *I do not know of anything which caused me more regret than your defeat at the Polls yesterday. Although we are on different sides of politics, I, like many others, have admired the place you have made*

for yourself in political life and the ability which you have shown both in the House and outside.

Your defeat emphasizes the present landslide in women's public life everywhere. I never knew a time when, as it seems to me, women were more needed on public bodies, and when there was a more determined stand to oust them.

I have always hesitated to raise the women's party cry, and have always claimed that I represented both men and women in my Ward, but it does appear to me as if the women must more definitely work together if they are not to be entirely eliminated from public life. With all good wishes for whatever work you may decide to take up.[11]

From lawyer Margaret Hyndman:

I have seldom regretted an occasion for writing a letter as I regret this one. I am very sorry and disappointed that you will not be in the House of Commons and I am sure that there are thousands of women all over Canada who feel the same way. However, these be the fortunes of war and I hope that in the next election you will come back stronger than ever. I do not know whether I have ever said it to you (because being Scotch I find it hard to say complimentary things to my friends) but I have said it on the public platform and to other women hundreds of times: I think every Canadian woman owes you a debt of gratitude which can never be repaid because you have so conducted yourself as to make it easier for women members of Parliament who come after you. Never once have you asked, or left any room for anyone to say that you have asked, any quarter because you are a woman. That in itself is something of inestimable value to all of us.

When you get rested and have some time to spend I hope you will give me an opportunity to have a chat with you. And I hope it may be soon.[12]

And H. L. Keenleyside, Department of External Affairs, wrote:

While few of us were surprised by the general result of the recent election, I have spoken to no one who was not surprised and distressed by the report that you would not be a member of the next House of Commons. This feeling of regret and disappointment seems to be universal; and certainly, among us who can claim some small measure of your friendship, your absence will be very deeply regretted. My own hope is that the Prime Minister will accept certain advice that is being tendered to him and that you will shortly appear either in the Senate or as a member of the Penitentiaries Commission. Our choice, as a matter of fact, would be the latter, as Katherine and I both hope that your absence from the House of Commons will prove to be only temporary.[13]

Agnes had "no plans for the future," she told the *Durham Review*, but would not return to school teaching. She was sorry the people had rejected her after so many years. "I told the people the truth at all times," she said, "and they say the truth will make you free. Well it certainly set me free."

She had "loved every day" in the House of Commons and would recommend it as a career for any woman who had the mental and physical stamina to endure it. "To get a job and hold it," she said, "means that I must entirely alter my way of thinking. I must start thinking about Agnes Macphail." [14]

Agnes worked hard over the years in establishing farm co-operatives. Her enthusiasm and support were big factors in getting them underway, and she had served on the board of directors of several, including the First Co-operative Packers of Barrie and the United Farmers Co-operative Company.

It was natural, therefore, for her to turn to the co-operatives now that she desperately needed a job. She soon found that there was no place for her in the movement.

She ran in a by-election in Saskatoon for the United Reform Party. She lost to lawyer A. H. Bence, a Conservative. She applied for a job in the Federal Government. None was available. She had to content herself with activity in local co-ops and the CCF Party. She felt very much out of things.

After a year of no regular income she was hired by the *Globe and Mail* at fifty dollars a week to write a thrice-weekly column on agricultural topics. It ran from April 1941 until March 1942, a long time considering that she and the publisher had very different political views.

In 1942 she rejoined the CCF [15] at the request of its new provincial leader, E. B. Jolliffe. On June 11, 1943, she was nominated CCF candidate in York East and was subsequently elected to the Twenty-first Legislature of the Province of Ontario, now led by George Drew and the Conservatives. She and one other woman, Mrs. R. Lulock, shared the distinction of being the first female members elected to the Ontario Legislature.

The Legislature opened on February 22, 1944, and on March 2, Agnes rose "amidst warm applause" to make her first speech, in which she criticized Canada Packers for their excessive profits and said she did not wonder that the President couldn't read his own balance sheets. "They are difficult to understand." [16]

In 1945 the CCF was almost wiped out in Ontario, and Agnes was among those who lost her seat. She wrote to James Palmer who was overseas and described her "run of bad luck," which included a severe cerebral thrombosis: [17]

> *My intentions were good — but the flesh has been very weak. It seems hardly possible that anyone in this remote and safe Canada could have such a run of bad luck as I have had lately — yet this warm Sunday morning finds me comfortable and reasonably happy, so it isn't so bad. However I will be happier when you get home and I hope that it won't be long.*
>
> *A week ago today I was in Dundalk (for a few days) and was talking to your Mother, Father and Helen and they said you were of the opinion when they last heard from you that it would be some time before you were home. I am sorry to hear that. I thought your Mother was looking much better than when I saw her some time ago.*
>
> *Now for the bad, or hard luck story — in a few months; the house we live in (210 St. Clair) was sold making it necessary for us to move before or by Sept. 30. Suye left and we had to stop giving dinners; I took seriously ill — cerebral thrombosis — a clot of blood in the artery of the brain; and I was defeated in York East although I*

got as many votes as two years ago, and the CCF were almost wiped out in Ontario — 7 M.P.P.'s all from the north. Now what do you think of that for a run of luck?

On the asset column is the great joy that the artery held and I am getting well, although it is doubtful if I can ever again work hard; and the further joy that a dear friend (Robert Gardiner ex M.P. farm leader) who left this earthly scene left me a legacy of $7,000, and my life insurance, on which I have been paying for many years matured and brings in $50.00 a month for life or $9000 in cash and wisely or not I chose the monthly payment. But Darling how am I going to live on less than $1000 a year? The Dr. says I must not teach school, make speeches or do political organizing or anything that is a mental strain. He says I can work physically, but the catch is can I earn a living that way? You teach and I can keep house for you — but the cooking might be too much for you.

Drew's Gov. had a secret branch of police which spent all its time digging up dirt about the C.C.F. and giving it to Sanderson the Bug man to use in ads all on the taxpayers' money, and if they could find nothing making it up. One of the Constables, Rowe by name, came to me, because he lived in York East and told me about this and asked me to arrange to have him meet Jolliffe in some secret place — which I did — the Prince George Hotel and from then on I had nothing to do with it. Ted broke the story about 10 days before the election, the first minute that he had the proof complete and believe it or not everybody (well almost everybody) voted for Drew and elected him with 66 or 67 (I forget which) in a 90 seat house. I feel very discouraged over the people being fooled. Why cannot they see that big business isn't spending money like water for their, the people's benefit? So far as I see, great changes must be made in the social structure, but probably not until after or during another election.

Gertha says she is going to send all the unemployed across the road to Conservative M.P.P.'s next time. I pray God there will be no other and people are safe in the hands of big business. Time will tell.

Most people, including Agnes, thought that the cerebral thrombosis had ended her career in politics. For two years she followed doctors' orders, holidayed in Mexico and rested a good deal more than she enjoyed. She finally decided that life on the sidelines was not for her and said: "So I don't live long. I'll live what's left doing what I want to do." That meant a return to politics.

In June of 1948 she was elected CCF candidate for the second time in York East, this time with the largest vote ever polled by a provincial candidate in Ontario. She moved back to Toronto from Ceylon and lived for a time with Mrs. J. Rowe, widow of the policeman who had testified at the "secret police" commission. Later she bought a duplex in East York. "Gardiner's money bought the duplex," said James Palmer, "but with wartime restrictions still in effect she had to go to court to get into it."

Interviewed by Helen Beattie for the *Canadian Home Journal*, Agnes said that her principles had not changed over the years.

If anything, I have become more radical. But on small things I have changed. I wouldn't make a fuss about little things any more. At one time it worried me terribly that Parliament opened Thursday and settled down to business on Monday. Those days in between were to me an awful waste. Now I feel that if it is tradition it's O.K. by me. I'll just amuse myself over the weekend and wait until the boys are ready. If I had had as much sense at thirty-one as I have now, I never would have had a breakdown in health.

I realize too that there is nothing so powerful as an idea whose day has arrived. Timing is the thing! For example, right now we are passing through an age of social consciousness and many things are being accomplished now that could not have been done a generation ago — no matter how hard a person worked. Look at family allowances. The time for them had come, and even those who originally fought against them finally voted for them.

Agnes speaking in the Ontario Legislature

She thought women did not go into politics because they thought it unlady-like. But government suffered because "we are only governed by half the human family." She defended women, though, stating that they paid such a high price for human life that they had little energy left for politics.

"Of course, women are no good to fight for themselves. The very fact they slave so hard for their husbands and children proves that. . . . And they aren't loyal enough to each other. Men have learned loyalty to their fellow-men through the years. . . . When I hear women talking it appalls me. They worry about their children's schools, their friends and their clothes — but they haven't the foresight to try to do anything about the kind of world their children are going to live in." [18]

Agnes' speeches in the Legislature were often rambling and not the concise, powerful speeches which had mesmerized members in the federal house. The stroke had taken a toll. Once in a northern town while making a speech she became so upset and frustrated at not being able to express herself that she burst into tears.

Impatient with herself and others, she was described as a "caged lion" by a reporter who watched her stride restlessly back and forth while waiting her turn to speak.

Life was no longer the joyous adventure it once had been. She missed Ottawa. She missed having the health and money to do what she wanted to do. She missed family and friends who had died. And in September of 1948 she must have felt her own precarious mortality when her childhood friend, Bob Tucker, died suddenly in Paisley. She wrote to his widow:

> It is with a sad heart I write to you today. I did not hear of Bob's sudden death soon enough to be at his funeral; and being there wouldn't have done anyone any good.
>
> The Macphail sisters were very grieved last Sunday, which we all spent at Lilly's home (Mrs. Hugh Bailey) in the Kingsway. We all knew Bob so well and liked him so much. My sympathy goes out to you Viola and to the three children — although they were grown up they will sadly miss their devoted father.
>
> It is a joy to me to remember that we had such an enjoyable visit the day after last Thanksgiving; I remember the good lunch we had of cold turkey and Bob was so cheery and I thought I had never seen him looking better.
>
> As a nurse you would know that the serious attack he had quite a few years ago was apt to re-occur but that does not make it any easier for you. My love and sympathy goes out to you and I commend you to One who knows the why and wherefore of life as we do not.
>
> Should you stay in Paisley I will look you up if I happen to be up that way at all.

In October Thomas L. Kennedy succeeded George Drew as Conservative Premier of Ontario; Ted Jolliffe was CCF Leader of the Opposition and Farquhar Oliver was Leader of the Liberals.

The Legislature opened in February, 1949. Agnes continued to fight for the weak and oppressed, for the "ordinary" man and woman. She said: "My interest has been and is still — and will I think remain — the people, and the people least able to look out for themselves. I have never been interested in the powerful and the rich, because I think they get more than their share anyway, so I see no reason why I should bother about them."

She had seen a picture of men sleeping on a floor without blankets. "Many of those men were veterans of the Second World War. . . . When I saw that picture, and then went and saw again this line-up for the soup kitchens standing in the cold winds, waiting to get in, I suffered. I don't know what they were suffering — but I know I suffered. The Honorable Minister of Labour at Ottawa (Mr. Mitchell) said this was just 'seasonal unemployment.' Well, Mr. Speaker, that does not make the board any easier to lie on; that does not make them any warmer without a blanket. The difficulty is that we do not think about them as if they were ourselves." [19]

Fighting for higher pensions for teachers, she cited a seventy-five-year-old woman who had taught for forty years. Her salary for the first twenty years ranged from $250 to $900 a year; the second twenty years had started at $1,400 a year and remained at that rate. She had contributed to the support of her widowed invalid mother

> and had had heavy hospital expenses herself (in connection with her arthritis). She gets the magnificent pension of $57.94 a month. By the time she pays her board, which costs $50 a month, she has $7.94 for the amenities, the luxuries of life. She is a very foolish woman because she pays out 3.50 monthly in order that her burial expenses may be covered by insurance. I would not care about that — I would go out to a show and have a good dinner — eat, drink and be merry.
>
> I would like to quote one sentence from her letter which says: "I can only pray that when the summons comes, the call will be clear and swift." Well, that does not make me very happy or proud of Ontario with its boasted resources and well-fed people. [20]

She fought for improved prisons for women. "Naturally there is nothing like the number of women prisoners there is of men . . . [but] what I want is more attention put on the few women there are." [21]

She fought for the elimination of the means test for pensioners. "I have known cases where their pride is so great where people really needed the pensions greatly and yet would not apply for them because they thought it was accepting charity."

She fought for hospital insurance, civil marriages, bursaries for normal school students, equal pay for women.

On the latter subject she quoted "two or three of the funniest bits" of a *Maclean's* magazine article by Charlotte Whitton: [22]

> The best one is the last one, so maybe I had better read it so as to keep everybody cheered up. It is about men and women stuffing sausages in a packing plant, and Charlotte says: "And why a man draws 50 to 77 cents an hour stuffing sausages beside a woman who draws 40 to 53 cents, only the sausages can tell." . . . [23]
>
> Looking at this question simply from the point of view of justice . . . you could not argue against it — there is no argument. It is just custom, and the dominant group governing society. Sometimes I think it is a pity the men could not have the children; they could just have this world all to themselves. . . . They could have all the jobs and all the pay and all of everything.

Agnes during her years in the Ontario Legislature

It should not matter whether one had children to support. "I will think that argument has some meaning when bachelors are not paid as much as married men for doing similar work; when a man with five children gets higher wages for certain work than a man with one. That does not happen; they are paid for the work, and rightly; why should not women?"

The Honorable C. Daley, Minister of Labour, conceded that it had been a contentious issue for years and that "a lot of work in the industrial sphere could be done better by women than men." Agnes interrupted to ask if they got better pay for it.

Daley said the point had been made that Miss Macphail "got the same pay for work in the Legislature. From my own observations over the years, I would say that is probably wrong. Miss Macphail probably should get a little more than some of the men." Agnes said: "You and I agree on that."

Daley said "girls entered industry but tended to stay a shorter time than men." Agnes asked: "Do not men move around from one job to another?"

She thought it was a "disgrace to men that they [were] not willing that women should get the same pay for doing the same work." But some day we would realize that if work was well done, it would not matter if a person were "a man or a woman, white or black, yellow or brown, he or she [would] be paid for the work he or she [did]." [24]

The fall session of the 1951 Legislature was short. In October an election was called. Agnes was defeated along with all but two members of the CCF Party. Her "brave and glorious adventure" was over.

The last two years, however, had seen two of her greatest victories. The government had passed two bills for which she had fought: one the bill granting equal pay for equal work for men and women in Ontario — the other a bill granting old age pensions at age seventy without a means test and at sixty-five to sixty-nine with an eligibility test. She had helped found the Elizabeth Fry Society to rehabilitate female prisoners. John Foote, V.C., Minister of Reform Institutions and member for Durham, had sent her to West Virginia to see how a model reformatory at Alderston was run. [25] On her return she was asked to speak to a group of women, members of the First Unitarian Church on St. Clair Avenue in Toronto. Dorothy Dennison recalled the meeting.

> I was invited to attend one of their meetings around 1950 I believe, where Miss Agnes Macphail was to be guest speaker. I never missed a chance to hear Agnes speak, as ever since I was a girl in my teens when my father Isaac Bainbridge took me to hear this first Canadian woman member of Parliament speak I had been a great admirer of this beautiful, intelligent woman. . . .
>
> The meeting was held in the parsonage on Spadina Avenue, south of St. Clair near to Casa Loma. . . . There was a group of about 30 probably, women assembled to hear Miss Macphail. . . . She spoke movingly about the plight of women in the penal system and deplored the fact, that while there was a John Howard Society to take active interest in the lives of former male jail inmates, there was no corresponding group to help women convicts rehabilitate themselves. Then she suggested that the women's group take initiative in forming such a group! After much discussion several women were chosen to

further pursue the idea. As a result of this meeting the Elizabeth Fry Society was formed. [26]

In spite of her accomplishments, Agnes had no illusions about fame, recognizing it as "short-lived at best." In 1950 a letter was returned from Ottawa, stamped "Not known here."

At a memorial dinner for J. S. Woodsworth in Windsor in 1952, Agnes had another attack of cerebral thrombosis. She was in hospital in Windsor and then in Toronto for the next two months and never fully recovered. Her balance was not good and she was forced to use a cane. She was increasingly unhappy, restless and abrupt even with friends.

Her financial position was as poor as her health, and when the government finally passed a member's pension bill, she just missed qualifying because of time taken off for a previous illness. She did not have the money to buy her way into the plan.

Friends were shocked that she had little money. "The last time I talked to her, in 1950," said William Bierworth, "she told me she couldn't afford a refrigerator — she had an old half-size one." She had been too open-handed with others, including the government; she was a "generous spendthrift who had always had trouble making money spin out to do all she wanted to do." A guide at the federal Parliament buildings said that no one knew half of what she had done for those in need.

At the opening of Agnes Macphail Public School in Scarborough, Agnes' niece Lena McCracken said, "We remember her love of beautiful things. When she was a member of the provincial house, a gentleman gave her a very beautiful hand-carved wooden horse. She treasured it for many years but, in the last years of her life, she encountered financial difficulties. On the Christmas before she died, feeling that she could not afford a suitable gift, she gave the horse to my father along with a card that said, 'I can't afford to feed the old nag any longer.' It was a hard gift for my father to accept." [27]

E. B. Jolliffe said she was "disappointed she was not appointed to the Senate" as a senate appointment "would enable her to continue politically active without going through the elections forbidden by doctors." [28] She had often criticized the Senate, calling it a "nice club for nice people," and a "retiring chamber for people who want to rest." In 1925 she was quoted in the *Flesherton Advance* as saying: "I would lock the door and throw away the key. . . . And I don't know that I would care very much whether the dear old Senators were inside or not but perhaps it would be just as well to have them out. The Senate is just a house of refuge for worn out politicians." [29]

When she visited Ottawa the year before she died, illness had changed her so much that friends did not recognize her. But the old spirit sometimes flashed out, "I hope," she told them, "I do get into the Senate just long enough to make a motion to abolish it!" [30]

Ironically, many years before, she had become the first woman to be offered a seat in the Senate. On October 18, 1929, England's Privy Council had reversed the decision of Canada's Supreme Court and handed down the decision that the word "person" should include females — which meant that females were now qualified to become members of the Senate in Canada.

The government, no doubt tired of her constant criticism, had offered Agnes a vacant seat in the Senate at that time. The *Toronto Star Weekly* commented: "There are about 100,000 women in Canada who could meet the property qualifications necessary for a Senatorship. One of them — Agnes Macphail — declined the honor with the comment that she was more interested in the abolition of the Senate than in appointment to that body. . . . There is no record in recent years of anyone refusing a Senatorship."

When she had said that, Agnes was still only in her thirties, healthy, and at the height of her personal and political popularity. Now, with parents and many friends gone, health and finances poor, the concept of a reward for services rendered seemed not a bad idea. And there is no doubt if she had been appointed she would have rattled the elegant rafters of the Senate Chambers as they had never been rattled before.

Efforts *were* made to get her into the Senate near the end of her life but when she died in 1954 Prime Minister Louis St. Laurent was still "considering" the matter.

On Thursday, February 11, 1954, Agnes Macphail had a heart attack. She died in Toronto's Wellesley Hospital two days later, a few weeks short of her sixty-fourth birthday.

Tributes poured in from people in every walk of life. Old friend and political leader E. B. Jolliffe said that while she had returned to Grey County, everyone knew that now "she belonged to all Canada. . . .

"When we stood beside her grave, the swift driving snow was lashing the Grey County hills all around us and so fierce was the wind that the voice of the minister could scarcely be heard. Agnes had left the storm-troubled world in which she had done so much for peace and justice. . . .

"No one in the public life of Canada ever had a wider circle of real friends, and her acquaintances were legion. She had friends in prison and friends in high office, friends who were pacifists and friends who were professional soldiers. To her they were all human, all people, and she loved them for their mistakes and their weaknesses as much as for their more admirable qualities." [31]

The March, 1954, issue of the *Pathfinder* (published by men confined to federal prison at Prince Albert, Saskatchewan) wrote a column headed, "We Lost a Friend." It said in part, "On February 14 [*sic*], 1954, this woman whose life was the very embodiment of right and service and enlightened purpose passed to her reward. The man behind the bars lost his greatest benefactor and gained a patron saint.

"May you rest in peace, Agnes Macphail."

A column, identified only as written "by Joan," recalled Agnes' school days when as a "country kid . . . a young clever-faced girl in a prim black dress and big hair-ribbons," she had come up against the "maddening superiority of the urban students. . . .

"Then the young schoolma'am, lively, popular and fun-loving, who often danced until daylight and then went to school to teach all day, who had plenty of beaux and might have settled down happily, like hundreds of other young school teachers — except that she seemed to hear a call, one of those Highland Scot's 'second sight' calls."

She described the years in Parliament where Agnes fought mostly for unpopular causes, because when they became popular she felt she could hand it over to someone else.

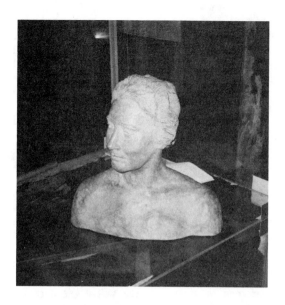

Bronze bust of Agnes, by Felix de Weldon, in the House of Commons

Agnes' grave in McNeill Cemetery, Priceville, Ontario

In conclusion the writer said, "But it is not as a fighter for decency and justice, not as a brilliant speaker nor an able politician that Agnes Campbell Macphail will be best remembered by those privileged to call her friend. She will be remembered as a woman, a real woman with a warm and generous heart, a side of her personality that some of her political opponents never saw. A woman who long ago put self in the background and buried deep in her heart those girlhood dreams . . . in order to aim for a shining goal that could only be reached by a rough and difficult path."[32]

Three funeral services were held for Agnes Macphail, the first on Monday, February 15, at Don Mills United Church where she had taught Sunday School for a time; the second the same evening at Richards Memorial Chapel in Flesherton; the third at St. Andrews Presbyterian Church, Priceville, the following day.

At the Priceville service, Reverend John Watt of Don Mills United Church said that Agnes Campbell Macphail had "returned with honour to the county in which she was born. . . . There had been little good social legislation in the past 30 years in which she had not had a considerable part. . . .

"When the score of her accomplishments is added up and compared with other political records, it will be found that there is no greater man or woman, and that there are few who have been as great. . . . She was a friend of the weak, champion of the underprivileged and a protector of the unfortunate."[33]

An editorial of the day said that "high purpose and sincerity of motives" were combined in Agnes Macphail "with a genuine talent for politics in such measure as to set her career apart." She was an "idealist" but with "practical talents" who had "performed exceedingly useful service through five Parliaments. She was a formidable critic, as three Prime Ministers and many cabinet ministers had found out. They listened to her with respect, and she left the imprint of her thinking and her personality upon many legislative measures. . . . She was never satisfied with the gratuitous distinction of being the first female Member of Parliament in Canadian history. As the House of Commons came to realize, she possessed the talent of compassion and the gift of human insight. In her death, Canada and Ontario lost an industrious servant of the public interest whose example elevated our political life."

In hospital, shortly before she died, Agnes filled in biographical information for the new Encyclopedia of Canada. An attached note says: "Filling out this form may well be the last thing Miss Macphail wrote as the paper was found and mailed to Mrs. Keith from the hospital two days after her death." The last item on the form asked for "Special honors, or other important facts." Agnes wrote: "No special honors except the love of the people which I value more than any other."[34]

Notes

Chapter I

1. *Durham Chronicle*, Obituary, February 18, 1953.

2. Agnes Macphail, "My Ain Folk," unpublished autobiography, written shortly before her death.

3. Agnes Macphail, "Women Pioneers of Proton," *Dundalk Herald*, December 1920 and January 1921.

4. Macphail, "My Ain Folk."

5. Kate I. Connolly, "Miss Agnes Macphail, M.P., Friend of Farm Women," *London Advertiser*, April 5, 1926.

6. Macphail, "My Ain Folk."

7 *Ibid.*

8. "From Milking Stool in Grey to Peacock Alley in Ottawa," *Toronto Daily Star*, October 7, 1921.

9. "Canada's First Woman M.P.," *Woodstock Daily Sentinel Review*, December 20, 1921.

10. Marion Wathen Fox, "Canada's Only Woman M.P.," *Family Herald and Weekly Star*, May 2, 1928.

11. *Ibid.*

12. Connolly, "Miss Agnes Macphail."

13. *Durham Review*, May 25, 1933. Reprinted from *Toronto Daily Globe*, "Under the Gallery Clock."

14. Archives, CBC, Toronto.

15. Ontario Hansard, April 5, 1950.

16. James Palmer, "Agnes Macphail — a Biographical Sketch," *The Quarterly*, McMaster University, January, 1936.

17. *Farmer's Sun*, letter to the editor, April 7, 1920. It seems likely that this is the letter which drew Agnes to the attention of Mr. Ross. In 1920 Agnes was teaching at Sharon, County of York. While she signs herself "A North York Teacher," she says in the letter that she is beginning her third year in York. Newspapers of the time also refer to her as a "North York Teacher" (*Woodstock Daily Sentinel Review*, December 20, 1921). Friend and protégé Farquhar Oliver, said: "The letter re teaching tenure is I believe correct, including the Wellington reference. I don't find it unusual that the letter referred to was signed this way" (rather than signing her own name). The letter reads:

> It is simply great to read the Farmer's Sun. I look for it with much the same feeling as one looks for a letter from home.

I want to talk about the letter of a Huron County Teacher. [The March 6th, 1920 issue contained a letter from this teacher complaining of the lot of a country teacher in rural boarding houses.] *I never taught in Huron, but I was 3 years in Bruce, one near Burgoyne and two at Kinloss. I was going to say that I was used as a daughter in both boarding houses, but I was in a way used better, because I hadn't the work and worry of the household but I reaped the benefits. The whole community in each case did everything to make me feel at home and Bruce County will always hold a big place in my mind and heart.*

I think a country teacher at 800. or 825. is better paid than most small town teachers.

Now you may think Bruce some extra special county but I supplied in Grey for 3 months, I taught in Wellington for 1 1/2 years and I am beginning my third year in York, and everywhere I have found the most delightful people and the most generous hospitality.

There are snags, I know, but they can be found in every walk in life. I find people give me credit for more wisdom, knowledge and goodness than I possess.

Huron County Teacher, if you want to have an appreciative section, a trustee board without peer, the most gracious P.S.I. I ever met, a home for $5. per and 30 normal, healthy, mischievous, good-hearted pupils, be my successor. Will you?

"A North York Teacher"

18. Marion Wathen Fox, "Canada's Only Woman M.P.," *Family Herald and Weekly Star*, May 2, 1928.

19. "Will Be No Coalition For Miss Macphail," *Toronto Star*, December 19, 1921.

20. "Ceylon Lady Declines Nominations For Commons," *Toronto Globe*, April 15, 1920.

21. "Altered Tariff of the States Aided Farmers," *Toronto Star*, December 3, 1920.

22. "Miss Macphail at Orono," *Dundalk Herald*, August 5, 1920, reprinted from the *Farmer's Sun*.

23. Marion Wathen Fox, "Canada's Only Woman M.P.," *Family Herald and Weekly Star*," May 2, 1928, reprinted from the *Durham Review*.

Chapter II

1. "Farmer-Labor Convention chooses Miss Agnes Macphail as the Candidate," *Durham Review*, July 14, 1921.

2. Marion Wathen Fox, "Canada's Only Woman M.P.," *Family Herald and Weekly Star*, May 2, 1928.

3. "A Farmer's Daughter in the Canadian Parliament," *St. Louis Post-Dispatch Daily Magazine*, June 10, 1929.

4. "Walter Hastie in South Grey," *Owen Sound Sun Times*, October 20, 1921.

5. "Canada's First Woman M.P. Tells How She Won Her Election Fight," *Toronto Star*, December 19, 1921.

6. "Agnes Macphail Would Return 'Dirty Money,'" *Owen Sound Sun Times*, November 1, 1921, reprinted from *Hanover Post*.

7. "UFO Directors Uphold Miss Macphail," the *Durham Review*, November 17, 1921.

8. Letter to the editor, *Durham Review*, November 28, 1921.

9. "Reply of Miss Macphail to John Cooper's Charge," *Owen Sound Sun Times*, November 15, 1921.

10. Marion Wathen Fox, "Canada's Only Woman M.P.," *Family Herald and Weekly Star*, May 2, 1928.

11. "Canada's First Woman M.P.," *Woodstock Daily Sentinel-Review*, December 20, 1921.

12. *Durham Review*, November 24, 1921.

13. "Women Pioneers of Proton," *Dundalk Herald*, December 1920 and January 1921, reprinted from the *Farmer's Sun*.

14. "A Farmer's Daughter in the Canadian Parliament," *St. Louis Post-Dispatch Daily Magazine*," June 10, 1921.

15. "Old Faces and New," *Toronto Globe*, December 7, 1921.

16. "Cleveland Saw Grey's Star Rise," *Beaver*, November 7, 1929.

17. "South Grey Elects Agnes C. Macphail," *Durham Review*, December 8, 1921.

18. "Notes and Analysis," *Durham Review*, December 8, 1921.

19. "Canada's First Woman M.P.," *Woodstock Daily Sentinel-Review*, December 20, 1921.

20. "Miss Macphail Pays Visit to Ottawa," *Durham Review*, February 2, 1922, reprinted from *Ottawa Journal*.

Chapter III

1. Hansard, March 1922. Welcoming speeches from colleagues in House.

2. James Palmer, "Agnes Macphail — a Biographical Sketch," *Quarterly*, McMaster University, January, 1936.

3. Thelma D. Williams, "Canada's Only Woman Member of the House of Commons," *Zontian* (Saint Paul Minnesota), 1929.

4. Arthur Hawkes, "Agnes Macphail's Geneva Gown," *Beaver*, November 7, 1929.

5. "A Farmer's Daughter in the Canadian Parliament," *St. Louis Post-Dispatch*

Daily Magazine, June 10, 1929.

6. "Page About People," *Toronto Star Weekly,* February 5, 1930.

7. "A Farmer's Daughter in the Canadian Parliament," *St. Louis Post-Dispatch Daily Magazine,* June 10, 1929.

8. Archives, CBC, Toronto

9. The *Toronto Star* said in its obituary: "Her fight for women's rights was probably her most abiding battle" ("Schedule Three Services for Agnes Macphail, M.P.," February 15, 1954). In Dundalk during her 1935 election campaign she told an audience of 300 women that "she never forgot that as the only member of her sex in Parliament she was and still is the 'torchbearer' of women" ("Miss MacPhail Spoke to Ladies," *Durham Review,* September 12, 1935).

10. Genevieve Lipsett-Skinner, "Montreal Paper Tells of Miss Macphail on Duty in Ottawa," the *Durham Review,* April 27, 1922, reprinted from the *Montreal Star.*

11. National Archives of Canada, Macphail files, letter dated May 4, 1922.

12. *Ottawa Evening Citizen,* editorial, April 6, 1922.

13. John McHugh, "Substitute for Party Rule Is Offered by Miss A. Macphail," *Boston Herald,* April 4, 1928.

14. *Ottawa Evening Citizen,* editorial, April 7, 1922.

15. Kate Connolly in her article in the *London Advertiser,* April 5, 1926, noted the titles of several books in Agnes' bookcase: *Tolstoy and His Politics,* A *History of Modern Europe* and *Co-operative Democracy.*

16. *Durham Review,* March 23, 1922. Reprinted from the *Ottawa Journal.*

17. A reporter once said she could talk on any subject from alfalfa hay to the gold standard and command rapt attention.

18. Sir James Matthew Barrie, 1860-1937, British author.

19. "Substitute for Party Rule Idea Is Offered by Miss A. Macphail," *Boston Herald,* April 4, 1928.

20. "Canada's Only Woman M.P.," *Family Herald and Weekly Star,* May 2, 1928.

21. Ed Ruthven, "Parliamentary Sketches, Miss Agnes C. Macphail," *Labor Advocate,* January, 1931.

22. *Flesherton Advance.*

23. "The Woman in Parliament," *Ontario Farmer,* Toronto, November 21, 1925.

24. "Maxine Lyons Brightly Relates Her Trip to Ottawa," *Durham Review,* February 19, 1925.

25. The topic of the essay was "Unemployment — Some Causes and Remedies."

26. Editorial, "Miss Macphail and China," *Toronto Sun,* April, 1927.

27. "Miss Macphail Stands by Her Letter," *Toronto Star*, April 13, 1927.

28. Hansard, 1927.

29. Dr. Sherwood Eddy, quoted in the *Globe*, March 5, 1923.

30. Hansard, 1927.

31. James Palmer, "Agnes Macphail — A Biographical Sketch," the *Quarterly*, McMaster University, January, 1936.

32. Archives, CBC, Toronto.

33. John Kidman.

34. "If the Nova Scotia miners are not Reds they have at least done their best," said Greg Clark in the *Toronto Daily Star*, July 4, 1923. Agnes herself was tired of the ridiculous accusation that she was Red and once shot back: "I'd rather be Red than yellow."

Chapter IV

1. *Flesherton Advance*, September 16, 1925.

2. *Durham Review*, January 14, 1926.

3. J. H. King, North Huron, was the other survivor.

4. Agnes corrected her opponent, Edwards, in a note to electors in the *Durham Review*, September 8, 1926. She said she had not had time to answer him in her allotted time during the nomination meeting. She wrote: "I favor as intensive an industrial development as is healthy for other classes in Ontario. I am always glad when factories are running full time, then I know the workers are busy and happy, and that Canadian citizens elsewhere are prosperous enough to buy the products of their labor. I know that the cheaper goods are, the more will be sold, and the busier the workers will be. I know high tariff makes dear goods."

5. F. G. Griffin, "How Aggie Did It," excerpts from the *Toronto Star Weekly*, November 14, 1925, reprinted with permission, *Toronto Star* Syndicate.

6. "From a Woman's Point of View," *Durham Review*, January 21, 1926, reprinted from the *Toronto Telegram*.

7. Julian Hedworth, George Byng, First Viscount Byng of Vimy, 1862-1935, British general; Governor-General of Canada 1921-1926.

8. "F. Oliver for Local House — Miss Macphail for Dominion," *Durham Review*, July 8, 1926.

9. "Who Will Oppose Miss Macphail?" *Durham Review*, July 22, 1926.

10. "Crowded Hall Hears Miss Macphail in Durham," *Durham Review*, September 2, 1926.

11. "Biggest Nomination Crowd Ever in Durham," *Durham Review*, September 9, 1926.

12. Her political creed was recorded in Hansard, June 29, 1926: "I have a political creed, and it may be of interest to the House to know what it is. I

believe we need a change in the form of government which will allow questions
to be debated on their merits, and in which the cabinet will be a committee of
the House. I believe in good will and the creation of a peace psychology to
replace war and militarism. I believe in social credit; I believe that humanitarian-
ism should be expressed in our social laws. I believe in the low tariff. I believe
in enabling laws for co-operation. I believe in electoral reform."

13. "Agnes Macphail Is Today a Busy Lady," *Toronto Evening Telegram*,
September 14, 1926.

14. "1722 Majority for Miss Agnes C. Macphail. Liberals Will Form New
Government," *Durham Review*, September 16, 1926.

15. "Farewell Gathering Ere Moving to Ceylon," *Durham Review*, November 24,
1926.

16. Hansard, April 6, 1927. Debate on naturalization of women. Under the
Canadian Citizenship Act of 1947, people born in Canada and immigrants who
chose naturalization became Canadian citizens. However women who had lost
their status when they married before 1947 remained non-citizens. Only in 1977
did Parliament amend the law to allow such women to regain their citizenship
and it is still not automatically restored. The woman must apply to get it back.
There are still women in Canada who may not even realize they are stateless.

17. Hansard, April 9, 1927. Debate on cadet training. The following year, Brady
invited Agnes to go with him to the Royal Military College in Kingston so that
he could change her feelings toward the military. In her weekly letter Agnes
quoted "a rhymster in the Press Gallery":

> *Come visit the nest of the blue-blooded snobs;*
> *And treat them to some of your pacifist sobs;*
> *Let's take a day off and consort with the nobs,*
> *Says Jim Brady to Agnes Macphail.*
>
> *If you'll come down to the RMC*
> *And take a toddle around with me,*
> *You'll be fair astounded at what you see,*
> *Says Jim Brady to Agnes Macphail.*

(Two of several verses.)

18. Hansard, April 28, 1928. Debate on annual financial statement of Minister of
Finance.

19. Dunning was Minister of Canals and Railways at this time.

20. *Hanover Post*, March 15, 1928, reprinted from *Saturday Night* editorial.

21. In 1929 Agnes told the Erie County Women Voters of Buffalo during an
armistice day speech that President Coolidge had urged increased armaments, thus
weakening the effect of the Briand-Kellogg Pact, which had condemned war and
agreed to the peaceful settlement of international differences. She said: "As a
Canadian I feel that the whole world owes a debt of gratitude to the country that
produced a Woodrow Wilson. We never could understand why his own nation
did not back him up in his great idealistic dream of world co-operation. Mr.

Kellogg is another like Wilson — a splendid man. But we cannot see how the same country that produced a Wilson and a Kellogg could produce a Coolidge".

22. F. E. W. Bright, "She's the Only Woman in Canada's Parliament," *Detroit News*, 1928.

23. "Crowd Hears Woman M.P. Preach Pacifism," *Border Cities Star*, Windsor, Ontario, February 1, 1928.

24. Hansard, March 26, 1928. Debate on international peace.

25. *Ibid.*, March 28, 1928.

26. "The First Woman in Ottawa," *Alberta Labor News*, February 23, 1929.

27. Excerpt from weekly letter, *Durham Review*, January 31, 1929.

28. *Ibid.*, *Flesherton Advance*, February 27, 1929.

29. Debate on international peace and the Kellogg Pact, Hansard, February 19, 1929.

30. Paraphrase of Lord Byron's *Childe Harold's Pilgrimage*, Canto 31, stanza 21:

> *There was a sound of revelry by night,*
> *And Belgium's capital had gathered then,*
> *Her beauty and her chivalry, and bright*
> *The lamps shone o'er fair women and brave men.*

31. Excerpt from weekly letter, *Flesherton Advance*, March 6, 1929.

32. *Ibid.*, *Durham Review*, April 18, 1929.

33. Sir Robert Laird Borden, 1854-1937. Prime Minister of Canada from 1911 to 1920.

34. Excerpt from weekly letter, *Durham Review*, April 25, 1929.

35. Debate on the budget, Hansard, March 19, 1929.

36. The little red schoolhouse made famous by the poem "Mary had a little lamb" was restored and moved to Greenfield Village in Dearborn, Michigan, by Henry Ford. The small book, available in the village inn, tells of how the lamb was abandoned by its mother and how Mary (Sawyer) looked after it. She took it to school one day on the suggestion of her brother and hid it under her desk wrapped in a striped blanket. The teacher, Miss Polly Kimball, discovered the lamb. Everyone enjoyed the story, which spread through the area. Mary lived to be eighty-three and often told the story at gatherings in the area.

37. Weekly Letter, "Entertained by Detroit's Own Henry Ford," *Durham Review*, April 29, 1929.

38. Debate on domicile in divorce, Hansard, May 7, 1929.

39. Excerpt from weekly letter, *Durham Review*, May 9, 1929.

40. *Ibid.*, May 16, 1929.

41. Excerpt from weekly letter, *Durham Review*, July 16, 1929.

42. William Howard Taft, 1857-1930, President of the United States, 1909-1913; Chief Justice of the United States, 1921-1930.

43. William Jennings Bryan, 1860-1925, American political leader noted for his oratory.

44. Excerpt from weekly letter, *Durham Review*, August 1, 1929.

45. *Ibid.*, 1929.

46. Excerpt from weekly letter, *Durham Review*, August 15, 1929.

Chapter V

1. *Ibid.*, August 15, 1929.

2. Excerpt from weekly letter, *Flesherton Advance*, September 4, 1929.

3. *Ibid.*, September 18, 1929.

4. James Ramsay Macdonald, 1866-1937, British statesman. Founded Labour Party. First Labour Prime Minister, 1924. Premier of 2nd Labour Cabinet in 1929.

5. Gustav Stresemann, 1878-1929. German Chancellor, 1923, and Foreign Minister 1923-1929. Shared Nobel Prize with Briand in 1926.

6. Aristide Briand, 1862-1932. French statesman; ten times premier of France. Foreign Minister, 1925-1932. Chief architect of Locarno Pact and Kellogg-Briand Pact.

7. Arthur Henderson, British Labour statesman, 1863-1935. Nobel Peace Prize, 1934.

8. Excerpt from weekly letter, *Durham Review*, September 11, 1929.

9. Fridtjof Nansen, 1861-1930, Norwegian statesman. Nobel Peace Prize, 1922.

10. Excerpt from weekly letter, *Durham Review*, September 19, 1929.

11. *Ibid.*, October 3, 1929.

12. During the Second World War, Whittaker was forced to flee France, leaving all his possessions behind, when the Germans invaded the country. Back in Canada he and Agnes visited their friend Bob Tucker in Paisley. Whittaker and Tucker had not met since their service together in the First World War. Whittaker threw his arms around his friend and kissed him on both cheeks, much to Agnes' amusement.

13. William Ewart Gladstone, 1809-1898, British statesman, Liberal Party. Prime Minister four times; noted orator.

14. William Pitt, 1708-1778, English statesman, head of coalition government in 1757. Known as the Great Commoner. His son William (1759-1806) was Prime Minister 1783-1801. Established general elections.

15. Sir Robert Peel, 1788-1850, English statesman. Twice Prime Minister of Great Britain.

16. Excerpt from weekly letter, *Durham Review*, October 10, 1929.

17. "Agnes Macphail's Geneva Gown," *Beaver*, November 7, 1929.

18. "Canada's Only Woman Member of the House of Commons," *Zontian* (Saint Paul, Minnesota), 1929, reprinted from the *London News*.

19. Dorothea Price Hughes, "The Dawn of a New Era in the League of Nations," reprinted from *New Outlook*, official organ of the United Church of Canada. "Made Impression at Geneva," *Durham Review*, October 17, 1929.

20. "Cleveland Saw Grey's Star Rise," *Beaver*, November 7, 1929.

Chapter VI

1. Agnes Macphail, "Go Home, Young Woman? Ha! Ha!" *Chatelaine*, 1929.

2. "Well Known Auctioneer Receives Last Call," *Durham Review*, January 23, 1930.

3. National Archives of Canada, Macphail files.

4. Two valentines were typed on plain paper and signed "Your Valentine." The signatures were typed in the same distinctive way. The first is undated, the second is dated February 14, 1946.

To Miss Agnes Macphail, M.P.

Oh "isolationist," fair Agnes sweet,
However can a swain sit at your feet
If "isolated" you are to remain? —
'Twill drive admirers mad, yes, quite insane.

Restrain your "isolation" to the role
Of politics — Your wisdom we'll extol
If so you'll curb it, circumscribe it quite,
But leave to us yourself, for our delight.

And this you'll do, unless I miss my guess,
For you've a kindly heart as all confess —
To gen'rous deeds you ever do incline,
You'd never, never wound your valentine.

To Miss Agnes Macphail, M.P.

I may be a Grit, I may be a Tory,
A Stevenite bold, or a Communist gory,
A very small fish, or a very big whale —
Whatever I am, I'm for Agnes Macphail.

(The first of five verses, signed again "Your Valentine.")

National Archives of Canada, Macphail files.

5. National Archives of Canada, Macphail files.

6. *Ibid.*

7. *Ibid.*

8. *Ibid.*

9. Mrs. Dorothy Dennison, wife of William Dennison, one-time Mayor of Toronto and MPP with Agnes. Letter dated July 11, 1982, Macphail family files.

10. T. C. Douglas, CCF and NDP premier of Saskatchewan for seventeen years. Federal member, 1934-1944.

11. "Miss Macphail Wants Justice for Disabled Soldiers," *Durham Review*, March 6, 1930, reprinted from Hansard.

12. Debate on divorce, Hansard, May 9, 1930.

13. Excerpt from weekly letter, *Durham Review*, April 17, 1930.

Chapter VII

1. "Bouquet for Miss Macphail," *Durham Review*, July 10, 1930, reprinted from the *Toronto Daily Star*.

2. Campbell advertisement, *Durham Review*, July 10, 1930.

3. "Over 2000 Hear Nomination Address," *Durham Review*, July 17, 1930.

4. "Liberals Will Support Miss Macphail," *Durham Review*, July 24, 1930.

5. "South East Grey Returns Miss Macphail," *Durham Review*, July 31, 1930.

6. *St. Thomas Times-Journal*, July 30, 1930.

7. Ed Ruthven, "Parliamentary Sketches," *Labor Advocate*, January, 1931.

8. Excerpt from weekly letter, *Durham Review*, September 18, 1930.

9. "Crowd Hears Woman M.P. Preach Pacifism," *Border Cities Star*, Windsor, February 1, 1928.

10. Excerpt from weekly letter, *Durham Review*, September 25, 1930.

11. *Ibid.*, November 6, 1930.

12. Eva Le Gallienne, born 1899, American actress and producer; founder of the Civic Repertory Theatre in 1926 and with Margaret Webster of the American Repertory Theatre in 1946.

13. Excerpt from weekly letter, *Durham Review*, November 20, 1930.

14. Sir Rabindranath Tagore, 1861-1941, Indian author and philosopher. Won 1913 Nobel Prize in literature.

15. Mohandas Karamchand Gandhi, 1869-1948, revered Indian leader; led struggle for India's independence; espoused non-violent resistance.

16. Jane Addams, 1860-1935, noted American social worker. Nobel Peace Prize, 1931, shared with Nicholas Murray Butler.

17. Excerpt from weekly letter, *Durham Review*, December 1, 1930.

18. *Ibid.*, March 20, 1931: "Parliament Opens with R. B. Bennett at Helm."

19. Excerpt from reply to Speech from the Throne, Hansard, March 16, 1931.

20. Hansard, April 21, 1931.

21. Denton Massey, member for Greenwood, Toronto, had led a successful Men's Bible Class in Toronto.

22. Excerpt from weekly letter, *Durham Review*, August 6, 1931: "Beauharnois Scandal."

23. *Ibid.*, *Durham Review*, March 17, 1932: "Agnes Meets Right Hon. Winston Churchill"

24. Excerpt from weekly letter, *Durham Review*, April 7, 1932.

25. *Ibid.*, April 21, 1932.

26. Partial text of speech on budget, Hansard, October 13, 1932.

27. Excerpt from weekly letter, *Durham Review*, November 17, 1932.

28. The Honorable Paul Martin (b. 1903), MP East Essex, 1935-1968; then appointed to Senate.

29. Excerpt from weekly letter, *Durham Review*, November 24, 1932.

Chapter VIII

1. Kurt von Schleicher, 1882-1934. Appointed Chancellor of Germany in December, 1932; tried in vain to stem Nazis. He resigned and Hitler became Chancellor in January, 1933. The Nazis murdered von Schleicher in 1934.

2. Excerpt from weekly letter, *Durham Review*, January 5, 1933: "Miss Macphail Speaks in the Sunny South."

3. "CCF in Action," *Montreal Herald*, January 17, 1933.

4. E. C. Buchanan, "Will Miss Macphail Oust Woodsworth and Become Next Premier of Canada?" *Durham Review*, January 12, 1933, reprinted from *Saturday Night*.

5. "Debate on Criminal Code — Unlawful Associations," Hansard, February 16, 1933.

6. Excerpt from weekly letter, *Durham Review*, February 18, 1933.

7. *Ibid.*, March 2, 1933: "CCF Leader of United Empire Loyalist Stock," *Durham Review*.

8. *Ibid.*, March 9, 1933: "Liberal Leader Discusses the CCF in House," *Durham Review*.

9. Editorial, *Saturday Night*, April 15, 1933.

10. Excerpts from weekly letter, *Durham Review*.

11. *Ibid.*

12. *Ibid.*

13. *Ibid.,,* November, 1933.

14. *Ibid.,* February 22, 1934: "Lady M.P. Visits Texas."

15. Debate on penitentiaries, Hansard, February 14, 1934.

16. Excerpt from letter dated Ottawa, March 28, 1934, to Edward Baynes, Antigua, B.W.I. National Archives of Canada, Macphail files.

17. Excerpt from letter dated April 27, 1934, to Agnes Macphail from Edward Baynes. National Archives of Canada, Macphail files.

18. Excerpt from letter sent to newspapers of Grey-Bruce, February 24, 1934. National Archives of Canada, Macphail Files.

19. Debate on penitentiaries, Hansard, July 3, 1934.

20. Debate on supply-justice-penitentiaries, Hansard, April 4, 1935.

Chapter IX

1. "Miss Macphail Has Big Meeting," *Durham Review*, October 10, 1935.

2. "Miss Macphail Starts Campaign," *Dundalk Herald*, July 11, 1935.

3. Marguerita Nuttall was a well-known coloratura soprano from Toronto. She and Agnes met when both performed at Chautauqua.

4. Gladys Howey was a pianist from Owen Sound. She accompanied Marguerita Nuttall. Nuttall and Howey performed free at Agnes' political meetings.

5. Agnes told a *Toronto Star* reporter that she belonged to the "plain people — you can see that."

6. National Archives of Canada, Macphail files, dated Ottawa, February 12, 1936.

7. *Toronto Star* weekly editorial, February 28, 1936. Reprinted with permission, the *Toronto Star* Syndicate.

8. The boundary between Pennsylvania and Maryland. The term is popularly used to distinguish the South from the North.

9. "Miss Macphail Writes of the Stay in the Southern States," *Durham Review*; article is dated Ceylon, Ontario, February 1, 1936.

10. Excerpt from weekly letter, *Durham Review*, February 13, 1936.

11. National Archives of Canada, Macphail files.

12. *Ibid.*

13. Debate on retiring allowances, Hansard, February 20, 1936.

14. Debate on vocation education, Hansard, March 8, 1936.

15. Hansard, June 20, 1936.

Chapter X

1. Excerpt from weekly letter, *Durham Review*, March 12, 1936.

2. *Ibid.*, March 15, 1936.

3. *Ibid.*, *Durham Review*, March 19, 1936.

4. *Ibid.*, *Durham Review*, March 27, 1936.

5. *Ibid.*, April 25, 1936.

6. National Archives of Canada, Macphail files. Letter signed T. R. MacIntyre.

7. *Ibid.* Letter signed W. Bentley Plimsoll.

8. "Privilege Miss Macphail," Hansard, June 8, 1936.

9. National Archives of Canada, Macphail files.

10. *Ibid.*

11. *Ibid.*

12. *Ibid.*

13. *Ibid.*

14. *Ibid.*

15. Archives of CBC, Toronto, 1948.

16. *Ibid.*

17. National Archives of Canada, Macphail files.

Chapter XI

1. Excerpt from weekly letter, *Durham Review*, February 4, 1937.

2. *Ibid.*, February 11, 1937.

3. *Ibid.*, February 18, 1937.

4. Debate on housing policy, Hansard, February 10, 1937.

5. Excerpt from weekly letter, *Durham Review*, February 26, 1937.

6. *Ibid.*, March 11, 1937.

7. *Ibid.*, March 18, 1937.

8. John Buchan, first Baron Tweedsmuir, 1875-1940, Scottish author and statesman; Governor-General of Canada, 1935-1940.

9. Excerpt from weekly letter, *Durham Review*, March 25, 1937.

10. *Ibid.*, April 1, 1937.

11. Debate on pensions for soldiers' widows, Hansard, February 25, 1938.

12. Debate on old age pensions, Hansard, February 28, 1938.

13. National Archives of Canada, Macphail files. Letter dated March 21, 1938.

14. R. B. Bennett was succeeded by Dr. R. J. Manion as leader of the Conservatives.

15. Excerpt from weekly letter, *Durham Review*, March 17, 1938.

16. *Ibid.*, February 9, 1939.

17. *Ibid.*, March 24, 1938.

18. National Archives of Canada, Macphail files.

19. Excerpt from weekly letter, *Durham Review*, March 31, 1938.

20. *Ibid.*, *Durham Review*, April 14, 1938.

21. Miss Agnes Macphail and Mrs. Martha Louise Black, "How Far Can Women Help Solve National Problems?" CBC, May 21, 1939. National Archives of Canada, Macphail files.

Chapter XII

1. Excerpt from weekly letter, *Durham Review*, January 19, 1939.

2. Reply to Speech from the Throne, Hansard, January 27, 1939.

3. Excerpt from weekly letter, *Durham Review*, February 2, 1939.

4. *Ibid.*, *Durham Review*, March 16, 1939.

5. *Ibid.*, February 9, 1939.

6. *Ibid.*, April 27, 1939.

7. *Ibid.*, February 16, 1939.

8. Agnes once told a reporter she would like to take charge of Canadian prisons. "I want . . . to show that prisons can be changed from penal institutions into reformatories. Conditions in Canadian prisons are appalling. I think that a woman could reform the system. I should very much like to have the chance but I have little hope. It has not yet become the custom in Canada to appoint women to high administrative office." R. P. Brandt, "A Farmer's Daughter in the Canadian Parliament," *The St. Louis Post-Dispatch Daily Magazine*, June 10, 1929.

9. Excerpt from weekly letter, *Durham Review*, March 16, 1939.

10. Arthur Neville Chamberlain, 1869-1940. Prime Minister of Britain, 1937-1940. He signed the Munich Pact, which permitted Germany to occupy part of Czechoslovakia. He believed his appeasement policy would avert war.

11. Excerpt from weekly letter, *Durham Review*, March 30, 1939.

12. *Ibid.*, April 6, 1939: "Ottawa to Vancouver in 14 Hours by Plane."

13. *Ibid.*, May 4, 1939.

14. Debate on farm problems and world hunger, Hansard, May 8, 1939.

15. Debate on supply and national defence, Hansard, May 13, 1939.

16. Excerpt from weekly letter, *Durham Review*, April 27, 1939.

17. *Ibid.*, May 18, 1939.

18. *Ibid.*, June 1, 1939: "Impressions of Royal Visit to Ottawa."

Chapter XIII

1. *Ibid.*, June 8, 1939.

2. "Miss Macphail Again UFO-Labor Candidate," *Durham Review*, February 15, 1940.

3. *Durham Review*, March 14, 1940.

4. *Ibid.*, March 21, 1940.

5. "Grey Bruce Swings to Liberal Ranks," *Durham Review*, March 28, 1940.

6. "Miss Macphail Out of Parliamentary Life," *Durham Review*, March 28, 1940.

7. Archives, CBC, Toronto.

8. *Durham Review*, March 21, 1940.

9. National Archives of Canada, Macphail files.

10. *Ibid.*

11. *Ibid.*

12. *Ibid.*

13. *Ibid.*

14. "'Loved Every Day of It,' Said Miss Macphail," *Durham Review*, April 11, 1940.

15. When the CCF was formed in 1932 with J. S. Woodsworth as leader, Agnes led the UFO into the party. The next year the UFO pulled out. The *Dundalk Herald* reported: "Heads of the Co-operative Commonwealth Federation on Monday moved toward reorganization of the body in Ontario, ridding the ranks of Communism the main object of the step. Along with announcement of reorganization by J. S. Woodsworth . . . President of the CCF and member of the House of Commons for Winnipeg North, came the breaking away from the CCF of the United Farmers of Ontario. Withdrawal of the UFO from the CCF removed Miss Agnes Macphail, UFO member in the House of Commons for South East Grey, from the executive council of the CCF," March 15, 1934.

16. Ontario Hansard, March 2, 1944.

17. A note in the Macphail files, National Archives of Canada, dated May 4, 1945 says: "Had bad attack — went to bed. Cerebral thrombosis encephalopathy."

18. "Old Warrior," Helen Beattie, *Canadian Home Journal*, February, 1949.

19. Ontario Hansard, March 1, 1950.

20. *Ibid.*, February 24, 1949.

21. Debate on reformatories, Ontario Hansard, March 31, 1949.

22. Dr. Charlotte Whitton, first female mayor of a Canadian city, five times mayor of Ottawa.

23. *Macleans Magazine*, April 15, 1947.

24. Ontario Hansard, April 7, 1949.

25. Lt. Col. (retired) John W. Foote, V.C., died on May 2, 1988 at eighty-four years of age. After the war he was Chief Commissioner of the Ontario Liquor Control Board, MPP for Durham, Minister of Reform Institutions in the Ontario government, and Sheriff of Northumberland County from 1960 to 1969.

26. Macphail family files.

27. *Ibid.*

28. CBC Archives, Toronto.

29. "Miss A. C. Macphail, M.P., Choice of Progressives," *Flesherton Advance*, September 16, 1925.

30. Macphail family files.

31. E. B. Jolliffe, "Agnes," *CCF News*, March 1954.

32. Macphail family files.

33. *Owen Sound Daily Sun Times*, February, 1954.

34. National Archives of Canada, Macphail files.

Index

"In this, the centenary of the birth of Agnes Macphail, we are fortunate to have a new, well-illustrated biography of her exceptional career.

"Doris Pennington has done a painstaking job in assembling the documentary sources that reveal an extraordinarily full life. The book relies heavily on Macphails's own words from her speeches, letters and newspaper columns, and might almost be considered a book of readings. With her gift for both the written and the spoken word, it makes extremely good reading. . . .

"Agnes Macphail's quest for peace and justice continues as an example today, and underlines our celebration of her life."
— Audrey McLaughlin, MP, in *Canadian Forum*

"Biographer Doris Pennington knew the reformer from childhood. Her personal knowledge is combined with careful research and skilful writing to shape an authentic portrait of a strong woman and her constituency."
— Patricia Morley, in the Ottawa *Citizen*

"Agnes Macphail, Canada's first female MP, was not only energetic, ambitious, and driven by idealism — she was also a brilliant orator and writer. In **Agnes Macphail: Reformer**, Doris Pennington lets Macphail do most of the talking. . . . Macphail emerges from the pages with her warts, her sarcasm, and her ability to laugh at herself intact."
— Laurel Boone, in *Books in Canada*

"With an influx of women seeking leadership of political parties, it is timely for author-editor Doris Pennington to present the life of Canada's remarkable Agnes Macphail. . . . Black-and-white photos, extensive notes, bibliography and index add to the book's usefulness.

"I highly recommend the book to students of Canadian history or women's studies."
— Jean Farquharson, in *Canadian Materials*